The Way
of Merlin

The Way of Merlin

R.J. Stewart

The Aquarian Press
An Imprint of HarperCollins*Publishers*

The Aquarian Press
An Imprint of HarperCollins*Publishers*
77–85 Fulham Palace Road,
Hammersmith, London W6 8JB

Published by The Aquarian Press 1991
3   5   7   9   10   8   6   4   2

A catalogue record for this book
is available from the British Library

ISBN 1 85538 113 3

Typeset by Harper Phototypesetters Limited,
Northampton, England
Printed in Great Britain by
Mackays of Chatham PLC, Kent

Contents

Acknowledgements

A version of the visualization in Chapter 10, 'The Mystery of Merlin', was first published in *Advanced Magical Arts* by R.J. Stewart (Element Books, Shaftesbury, 1988); a version of the visualization in Chapter 12, 'The Cry of Merlin', was first published in *Psychology and the Spiritual Traditions*, edited by R.J. Stewart (Element Books, Shaftesbury, 1990). Both are included here by permission of the original publishers.

Extracts from the *Vita Merlini* are based upon the translation by J.J. Parry (University of Illinois, 1925) with variations according to my own understanding of the Latin text published by Basil Clarke (University of Wales, 1973). Extracts from *The Prophecies of Merlin* are based upon the translation by J.A. Giles (1896). Appendix 8, 'Mabon, the Celtic Divine Child', is reproduced by permission of the author, Caitlín Matthews, and was first published in *Merlin and Woman* (Blandford Press, London, 1988).

Foreword

The Way of Merlin is divided into two parts: the first is general discussion and theory, and the second involves practical work. I would recommend that you read the first part before working with the second, but this is not essential. You may be one of those wild souls, like Merlin and the seers and seeresses in the old Merlin tradition, who plunge straight into the cave, into the forest, not knowing what will come to pass. The old initiatory traditions frequently enabled changes, sometimes profound and shocking changes, with no preliminary explanation. Exposition came after the realization, not before it. Sometimes it did not come at all – explanation does not necessarily bring understanding.

This is not a 'complete-system' book, although I know that publishers love to describe esoteric or transformational books in such terms. The Mystery of Merlin is a wandering spiralling path through the forest, a circling dance that suddenly pauses and changes direction, a descent into a lightless cave to find the stars. These are not whimsical allegories or poetic phrases, but literal descriptions of the pattern and effect of working with this primal tradition.

Like the legends, myths and traditions from which it is drawn, this book has loose ends. The loose ends are woven into new patterns by you, by me, by us all. Then they are unwoven again, even as far as the stars, unwoven by the Goddess Ariadne, who is the universal power in the Mystery of Merlin.

It is difficult to avoid such images, for without them we reduce our description to jargon or seemingly technical but possibly meaningless esoteric vocabulary. You probably know the kind of thing: rays and thought-forms, sub-planes of etheric vibration, glowing cosmic rainbows of flashing colour in neatly defined pseudo-scientific spectrums, sub-personalities, regressions, and root-races. There is not much of this in the Way of Merlin, either in the book or in the experiences that it seeks to offer.

Much of the practical work is given in detail, including several visualizations and a ritual. Nothing that is offered is untested – everything suggested for you to work with has been tried by others and found to be powerfully effective. But do not think that you can sit back and find it all in these pages; some of the exercises are left open for you to make for yourself. Many of the processes described need regular work, and only the barest means of accessing them are given here. No author can do your soul-work for you.

If you seek a wise old Merlin to guide your every step, he is not in this book. Long ago (according to his biography written in the twelfth century but deriving from much earlier sources), the aged Merlin retired from active service, refusing to judge or advise the young warrior chiefs of Dark Age Wales. But if you seek the young prophetic child inflamed by the Red and White Dragon, or the wild seer or seeress of the woods, or those men and women who entered the bones of the land to enhance its awareness, and passed into Otherworlds to contact the beings therein, you might find such Merlins by working with the methods found in the following chapters. You might *become* such a one, though no claims are made or guarantees offered.

There is something of a detective story in all this – loose ends to be woven and unwoven, clues, scenes to be re-enacted, many people to trace, find, meet, question. That is how Mysteries, in the initiatory sense, tend to work. Forget about formal temples, masters in robes and grand eloquent rituals and grave speeches. Look instead for the fleeting glimpse of Merlin in the forest, the enigma of his sister, the radiance of the Child of Light. All of these and many more are real beings to track down, to encounter, to talk to. They are also within ourselves; yet, paradoxically, only when we realize that they are beings in their own right do we truly find them within.

Merlin is first and foremost a prophet; people on the Way of Merlin may become seers and seeresses. We need not covet this, for it is a type of seership that is hard, painful. Its first stirrings come from grief, from compassion at the suffering of others, and through disorientation and dissolution of regular consciousness.

The whole assembly of the Way of Merlin is defined to bring these wild forces into a holism, a vision of a unified Being. That being is also within, yet is the universe itself. And where does it all begin? Not in the mythic forest or the druidic circle, not in the stellar realms, but at home. The Mystery of Merlin is a back-yard mystery, for it declares the smallest, most local space to be sacred, to be alive, to be aware. If this resonates within you, read on.

Introduction

This book combines material from my earlier books on the Merlin tradition with other sources to create a coherent presentation for the modern reader. It is not, however, a reworking or cut-down version of the earlier books, and contains much that is not found in them, nor in any other modern publication. *The Prophetic Vision of Merlin*[1] and *The Mystic Life of Merlin*[2] were interpretations based firmly upon two medieval texts; these texts were drawn from bardic or Celtic oral tradition, expanded and set into Latin by Geoffrey of Monmouth in the twelfth century. *The Merlin Tarot*[3] defines the images found in the Merlin tradition as a deck of cards, and its accompanying book deals with techniques of using these as harmonic images for insight, farsight and divination. *The Merlin Tarot* book also describes the relationship of Merlinic images to the subsequent development of the Tarot in Europe during the Renaissance, suggesting a common ground in oral story-telling and mythology.

In *The Way of Merlin* the emphasis is rather upon practical applications of the core of the Merlin tradition, both for today and for the future. It does not include full translations of texts, and does not rely heavily upon historical discussion, as I feel that this has been given ample attention already.[4] Far from being an obscure or quaint subject, the Merlin tradition is vibrant and active. It contains deep insights into the nature of human consciousness, and suggests a series of techniques for inner transformation.

Much of this tradition, however, is not related to the popular stereotype of Merlin as found today. During the six years in which I have written the three books mentioned above, and edited the annual anthology published as a result of the Merlin Conference, it has become clear to me that the stereotype of Merlin as wise elder or, as is more fashionable now, channelled master, is still firmly rooted in popular entertainment. The New Age Merlin seems more the product of Disneyland than of tradition, history, or esoteric and spiritual sources. I have received portentous letters on mauve paper spangled with silver stars, sheaves of historically inaccurate notes on past-life regressions from various sources, and deeply vague writings full of almost meaningful declarations. These are all supposed to be connected to Merlin . . . the old man in the pointy hat. There is also a wide range of books now in publication that all follow this stereotype in various ways. Yet the solid and real Merlin texts and traditions, handed down and preserved from the culture in which Merlin lived, and in which the idea of Merlin permeated, play little or no part in such offerings.

I do not claim to be in regular touch with Merlin, and do not propose that I have sole contact with the Merlin tradition. Any such claims are pompous nonsense.

This book is designed to integrate many aspects of that Celtic and pre-Celtic tradition that is embodied by Merlin, within and beyond historical or inspirational sources. It aims to provide the means by which we might apply such material today. The discussions, visualizations and techniques are essentially my own interpretation and re-creation of what is present in the genuine sources of the Merlin tradition. Although I cite various sources from time to time, you will find the main body of evidence and textual material in other books, such as those listed in the Notes to the Main Text. There is, of course, a wide range of academic texts associated with Arthurian studies, medieval literature, and so forth.

The Way of Merlin is not intended as a textbook in the academic sense, but as a handbook of techniques of psychic transformation, using visualization, sacred dance, ritual and meditation. I hope to show that the Way of Merlin is a viable path, and not limited to a pseudo-Celtic or antiquarian tradition of mysticism, magic or prophecy. Furthermore it is not a rigid tradition, and if you follow the example and patterns offered in this book, you can develop methods of working that are unique to yourself or to a group and yet remain within the harmony or holism of the Way of Merlin.

The Way of Merlin is a manifestation of, or harmonic entity within, the Way of Ariadne, the Weaver Goddess. It is a powerful way because the truth of Merlin as a collective image, even with the primal levels buried deeply and hidden, as they are today, stills holds good. There is a hallmark of energy associated both with Merlin and, on a universal level, with Ariadne the Weaver Goddess to whom much of this book is devoted. If we use the Merlin tradition, if we adapt and regenerate for modern applications, we can bring that special energy through in forms that are of great use to us. Our inner Merlin is both a collective and individual image, merging with the ancestral Merlin or Merlins, who were living human beings.

This combination of ancestral and imaginative contact can generate a potent and enduring inner dynamic – something that boosts our individual or group effort, and amplifies it. Unless this boost or amplification really occurs, the Merlin tradition, and what I have called 'the Mystery of Merlin', is merely a literary curiosity.

In my own experience, and in that of others with whom I have worked, the transformations, the energy, and the reality of the inner forces are undeniable. Through the techniques and exercises in this book, and through the suggestions that you can develop on your own, you may also experience this power at work.

DEFINING THE WAY OF MERLIN

The Way of Merlin can be defined and affirmed in one simple phrase: 'Your true self and the land are one.' All Merlin's adventures, trials, experiences, transformations and teachings lead to this realization.

Today there can be few affirmations of greater importance than to rediscover and actively affirm the sacredness of the land. Whatever we do to or within the land we also do to ourselves: if the land is sacred, we are all sacred, if the land is disposable, pollutable, expendable . . . what are we? We cannot destroy parts of the planet and deplete vast areas of life and sustenance without such destruction unbalancing the whole.

Modern materialist science has suddenly admitted this to be the truth, a truth long affirmed as a central concept in the philosophy, religion and magic of the ancient world. Both the sanctity of the land and its potential destruction or beautification are clearly described in the medieval Merlin texts, which draw upon ancient oral traditional verses and teachings concerning Merlin. These texts represent a core teaching of the Western perennial spiritual tradition.

The Way of Merlin implies that we cannot be truly merciful, sympathetic and harmonious with one another until we relate properly to the land; people are not separate from the land, and lands are not separate from the planet. By 'land' we must understand firstly something very small, i.e. our immediate locality, wherever we happen to be. Without this immediate realization, this sacred locality, no greater vision and no wider consciousness can be achieved. Too many of us have wide yearnings to save the planet but ignore our own back-yards or simply use them as rubbish dumps. This is not a metaphor – in the Merlin tradition your own back-yard is as sacred as a sacred mountain . . .'Your true self and the land are one.' Merlin's visions, as we know them today from medieval sources, dealt exclusively with small localities in Wales, parts of England, and possibly southern Scotland. Yet if we consider the *Prophecies*, the awareness of the boy Merlin leaps from purely local and ephemerally political prediction to a universal apocalyptic vision. (Extracts from this vision are quoted in Appendix 1.)

Your true self and the land are one: relating to your immediate environment, however small, brings you to a universal awareness. This is the Way of Merlin. It begins within your own body – you become aware of your own physical location, your space, your apartment, your garden, your region. It can, under certain circumstances, which we will discover, leap to a universal vision, a transpersonal awareness of the relationship between the solar system and our true environment of the stars. But it begins in a very small way. Awareness of the planet and its wholeness comes after the lightning link between your immediate locality and the universal perception and awareness. In the mystical biography of the *Vita Merlini*, Merlin is instructed in the holism that arises from the Four Powers, Four Elements, Four Directions and Four Winds, all unified into a fifth that is at once the planet and the universe. (This vision is quoted in Appendix 2.) The universe is within the planet, within the land, in your own back-yard. This is the Way of Merlin.

Who or What is not Merlin?

Before we proceed any further with the practical aspects of the Way of Merlin, let us examine some of those attributes which Merlin does *not* have. If we look at the absence of certain aspects of inner development, certain techniques, ideas, types and methods, we can learn a great deal about what the Way of Merlin really does consist of. The sources for this brief exploration are in the primal Merlin legends and texts, which predate later literary or entertainment and fantasy sources by centuries. In other words, they are at the foundation of the popular notions concerning Merlin, magic, and that unique power to which even modern intuitions respond.

First of all, Merlin is not a warrior. He does not employ the skills of arms, endurance, physical arts or intense co-ordination. Indeed, as he is driven mad by grief and suffering when he sees his clan pointlessly killed in tribal warfare, it is clear that he rejects the ways of politics, war, conflict, and worldly power altogether. More subtly, he is not an individual in the 'martial arts' type of wisdom tradition, despite the fact that there is overwhelming evidence for a mystical warrior tradition in Celtic culture.

Merlin is not a person of intense discipline or strong will for much of the time, yet he has an intensity of purpose and a strength of openness. He is cast upon the cycle of the Wheel of Life, and passes through whatever deep changes arise as a result of his encounters. In many aspects, his legendary life reveals a spiritual acceptance, a crossing beyond personal will and personal boundaries into the unknown. It appears as prophecy, union with natural forces, inspiration by the Goddess of the Land, and contemplation of the Great Goddess and Universal Being.

Merlin is not, contrary to all popular belief, a formal or self-declared magician, though primal magic is inherent in the pattern of his life, encounters and transformations. This is very important indeed, and cannot be over-emphasized as an insight into the Merlin tradition. The Way of Merlin is a way of vision, acceptance, fluidity, prophecy, contemplation. It is not a way of dogmatic or systematic ritual magic as understood today, in which well-assembled systems are used in an inflexible manner to produce results according to will. We do not find Merlin conducting rituals, yet the background of his world, his holism, is identical to that of the deepest perennial magical and spiritual arts.

The Way of Merlin is found within Sacred Space, the Blessed Land, the living planet and singing stars. But Merlin does not stand before altars, manipulate magical implements or conduct invocations. His magic, which is the magic of transformation, arises spontaneously through letting go of outer forms and habits, and moving further into unity with other living beings.

In the earliest sources, Merlin is not an adviser or wise man. Although we have a vast assemblage of lore concerning his advice to King Arthur, this all comes within the body of Arthurian literature that is later (often much later) than the original Merlin tradition. In the early texts, Merlin seems to have little or no relationship to the reign of Arthur, being present only at his conception and non-death. In the works of Geoffrey of Monmouth[5] the child Merlin is summoned before the usurper Vortigern, upon which he prophesies. We later find that Merlin enables Uther to make love to Igraine by disguising his appearance (not through magical illusion as often suggested, but by cosmetics). This causes the conception of Arthur, later to be king. Then, in the *Vita*, we find a curious but important reference to the fact that Merlin was present when the undying but deeply wounded King Arthur was ferried to the Otherworld for healing by the priestess or goddess Morgen. (We shall encounter Morgen upon the Way of Merlin, as she is a major figure, embodying a power that is especially important for us today.) This theme of Merlin's absence from the life of Arthur, and his presence only at the turning points of conception and passage to the Otherworld, bears fruit in meditation.

Also, whereas we know that Druids advised, and frequently seem to have dominated, the ancient Irish kings, this is another aspect we do not find in the traditions of Merlin. In several parallel tales in various traditions, the mad Merlin or a mad saint or holy man appears at the court of a king not to guide or advise in a grave stately manner, but to utter wild confusing startling snatches of tangled insight. When the aged Merlin is asked, in the *Vita*, to counsel the young princes and chieftains of his land, in the manner of a Druid judge, he refuses. Indeed, the traditional wisdom teachings linked to his madness and his transformation are given by the bard Taliesin, acting under the guidance of the goddess Minerva. Merlin is of a different kind, the wild seer, the unpredictable prophet. He also represents that free spirit that appears at turning points or thresholds in a lifetime, a sudden inspiration or manifestation of deep forces that may enable powerful change, or bring such changes into manifestation. Little wonder that he is associated in legend with the conception and potential regeneration of the perfect king.

None of this body of tradition fits with the later idea of the sage Merlin gravely and knowingly steering the naïve young Arthur. So if you wish to be a grave, all-knowing patriarch, if you are determined to know more than anyone else, the Way of Merlin is clearly not for you. There are no 'Masters' upon the Way of Merlin, least of all Merlin himself, who is child, madman, fool and then withdrawn contemplative. And when Merlin withdraws into spiritual contemplation, his mantle of power is handed on to others.

It is interesting to find that in the *Vita* this mantle of prophecy is given to his sister Ganieda. While this may be a literary device to end the biography (by Geoffrey of Monmouth) it also reflects a whole range of old Welsh bardic verses concerning Merlin and his sister. The effect of Ganieda is to enable, to polarize, to balance certain energies in her brother. They take it in turns, so to speak, to mediate the power of the Goddess or God. When this power flows through a male it manifests in different ways to when it flows through a female.

Our life phases will also modulate the power. Upon the Wheel of Life (see Figure 1) we find four relative phases – Birth, Adulthood, Maturity and Age – while the primal Merlin tradition also uses a triple pattern of Youth, Adulthood and Age. This theme of polarity is found throughout the Mystery of Merlin, and we shall return to it frequently in this book.

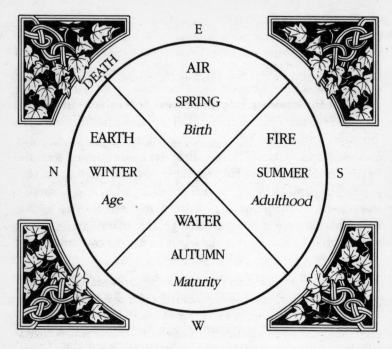

Figure 1: The Wheel of Life and The Four Directions

EAST:
Primary attributes: LIFE/Air/Spring/Morning/Childhood.

Creatures: Birds and other flying or airborne life. All creatures of morning and of swift motion.

Implements: Sword, Dagger, Arrow, Blades. All active, incisive, precise, swift implements.

SOUTH:
Primary attributes: LIGHT/Fire/Summer/Noon/Adulthood.

Creatures: Serpents or dragons, creatures associated with fire, the sun, hot environments. All creatures of midday and harmonious motion.

Implements: Rod, Staff, Spear, Lance, Wand. All outgoing, balancing, enabling, implements.

WEST:
Primary attributes: LOVE/Water/Autumn/Evening/Maturity.

Creatures: Fishes and other water creatures. All creatures of evening and gentle strength.

Implements: Cup, Cauldron, Bowl. All giving and receiving containers and vessels.

NORTH:
Primary Attributes: LAW/Earth/Winter/Night/Age.

Creatures: All four-footed beasts, night creatures, burrowing and earth-living beings.

Implements: Shield, Disc, Mirror, Lens. All protecting and reflecting surfaces.
Otherworld Associations:
EAST: All spirits, gods and goddesses of Life, inspiring energy from original Being and from expressed forms. Entities and Powers of breath, discovery, intellect, therapy, transition, spiritual birth, severance, change, purification, release.
SOUTH: All illuminating, enlightening spirits, gods and goddesses of Light, declaring and releasing form as energy. Entities and Powers of inner fire, balance, harmony, increase, radiance, perfection.
WEST: All spirits, gods and goddesses of Love, giving and receiving both energy and form. Entities and Powers of compassion, fruition, emotion, regeneration, cleansing, sustenance, transition.
NORTH: All spirits, gods and goddesses of Law, defining and limiting energy as form. Entities and Powers of manifestation, expression, realization, reflection, wisdom, grace.

REVERSALS

To reinstate practical developments for personal and trans-personal change within the Way of Merlin, we may need to reverse some aspects of the seeming order of legendary events. In the original legend, particularly in the detailed development that is found in the *Vita*, Merlin's life is intentionally set out as an allegory of the enclosed imprisoned human consciousness or soul; so much so that little or no guidance is given to him in a formal sense until close to the end of his experiences of adjustment. In short, we find that after a series of powerful catalytic experiences, Merlin is returned to balance, and to a new order of perception and awareness, by a holistic world-view, the perennial wisdom teaching concerning the spiritual and Elemental nature of the universe (this is quoted in Appendix 2).

This instruction, given by the bard Taliesin, is highly detailed, ranging from the Four Original Powers of the universe, to the Four Elements, the zones of the planet Earth and the countless living beings that inhabit these zones, defined and sustained by the four winds, four seas, and so forth. The exposition then leads into the Otherworld, and particularly focuses upon the Fortunate Isles, the Celtic proto-world or perfected land. This is not identical in concept to a reward-based paradise such as is found in Middle Eastern beliefs, but has some similarities to such concepts.

We should be aware that the exposition of the universe given to Merlin by Taliesin is not necessarily a revelation of the Mysteries in a religious sense, but is offered in a very practical down-to-earth manner. Merlin asks what is the origin of weather . . . and particularly why does it always rain on himself? This typically self-centred childlike human question is given nothing less than a universal framework for its answer, curiously reminiscent of the chaotic holisms found in modern weather prediction and computation of energy fields on a planetary scale.

The world-view does not suddenly set Merlin in balance by simply being talked at him, for it is not an intellectual lecture or dogmatic affirmation. One of the key events in the Way of Merlin is finding the right spring to drink from, and until that discovery is made, Merlin's energies are not set in proper balance for a new phase of life. This theme is shown in both the *Prophecies* and the *Vita*, and in a number of associated folk-tales and legends. It is only at the time of finding the spring that Merlin absorbs any formal teaching on the structure and pattern and rhythm of the universe. He realizes for himself that he has been out of balance because he has been upon the rim of the Wheel of Life which is inherent in this vast holism, and that only through a deep change of awareness can he find the centre of that Wheel.

Finding the right spring should not to be taken as a merely symbolic act, for it relates to actual springs or sacred water sources. We shall return to this subject in Chapter 6.

The original transformations of Merlin himself, as shown in our Tree of Transformation (Figure 2), are hard in the extreme, for at first there is no framework, teaching or background for the breakdown that he endures. He is alone, his barriers and protections collapsed, set spinning upon the Wheel of Life, the Seasons, the Elements.

This is typical of a number of primal methods leading to spiritual transformation: the individual is put through a harrowing series of experiences with little or no explanation . . . and he or she may or may not survive. To those who do, teaching is offered after the transformative events, as a type of clarification or structure into which the deeper realizations fit. This harsh method of spiritual initiation has great risks but also has great value, for by such means it is certain that the individual is not reacting out of any preconditioned source, and is truly

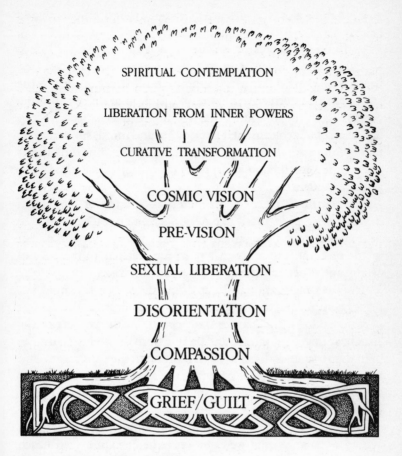

Figure 2: The Tree of Transformation

experiencing the unknown at first hand.

This 'shortened way', as it is often known, is a make-or-break initiatory pattern, based upon the concept that if we stripped our lives bare of all superfluous matters and self-importance, only a small number of key experiences would remain. If it is possible to initiate such key experiences directly, education and formal training are irrelevant. Ultimately it is the experience that matters, not the vehicle of tuition, or even the tradition in which the tuition is given form. The shortened way is found within the Way of Merlin, which originally was the path of the holy madman or madwoman, the wise fool, cutting across the highly structured and harmonically interwoven patterns of pagan Celtic myth and culture.

Traditional teachers of wisdom, initiators, magicians, seers, wise men and women tend to fall into two general categories: those who give preliminary training and instruction before the arousal of transformative power, and those that do not. It often occurs that during our inner life, in our spiritual changes, we leap far ahead of our conditioned personality and mind, subsequently taking long periods to catch up with ourselves. Thus the validity of extended instruction and preparation is often superseded by actual experience.

This entire subject is ultimately a matter of individual development, particularly as a personal human teacher is hard to find, never advertises, and never takes money for his or her instruction and initiation. Many of the teachers in the Way of Merlin and other branches of the Western Tradition exist upon the imaginative meditational inner dimensions, but this does not make them any less real or effective. We shall return to this subject of innerworld teachers again, particularly in the context of the visualizations of key images and people from the Merlin tradition.

In the absence of direct personal tuition in the early stages, and to build a renewed working form of the Merlin tradition, we may use the final holistic model (Appendix 2), that of the Five Zones, Three Worlds and Four Elements, as a guiding pattern from the very outset. It is a simple pattern with profound implications, and is used to balance us as we experience the encounters with each of the energies or images within the tradition. Figure 3 (page 54) shows this vision as a glyph or mandala. This figure will be referred to frequently as we progress, and has many levels of meaning accessible through meditation and visualization. It is a guide to the opening and activating of Sacred Space. From this simple pattern the Way of Merlin spirals open.

PART 1

The Merlin Tradition

CHAPTER 1

Finding the Way

Although almost everyone assumes that they know something of Merlin, mainly that he was a wizard who instructed King Arthur, very few people since the seventeenth century have really examined the true Merlin traditions in depth. This is not surprising, for in the West from the seventeenth to the twentieth centuries spiritual and magical disciplines were set aside for the development of an increasingly materialist society. Merlin, who was once a primal prophet and teaching figure of Western spiritual and magical tradition, pagan Celtic in origin but fusing pagan and early Christian wisdom in practice, is now a cartoon figure. He has become a stereotyped wise elder with flowing beard, presumably modelled upon the Victorian image of the Biblical prophets and the exaggerated and dangerous male-superiority of the period.

But if we seek to find the truth about Merlin, by examining the genuine early texts that derive from collective traditions, mainly in Wales and Scotland, but with counterparts all over Europe, we find several startling but valuable facts. These may be briefly summarized as follows:

1. The Merlin tradition predates the King Arthur legend, and has an entire mythology and proto-psychology woven around Merlin's life, in which Arthur plays almost no part, other than that described in two short references in the famous books of Geoffrey of Monmouth written in the twelfth century. The connections between Merlin and Arthur were all elaborated

upon and developed by later authors, and gradually draw well away from the original image and well-defined traditions concerning Merlin himself.

2. Merlin was the traditional figure-head or archetype of specific Celtic arts of prophecy and inner transformation; many legends tales, poems, and expositions of actual practical techniques were at one time associated with him.

3. The origins of Merlin may be traced to the prehistoric past, where the primal prophet and a youthful god of poetry and inspiration (similar in many ways to the young Apollo) were originally identical. Humans mediated the poetic prophetic power; such individuals were both the inspirers and the conscience-bearers of a community, a clan, a race and its land.

   Curiously, to the modern mind, we find that women mediated the god-power of prophecy in the ancient world, while men mediated the goddess-power. In the Merlin legends we find that Merlin is inspired by various goddesses, named and unnamed; they include Minerva, Goddess of Cultural Development, an anonymous 'Goddess of the Land', and Ariadne, the universal Weaver Goddess.

   In Welsh tradition we sometimes find the divine male figure called Mabon ap Modron, the Son of the Mother, and inscriptions from Roman Celtic Britain confirm his cult to have been active. The collection of Welsh legends known as *The Mabinogion*[6] is based upon this Son figure, though he never appears in any of the extant tales. There are inscriptions to Mabon as far afield as the eastern seaboard of the United States, if we are to accept the research of Professor Barry Fell.[7]

   This Celtic and Merlinic connection to a primal young god of inspiration is further reinforced by early writings from classical Greek historians concerning the origins of Apollo, the arts of prophecy, the Delphic oracle and the myth or mythic-history of the Hyperboreans. We also find resonance of similar traditions in early Irish epic poetry, which seems in part to preserve the pagan religion and legends of the Celtic bronze-age culture.[8]

4. Later and specifically Merlinic legends, from the medieval

period but preserving echoes of far older traditions, involve a prophetic child (Merlin himself), include carefully described methods of liberation from delusion, corruption and evil, and reveal a progression around the Wheel of Life towards spiritual maturity. This progression is accompanied by increasing knowledge of geomantic and stellar energies, and deepening understanding of many creatures, birds, animals, fishes, supernatural beings and divine forces, gods, and goddesses. The general content and impact of this progression, set out at length in the *Vita Merlini* and found in fragmentary form in parts of *The Mabinogion* and other texts drawing upon Celtic sources, is remarkably similar to the structure of an ancient Mystery, such as that of Orpheus.

The classical Mysteries took mythic tales and figures and expanded them into an initiatory system; there is ample evidence that the Merlin traditions also contain such mythic initiatory systems. It is probable that the material comes from bardic sources, preserving in a diffuse and elaborate form the traditions of the pagan Celts and Druids, but fusing these with both classical and early Christian spiritual impulses.

Most of this lore was combined by Geoffrey of Monmouth in the middle of the twelfth century into his *Prophecies* and *Life of Merlin*, drawn mainly from bardic oral tradition. Such traditions were active for many centuries in folklore, where the Mystery of Merlin was loosely preserved in poems, songs, tales and prophecies circulated around Wales, Brittany, Scotland and various other parts of Europe. Tales of Merlin are found even as far afield as Iceland, showing significant Norse/Scandinavian connections between the traditions of Merlin and those of Odin, just as there are classical connections between those of Merlin and those of Apollo.

All this is a fascinating detective story, supported by a mass of evidence that has simply been swept aside, partly forgotten, or ignored in the recent usage of Merlin as a character in popular entertainment. Clearly the doddering but wise Merlin of the nineteenth and twentieth centuries is very different from the original youthful Merlin inspired by an irresistible force of prophecy. Has his image aged as our culture has degenerated? Is the ever-young Merlin, the Divine Child that is both female and male, still at the heart of a land and in the heart of human beings? Can Merlin, you or I, be all of the life-phases simultaneously?

In early sources we find that Merlin passes through three life phases, that of prophetic youth, that of madman living close to nature, and that of wise elder retiring to spiritual contemplation. As already mentioned, even in the last stage he does not appear at Arthur's court or advise the king – in the *Vita* Arthur is already lost by the time Merlin retires into contemplation. Arthur must remain awaiting a potential cure at the hands of a mysterious goddess-figure called Morgen, the mistress of all arts of therapy and shape-changing, which we might interpret today as transformation in all senses of the word.

We shall return to this motif in depth in a later chapter, but should say, for the present, that this beneficial and goddess-like Morgen should not be confused with the 'evil' figure of Morgana or Morgan le Fay in later Arthurian literature, even though both have their roots in an ancient and savage goddess known in Ireland as the Morrigu or Morrigan.[9] The change from beneficial to destructive image is part of the Mystery, though its crystallization and propagandizing in literature has been, to say the least, unfortunate.

WHAT IS THE MYSTERY OF MERLIN?

If there is a coherent Mystery of Merlin, if the legends do indeed contain a system of inner development, preserved in a poetic and, to the modern mind, a confused form from a very early period, how might we apply such a tradition in modern use? And before we ask how, we might ask why. Why should we bother with this Merlin lore? Is it not simply the detritus of a forgotten age?

There are several interconnected answers to these questions. Some of the answers are intellectual, others are intuitive, and many are to be found within ourselves, rather than in words upon a printed page. Let us first consider, briefly, the intellectual answers.

The close of the twentieth century has seen an astonishing revival of interest in esoteric, magical and spiritual arts and disciplines, and while most of this is fashionable trivia, there can be no doubt at all that many issues inherent in ancient magical and spiritual traditions now manifest as literal or general concerns for people at large. While ethereal movements and cults abound, the general consciousness requires something very specific and rooted into the land, the planet. Environmental awareness, that was once the mysterious yet practical property of meditators and initiates into minor traditions of magic, witchcraft, shamanism and the like, is now firmly present, in a new form, in the consciousness of millions of people.

This new awareness, on a political, economic and ecological level or scale, has come hand in hand with an increased specialist interest in the primal chthonic, magical and shamanistic arts, all deeply concerned with the sanctity of the land. The Merlin tradition is a major vehicle for this type of awareness: it taps into mythic roots that run deeply into our ancestral memory, in which the Goddess and the land are one. Today we talk increasingly of the planetary environment, so the consciousness of the sacred land has turned a spiral, appearing in a new or higher form.

The methods of the Merlin tradition, preserved in various early texts and in oral teachings, have the potential to attune the modern psyche to the ancient ancestral ideas of a sacred land, the sanctity of the interrelated orders of life, and the relationship between humanity and divinity. The Merlin cosmology is a harmonic and holistic one, such as has been rediscovered, although with a different technical vocabulary, by the most modern and advanced physics.

Many other spiritual traditions claim something similar, so this is not a unique characteristic. Indeed, the Merlin tradition is but one part of a perennial holistic spiritual tradition that includes many specific branches. Its value as a specific branch lies in its powerful effect, its individual techniques and results, many of which are virtual hallmarks of psychic transformation.

If, as seems likely, the Merlin tradition reaches back to prehistoric times and to the primal relationship between geomantic, environmental and cosmic forces, manifesting through human consciousness, then there is a strong case for working with it. Not for working with it in the sense of idle experiment or sensation-seeking, but to bring such techniques and traditions to bear upon our new cycle of holistic awareness.

Such awareness, rediscovered after centuries of neglect, has reappeared under extreme duress, now that we are suddenly aware of the potential destruction of our planet.

To this very substantial broad argument, we might add the more limited but important fact that the Merlin tradition contains many elements that seem integral to Western consciousness, and that its application and development may, therefore, gain very rapid results and transformations. It resonates to what is already within us, just as the profound traditions of the East resonate to the collective awareness of their people. Ultimately all such traditions merge, but the transcendent level of realization is often the last to be found, coming during the age of spiritual contemplation when all other turnings of the Wheel of Life and Transformation have been undertaken.

Moreover, the triple aspects of youth, adulthood, and maturity, as defined in the Mystery of Merlin, need not necessarily relate to physical age, and have collective racial or planetary harmonics as well as individual.

So much for the briefest possible summary of the argument which states that the fundamental ideas, the images and archetypes, and the techniques of the Merlin tradition are highly suitable and potent for restatement today. The intuitive arguments, however, cannot be written out, but rest with the individual's own response to the tales, the images, the energies inherent within the Merlin tradition itself.

Because the tradition is rooted in Western consciousness, it is more accessible for the individual to work with and try for him or herself than many Eastern techniques. Thus it poses the rare opportunity of enabling the individual to test the tradition in a fairly short period, rather than the many years required for most of the inner disciplines. I would not want to stress this rapidity too strongly though, as there is no easy way to inner development and transformation, be it Eastern or Western, chthonic, shamanistic, or transcendent.

In the last decade, however, there have been an increasing number of people who realize that techniques of spiritual development cannot simply be a matter of sweet calm meditation and good thoughts – these are only one preliminary and lesser aspect of any spiritual tradition. The truth is that spiritual transformative traditions are always, without exception, hard and painful, for they enable the process of growing and maturing upon a higher octave than that of habitual outer life. The Merlin tradition, particularly in its extended presentation in the *Vita Merlini*, deals precisely with this growing process, and describes the pains and the pitfalls, the ecstasies and achievements, in considerable detail. Thus it provides a map, through the experience of Merlin and his associates, which we can follow.

How Does It Work In Practice?

One problem with the growing awareness of spiritual traditions outside the mainstream of orthodox religion is that people become rather hardened and pseudo-knowledgeable, as if some comparative information on techniques and symbols equates to actual inner experience. The first and last answer to the question 'How does it work in practice?' is that we must simply stay within the tradition (whatever it may be) and work through it and with it.

In regard to spiritual development, many modern books and methods take an analytical and scientific approach, giving specific labels, techniques, exercises, and so forth, in graded stages. This gradation and specialization is found in the Mystery of Merlin, but it is presented as an elongated story. The method of presentation is important, for myth-generation and story-telling are not merely matters of primitive entertainment or pre-scientific explanation but rest at the very roots of consciousness.[10]

Creation myths tell of the creation of the world (which is always a universal world in which the planetary world is reflected), and then proceed with the story of all the living beings in that world, right through to the smallest creature upon our planet. Prophecy is intimately connected to creation myth, using mythic imagery and characters that are often outside state or orthodox religion, stemming from older sources. If we are able to tap into this fountain of myth-generation, which is exactly what was done by Merlin, we are able to use its energies to transform ourselves. Our own lives, after all, are merely a collection of short stories.

So, having stated that we must remain within a tradition, and that the Merlin texts and their inherent techniques provide clear maps for such a route, we need to assess the basic requirements, particularly in the light of how they might be applied for modern use. Originally the mythic tales, the epic poems and the verses of prophecy were absorbed in poetic and collective oral form, that is, people heard them repeated and often knew them by heart. At that time people partly lived within the dream-like structure of the tales, which attuned to the seasons of the year and certain religious beliefs and practices. Clearly this collective level of tradition does not exist today. In later chapters we shall return to this idea, and discover how it may be empowered today, as part of the experience of mythic and ancestral awareness that forms a central theme in the prophetic traditions connected to Merlin. But for the present, we need to consider how we might attune to the Merlin tradition when it is no longer part of our general collective currency of imagination.

There is, of course, a layer of Merlin imagery in modern tales, books, films and popular conception. But as mentioned briefly above, this deals almost exclusively with the aged Merlin, and tends to twist into the Victorian stereotype of the all-wise, all-male elder. This image is something that would have been monstrous and abhorrent to those bards, seers and seeresses who preserved the oral Mystery of Merlin. Apart from the proper identity of Merlin himself, the Merlin texts place a strong emphasis upon women. Many major transformations within the initiatory tradition are connected to specific women, goddesses or the interaction between male and female archetypes or images and personae.

The secret of using such images as Merlin is that we must always try to move to the earlier or deeper levels of each image (be it god, goddess, hero, persona, or scenario), for if we remain at the first level of an image, it will often transform all consciousness to suit its most recent or obvious form. This rule has many exceptions, but is well known in modern psychology, and used to great effect in advertising, social and political conditioning, and general propaganda. For a long period it was used extensively in political religion, leaving us with disastrous results today.

We need to examine the basic elements of the Merlin tradition, separate them out initially, and then, having identified them, allow ourselves to become reabsorbed within the stories themselves. There is an infallible method for this, time-hallowed

and effectively used within perennial wisdom teachings: behave
as if the legends, myths or tales of the religion or Mystery are quite
true. This is a dangerous and often underestimated technique; we
use it in lesser ways whenever we watch a film or play, but when
it is applied to potent magical transformative material, it is far
more then mere suspension of disbelief. We have seen,
historically, the most negative aspects of this in dogmatic religion,
where people take ancient texts literally and murder those who
will not. But if we are able to balance our suspension of disbelief
with a proper understanding of the elements contained within
the multi-layered tales and myths of any tradition, we will find a
path towards transformation.

A summary of the stages used in this book, which form a
restatement of the stages inherent in the Merlin tradition itself,
can be given at this point. It should be said, however, that certain
of these stages would have been implicit for people of earlier
culture, such as the Wheel of Life, the Four Elements and the
attuning to mythic story-telling. Furthermore, there is no
suggestion that this is a rigid or dogmatic process, for many stages
are interchangeable, and they unfold in a spiral pattern, often
reappearing in higher harmonic levels of one another. We shall
return to this idea of harmonic levels of consciousness frequently.
The stages are as follows, and form the basis of a fivefold pattern
within this book, based upon the fivefold creation patterns in the
Merlin cosmology.

1. The Four Elements and Four Powers are encountered and
   experienced through meditation and training exercises. These
   Elements are Air, Fire, Water and Earth, and have their
   reflections and resonances throughout all existence. This
   pattern is clearly described in the Creation Vision of the *Vita*
   (Appendix 2). The Elements are reflected through the Four
   Seasons of the Year, the Four Winds, and the Four Directions
   of East, South, West and North. They are related to the Axis
   Mundi or the World Pillar by the ideas of Above (the stars) and
   Below (the Underworld). This is the framework within which
   the adventures and transformations of Merlin and his associates
   occur.

2. We people this conceptual and actual environmental and

cosmic model with personae and entities. These are initially Merlin himself, his mother, his sister Ganieda, his wife Guendoloena, and various other characters. It must be emphasized that this is not 'role-play' but the use of highly empowered magical images which embody and mediate very specific, recognizable and potent energies. The major characters may be used in meditation and visualization, and various exercises working in this way are given in our later chapters. Some of the exercises are detailed examples of ritual, imaginative visualization, sacred dance, and empowering Sacred Space. Others are deliberately left open for you to assemble, define, refine and work with yourself.

3. To the primal personae or people, we then add the creatures. Merlin is particularly associated with the wolf, the pig, the crow, the hawk or eagle, the salmon, the deer, the she-goat, and, in some traditions, the wren. Other personae have other creatures relating to them. The creatures are in turn related to the Seasons, the Directions, and the Elements. Thus we have already begun to define a comprehensive natural alphabet of living forms, some human, some animal, some like Merlin himself, partaking of both human and non-human origins.

4. We then move through the various related dimensions, as described in the early texts and methods. In the world Above are the various spiritual potencies, stellar and planetary deities, and orders of angels and archangels. In the world Below are the ancestors, the fairy people, and the gods and goddesses of the Underworld. We discover how these relate to the human characters and personae, and how they resonate as octaves or reflections of one another.

5. The fifth and final stage is learning to use the abilities and imagery developed through involvement in the Mystery, and how to apply them in practical work today. The main emphasis of this is within oneself, but the Merlin tradition is always concerned with actual locations – sacred sites, springs and wells. This is the least developed aspect of esoteric tradition today, and on a practical basis the Merlin techniques reveal many ways of revitalizing and harmonizing the environment.

We may also apply the polarities of the tradition, which are the ways in which the sexual energies and identities of the personae encounter and respond to one another. This is very important and effective work, for the Merlin tradition includes a primal pattern of polarized or sexual relationships, long predating that of materialist psychology, and revealing the connections between certain powerful images or god and goddess-forms, environmental forces and human sexuality, compared with the higher modes or abilities of consciousness.

A WORD OF CAUTION

It should be stressed at this introductory stage that these can be very powerful dynamic techniques. Once you have brought the Way of Merlin alive within yourself the mass of text and detail becomes less relevant, and takes second place to developing the techniques and experiencing the encounters embedded within the tradition.

The chapters that follow are designed to move progressively through various levels. First we relate to the Elements, to the Creation of the World. This begins with Sacred Space. We people the world with its major human or transhuman occupants, accompanied and enhanced by certain companion or spiritual animals. Only after these important guiding balancing and mediating entities are firmly established within our imagination, do we approach the higher and lower worlds, in which otherworldly beings are encountered. The last stage might seem to be that of reapplying the changes and energies concerned to transform our outer life, but this transformative process has been at work through every stage of the Mystery.

If you are looking for sweet and helpful spirit guides, or for easy answers to life's problems, then the Merlin traditions are not for you. Merlin himself repeatedly asks, in the *Vita*, why life is not easy, and the answers that come to him from various adventures and other people are often of the most surprising and convoluted nature. Many encounters with images in visualization are deeply disturbing, not in any sense of evil, but because they reach right to our roots of consciousness and entity. We usually fear true change, no matter how much we claim to be seeking it within ourselves.

The key to balance comes in the early exercises, those of the Four Elements, Four Seasons and Six Directions. If we work through these fundamental patterns, they will enable us to stay on course and not to be excessively disturbed by the more potent images. The images themselves are balanced by one another in polarized patterns, as many of our exercises and diagrams show.

FLEXIBLE WAYS

The methods suggested in this book are flexible; they may and should be changed according to our intuition. If they are taken too far out of their primal tradition of the Goddess and Merlin, they can become ineffective; but if we use the tradition rigidly or as dogma we lose its benefits altogether.

This balance, between form and content, is often difficult to assess intellectually. It is a matter for intuition, for development in meditation, in visualization and in movement, and in relationship to the sacred land. Three basic ways of achieving it are suggested here, and working examples given of each: ceremony, visualization and movement.

Ceremony

In ceremony we ritually re-enact and create afresh key mythic scenes from a Mystery. A 'Mystery' is a collection of mythic images, tales and traditions having a coherent identity. In the manner of the ancient Mysteries it may be brought alive through conscious effort, through instruction and through initiation. Today initiation is often gained through direct experience and not through any romanticized membership of a group, order or self-acclaimed organization.

On the surface ceremonial work might seem the most archaic or intentionally traditional way of working, using ritual and predetermined words and images, such as the example on pages 152–159. In truth it is a modern development, with no historical or formal connection to the old Merlin tradition, which was founded upon spontaneity and inevitable experience.

I say no formal connection because the idea of re-enacting myths and legends as group ritual is an emergency technique for those of us who are out of touch with primal themes. While people claim that such ceremonies are inherited from ancient tradition – and in spirit I would not disagree – the form and the content are quite modern. No one worked ceremonies of this sort when the traditions of the Goddess and seership were alive within our culture. As a rule, formal ceremonies, even in the ancient world, are the product of state religion. Great civilizations were held together by magical ceremonies or religious calendars – individual spiritual insight tends to dissolve such systems. The Merlin tradition, like many primal traditions, is revolutionary. There is an intentional pun here, a deep insight into the nature of language and consciousness. Prophetic and primal arts are revolutionary – they disturb and dissolve the status quo. They bring in new revolutions or spirals of the Wheel of Life and Change.

Our spiral for today is the dissolution of aggressive patriarchal materialism. Unless we can achieve this new level of awareness we will destroy our world. The spiritual traditions suggest that we can lose our rigid delusions. By doing so we seem to die inwardly; but if we do not, the change comes outwardly in a most devastating form. Much of the Way of Merlin is concerned with this willing self-change in contrast to the rigidity of unwilling selfishness.

There is a level of ceremony or ritual that is timeless, and not dependent upon the mental attitudes of society. It is the simplest and most powerful way of working ritual. When we visit a sacred spring, talk to a tree, climb a hill at night to view the stars, we are making powerful rituals that are at the heart of the Way of Merlin, and come directly from the Goddess. It is significant that these ceremonies are concerned with physical movement, with the relationship between our bodies and the locations of energy in the land. If we were able to strip away all the accumulated layers of our conditioned lives, the simple acts would be enough. Go to a spring, find a silent cave, sit still in the depths of the night. These acts with no further symbolism, meditation, words, images or window-dressing were and are the foundation of the Way.

The men and women who entered the deeper relationship with the Goddess of the Land, or with Ariadne, did so by attuning to places of power. They were instilled with a poetic tradition of verses and tales, and had no need formally to induce this in themselves as we do today. That potential of simple transformation is still within us all – books such as this one should be thrown away as soon as possible.

Visualization

There is a difference between visualization and vision. Visualization is a very recent development, part of our last-ditch collective attempt to retrieve something from the collapse of our creative imagination. Visualization is a formalized exercise, and its most powerful levels require practice, concentration and intent. Vision is spontaneous, arising in the consciousness from energies that stir the normal patterns of perception out of their habitual state.

The relationship between visualization and vision is important for modern people, for we do not always have a body of images from a living tradition. The old seers and seeresses had such a body of images, mythic and legendary themes and people, sometimes masking and revealing gods and goddesses, which in turn masked or revealed potent energies of life and death. Nobody learned these images as discipline, they were part of everyday life. Mythic images were woven into the fabric of a society that was based upon rhythm, music, oral wisdom and the cycle of the seasons and stars. We do not have these.

Despite our obvious separation from natural rhythms and from the sacred land, however, we may recover our relationship, for it is not merely a conditioned relationship, but an inherent one. The people and the planet are one; we are not separate from each other. Modern science has shown in the most materialist sense that if we destroy the land, the planet, we destroy ourselves. In truth the destruction began with our separation from the land.

The relationship can be re-established, however, through the special techniques outlined here. The key word always is 'intent'. Aimless use of these techniques, compulsive or sensational use, for fun and entertainment, will not bring us closer to truth. The inherent relationship between ourselves and the sacred land, and then the holism of time, space and energy represented by Ariadne weaving the Four Powers and Four Elements, is opened out by unwavering intent.

Intent, however, is not will-power. The idea of striving, muscular will-power is a delusion. Intent is fluid, flexible, and constantly dissolving and reforming. Its strength is its perpetual recreation, and not in rigid immobility or unnatural endurance. The Merlin legends show this amply in the theme of the boy Merlin and King Vortigern. The despotic king builds a tower that is doomed to collapse, while the youth whom he seeks to sacrifice for selfish ends is perpetually open to the powers and visions of the Goddess. Vortigern passes away because he strove to survive; Merlin survives because he sought neither passing nor surviving. His intent was to find truth, shown in the legends by his repeated childish questions and incessant motion around the Wheel of Life.

Visualization today should have a clear intent. In the Way of Merlin the intent is to attune to a small but powerful set of key images that bring through specific energies. We may not predetermine the effect of these energies, but we may induce them by the images traditionally associated with the Mystery of Merlin, rooted as it is in the power of the Goddess.

Movement and Sacred Dance

All life moves, and the key vision of the Merlin tradition is a holistic motion and interweaving in which the planet mirrors the universe and is embedded within it. Embedded within the planet is the Otherworld. All living beings are interwoven with one another in a perpetual dance. This understanding is the basis of ritual or mystical dance. The Way of Merlin contains a simple but powerful movement, a dance pattern involving the flow of energy in Sacred Space.

If we attune to Sacred Space, it alters the flow of energy within ourselves. The perfected way would be to combine movement to a spring, tree or cave with the energetic dance. The development of visualization or formal ceremonies beyond these simple basics is merely a way forward, a means and not an end.

I would like to offer a word of caution here, one that may arouse opposition. There are many types of sacred dance found within world cultures, religions, mystical sects, folklore and primal magic. All share certain fundamental characteristics, and these were summarized by the ancients as three primary motions of the universe: Circular, Straight, and Oblique or Serpentine. Movement and its relationship to sacred space is inherently powerful . . . our emotions and responses are perhaps irrelevant.

Sacred dance is not something merely to release emotion, to enter trance states, to earth energy. All of these things may happen, but the sacred dance is, in itself, a motion that mirrors universal motion. We may dance to release emotion, to eliminate accumulated energy and bring temporary relief, but this is not sacred dance. We may dance to raise wild energies within ourselves and seek escape from the deadening enslaving patterns of our daily lives, but this is not sacred dance. Yet all of these *are* sacred dance providing we do not set limits upon the sacred quality, and providing that our intent is always to experience a further reality, a truth that lacks self-gratifying motive.

In the Way of Merlin sacred dance is intimately linked to self-sacrifice. It is the dance of dissolution, and not the dance of gratification. This is not the doom-laden, corrupt, propagandized sacrifice of orthodox Christianity, but a dissolving in perfect love, a realization of unity. In the Merlin legends it is known as the Threefold Death, a theme found in mysticism, magic and religion throughout our world. It is found because it is inherent within each of us – the Way of Merlin is only one tradition that gives us methods and images to work with.

We will return to this aspect of the Way of Merlin in our later chapters, but I would like to say at this stage that there is no obligation or demanding burden in the Mystery of Merlin. You take into yourself and bring out of yourself only that which you choose freely; the people, patterns, places and powers of the tradition amplify and clarify your intent.

CHAPTER
2

Merlin and Woman

One question often asked is how the legend of Merlin and its inner content, assuming such inner content to be truly present, might be relevant to modern women.[11] If we accept that Merlin is a male superior master, a wise elder patriarch, a mysterious source of dogmatic dictated wisdom from another world, then he has little or no relevance to women of the twentieth and twenty-first century, or to men either.

More specifically we need to address the problem that in popular literary, film and cartoon versions of Merlin legends, and even in several modern books claiming spiritual insight, we find the prophet shown as an elder male. In his relationships with women, he is sometimes deluded by a power-hungry young woman (Merlin and Nimuë) or found battling against the wiles of an evil sorceress (Merlin and Morgan le Fay). These ideas, these images, must be realized for what they are: propaganda. They are the result of political Christian orthodox propaganda and conditioning, despite the quality of the works of art and literature in which they appear. The further we go back in time, reaching towards a more primal source, the fainter these imbalanced images become. They play no part in the primal Merlin legend, concerned as it is with a relationship between the life cycle of a human being and the sacred quality of the land, the environment in which that human lives.

With regard to the important question concerning the Merlin tradition and women, there are two potential answers, and if we are to give the Way of Merlin a practical emphasis for the present and future, these must be examined carefully. If the Way of Merlin is for men only, it is valueless.

The first answer is linked to historical evidence and tradition. Historical evidence alone suggests that the Way of Merlin was never for men exclusively, and that it preserved and vitalized much of the awareness of the sacred land and the Goddess that was forcibly excluded from political Christianity. A merely historical perspective is not sufficient for modern work, however – it only forms a partial foundation to suggest origins and continuity of a tradition; it is not necessarily the tradition itself.

With this in view, if we consider the early Merlin legends with an open mind, we find that every stage of the prophet's transformation was powerfully linked to the presence of a woman, either human or otherworldly. The extensive texts of the *Prophecies* and *Vita* repeatedly show this important link between Merlin as a seeker after truth and the presence of goddess figures. Sometimes the goddess figures are described overtly, like Morgen who presides over therapy and the liberal arts. This beneficial otherworld image, a goddess from Celtic tradition, was eventually misrepresented as the evil Morgan le Fay, yet in the *Vita*, perhaps the earliest description of her association with Merlin and Arthur, there is no suggestion whatever that she is anything other than good.

We should really begin not with Morgen, as she comes close to the conclusion of Merlin's spiritual quest, but at the very beginning with his mother. At the outset we find that Merlin has a human mother and an otherworld father – echoes of the myth that founded Christianity, but certainly not borrowed from it. It is the myth of the child of two worlds, human and spiritual: we are all such children. All human feelings, problems, pain and suffering are felt by Merlin as he progresses around the Wheel of Life; he is never shown as superior, elitist, all-wise, dictatorial.

In the *Vita*, Merlin's sister Ganieda plays an important role in helping him towards rebalance. She is another reflection of an ancient culture goddess, Brigid of the Celts, or Minerva/Athena of the classical world. She represents the brother-sister relationship between man and woman, and indeed between humanity and the Goddess. This is relationship in which inner forces leading towards harmony and development act through guiding but not dictatorial or compulsive beings. The idea of the Goddess as elder sister was very powerful in the ancient world, and we have not yet recovered enough of this aspect in modern Goddess revivals.

Where we do find the beginnings of Christian sexual propaganda in the *Vita* is the relationship between Merlin and his wife Guendoloena. She is the lover aspect, the Flower Maiden, the sensual feminine power of nature. While the venerable traditions of Minerva and the Great Goddess are clearly preserved in Geoffrey of Monmouth's texts, drawn as they are from bardic sources, the nature aspect of the Goddess in connection to love and sexuality is not so well represented.

Guendoloena is rejected by the mad Merlin, and marries someone else. She is a confused image, in which the original lover-goddess, the Lady of Nature, partner of the Lord of the Animals, still shines through, but has been suppressed by the Christian culture of the day, and possibly by the pen of Geoffrey of Monmouth as creative editor.

There is nothing wrong, however, in the legendary theme that a human, male or female, must abandon his or her sexual stereotypes and habits before realigning inner energies and reaching liberation. This aspect of Merlin and Guendoloena still comes through in the *Vita*, and is found in other variant legends and examples of the tradition.

In the *Prophecies* we find the more primal images of the Goddess of the Land, and the Great Goddess of the unweaving, the pagan apocalypse. This is clearly derived from an oral tradition, though it has certain literary parallels and shares a common source in the spiritual traditions of the world. Such traditions, religious or magical, always contain apocalyptic verses or tales concerning the ending of all things, just as they tell of the beginning of all things.

The great power in the visions of Merlin is the Goddess, and not any God, orthodox or otherwise. This is the keystone to the foundation of the Way of Merlin, for it derives from the holistic world view of the Goddess, eventually suppressed but not destroyed by orthodox Christianity. Merlin is someone inspired by the visions and insights given by the Goddess, who appears as sister, lover and taker. In this sense we can feel that the Way of

Merlin is clearly valid for modern women, for it preserves and restates the power of the Goddess, and runs counter to the suppressive delusion of male superiority.

But there is a second and more simple, more powerful answer to the question of Merlin's relationship to women. It is this: there is no reason why Merlin should be exclusively male. The word 'Merlin' is a descriptive term for an individual inspired prophetically by the Goddess of the Land. This individual appears as male in the surviving legends, but there is no ultimate requirement that the gender be male.

Indeed, we find that Merlin's sexuality is not always well defined, as a review of the Merlin legends in folklore will show. By far the greatest portion of the primal legend concerns a mysterious child, half-human, half-otherworldly. This reflects the myth of the Divine Child, the perfect innocence at the heart of creation. There is no sexual stereotype or gender definition here: that Divine Child is within each of us. It is the child Merlin that utters the *Prophecies*, not an elderly male.

Turning to the *Vita*, one of its central themes is the Threefold Death. This is preceded by a scene in which the mad seer is shown a youth in three disguises, both male and female, and predicts three different deaths for this single person. The Youth of Three Disguises is The Fool and The Hanged Man of Tarot imagery; he/she is also found in many folk rituals in which a central person is bisexual or changes sex. This central person also dies and is brought back to life again.

The adult Merlin is then prince among the north Welsh or southern Scots. Here there is a clear role and a male gender. Yet this is when he is weakest, for his situation as ruler, as male, is merely the preamble to a series of devastating changes, of breakdown of personality, of transformation leading to a new level of consciousness and energy. During his disorientation arising from grief and compassion, Merlin reverts to the wilds, merging with the ancient god of nature, Pan, Cernunnos, or the Lord of the Animals. His personal sexuality is replaced by a divine polarity, highly energized, non-human. It is during this phase that we find the connection between the Lord of the Animals and the Lady of Nature, although distorted in the *Vita* by a measure of Christian anti-feminine propaganda.

In a later phase, coming into a relationship between the holism of the planet and living beings within that holism, Merlin again becomes bisexual, or moves into a consciousness of spiritual reality that is no longer gender defined.

If we applied this cycle of changes to Merlin as a woman rather than as a man, we would see that much of it remains true . . . for it is to do with human changes rather than male changes. For example, in the stage of breakdown, leading to the identification with powerful natural forces, it is the physical body that defines (though not inevitably) the manifestation of an inner energy. The male Merlin becomes a man of the wildwood, taking on the image of the Horned God. A female Merlin would be likely to take on the image of the Goddess of Nature – and she can be as savage, powerful and irresistible as her male polarized counterpart.

Polarity is very important in the practical working out of magical and spiritual traditions. Today we are rediscovering the feminine powers and restoring a long overdue balance between men and women. Beyond this revolution and restoration is the next stage, that of polarity and exchanges of energy between men and women equally – which means a rhythmic basis with no superior or inferior roles. The Way of Merlin, even in its varied fragmentary ancient sources, reveals this rhythm, both in human relationships and in those between humans and otherworldly beings, natural forces, and spiritual realization.

TRAPS, PITFALLS AND OBSESSIONS

The story of Merlin and Nimuë, in which the old wizard is seduced and imprisoned by the magical young woman, his student, is a literary fabrication, drawn from orthodox sexist religious propaganda. Yet there may be some value in it, providing we assess it carefully. There are always connections between the levels or harmonics of a myth or legend, even when we are dealing with propaganda overlaid on the original patterns. These connections are valuable when we apply the legend in practice in order to change consciousness, and they often take surprising turns that are not accessible through a literary or historical approach.

The theme of an imprisoned or beguiled Merlin plays little or no part in the primal legends, which tend to emphasize freedom from sexuality and sexual stereotyping. In the *Vita* we find Merlin rejecting his Flower Maiden wife in a confused scene that involves sexual stereotyping and astrological symbolism, and later there appears the important motif of the poisoned apples, in which a scorned ex-lover features. She may be a mask over the original goddess of taking. This female figure poisons apples as a trap, seeking for revenge upon Merlin, but succeeds in driving other men mad. Thus the rejection of a sexual stereotype wife or lover, and the theme of destruction by a feminine power or ex-lover, are loosely connected through the figure of Merlin. Exactly how they are connected is curious, and not what we might expect. The two women are manifestations of two goddesses, or we might say of two aspects of one Goddess. In Celtic legend and religion we find various feminine personae embodying the light and dark forces, the giving and taking powers.

The Flower Maiden is the bright sexual woman-power, the spring power of life-giving. A visualization attuning to her power is found later on in Chapter 13. But this image cannot be fixed into one quality only, for like all other forms it moves around the Wheel of Life and Change, and may rotate at any time into that of the Dark Goddess. The dark power is inherent in the light, and the light power is inherent in the dark. Only through a change of direction and suspension of the Wheel can we encompass and realize this truth within ourselves. The Dark Goddess plays a more significant role in the Mystery of Merlin than the Light Goddess . . . but they are the same Goddess.

This major figure of the Dark Woman or Goddess is also represented as the Queen of Fairyland in Celtic tradition, and a sacred apple tree is dedicated to her. The historical bard and prophet Thomas Rhymer (Thomas of Erceldoune) is associated with initiation into seership in the fairy realm of the Underworld. The fruit of the Underworld apple tree may be poisonous or blessed depending upon ourselves. The variables are our understanding, our sexuality and our relationship to other beings and dimensions of energy. In a very direct sense this legend reminds us that sexual energy and imagery can be either a blessing or a curse within ourselves.

The development of Morgan le Fay and Nimuë in Merlin

literature and legend seems to relate to images of the Dark Goddess, the Fairy Queen. It is undeniable that the original Morgen (in the *Vita*) is a wholly beneficial therapeutic figure, and Nimuë, the seductive student of magic, does not appear at all. So what is the value of this gradual negation of feminine figures, as far as we are concerned today? It clearly cannot lie in orthodox propaganda regarding sex, sin, temptation, weakness in men, and so forth. We should reject this pernicious nonsense altogether.

If we set aside the chronology of characterization, the theme has some interesting inner aspects. It suggests that we may see the Goddess in a mortal lover, and if we do not relate to this power properly, it can be deadly dangerous. This is not a sexist or patriarchal subject, for any woman may see the God in a man, and be in equal danger of misidentification.

The situation is amplified if one partner is talented or skilled in imagery and invocation, and the other is not. Curiously the danger is more likely for the experienced partner (male or female) than for the inexperienced. If the deep power of God or Goddess is brought through an ignorant or wilful person in partnership, it can have shocking effects upon someone attuned to the power through meditation, visualization, or spiritual and magical disciplines. This difficulty only arises, however, if emotional identification takes place – if personal love is confused with divine love.

The possibility of this confusion arises equally for men and women. If we are to find anything of human, emotional or spiritual value in the various tales of Merlin imprisoned by his lover, it may concern this confusion of personal and transpersonal love. Wisdom and experience do not seem to apply to this situation – other than as warnings not to enter into it.

It seems that no amount of wisdom or power can liberate the besotted Merlin from the wiles of young Nimuë. This is, we are told, because she has learned his magic and uses it against him. The same might be said in a reverse situation, in which a handsome youth beguiles a wise experienced woman, and uses her magic against her. While this simplistic scene makes good literature – and good sexist propaganda when it is given a Christian overtone – it is not the full story.

What may occur is that the magic, which is nothing more nor

less than the application of energy and imagery, is routed through the physical and emotional image of the human lover. Here is where wisdom may not prevail, for this flow of energy is a trap that can only be broken rather than released. It is, in its worst potential situation, the inverse of the divine mystery of love. Ideally we may see divinity in a human lover, but this is different to feeling that the God or Goddess can *only* come through that lover.

This entire situation is horribly confused and warped by Christian conditioning, in which love and sex are linked with sin and retribution. Although we pride ourselves on being free of this type of propaganda, the damage runs deep and manifests in many ways. Both suppression and liberation rest upon our human potential for releasing and moving energy through images.

A very frequent version of this is found in the variable transference that occurs during therapy; a negative version is obsession with another person. But these are nothing compared to the location of a divine image and power upon or within a human lover who may or may not be able to mediate and relate to that image fully.

Magical groups of all sorts experience problems with this transference of power; in the old style, sexually repressed, magical orders of the nineteenth and twentieth centuries it was commonplace. People discovered that they were obsessed with one another, left their marriage partners, declared that they were reliving previous incarnations and so forth. This confusion has begun to clear in the modern practice of magic, but still occurs frequently.

The true resolution of this type of inversion is through perfect love. In the Merlin tradition perfect love is represented by the Threefold Death, in which all personal elements, the cycle of the Wheel, cease to turn, and flow in a different direction. In transpersonal or perfect love there can be no confusion between personality and divinity, sexual alignment and god or goddess images. The Hanged Man or Woman is in a state of unconditional love and acceptance.

This is not, however, the same as meekness and acceptance in an old-fashioned religious propagandist sense, or a contrived openness and sharing such as we find in many modern alternative techniques of interaction or meditation.

THE OTHER SACRIFICE

There is another level to this theme, one in which Merlin's imprisonment is a willing sacrifice. If you work with the Merlin tradition for any length of time, you will find resonances of the Threefold Death and the sacred land. We find in some tales that Merlin passes into the land as a redemptive act; his withdrawal into spiritual contemplation is, literally, materialized. The Underworld and the Stellar World are unified through this withdrawal and redemptive self-sacrifice. Merlin can talk to you from anywhere in the sacred land, though his presence is stronger at certain sites, associated with individual Merlins. We will return to this theme in later chapters.

The implication here is of a localized version of the redemptive sacrifice of Christ, which is said to be upon a planetary level. The theme of the Harrowing of Hell is much misunderstood, for it was a typical Underworld journey, such as other redemptive kings and heroes made in the pre-Christian religions. By pre-Christian we should understand, of course, the religions and religious Mysteries contemporary with Christ and with those who developed Christianity for several centuries after Christ's death.

Of these, the legend and Mystery of Orpheus is perhaps the most obvious example predating that of Christ, while the Mystery of Mithras also contained many elements similar to those of Christianity. There is something similar to the miraculous birth and redemptive death of Christ in the Merlin legend, but it is limited in its territory to Britain and parts of Europe. Yet as a process, an interaction between ourselves and the land, it can happen anywhere on the planet, yesterday, today, tomorrow . . . now.

THE APOCALYPSE OF ARIADNE

We live in a time of unweaving. Many people believe in, or long for, the coming of a New Age without the dissolution of the old. The visions of Merlin are indications of the transformation, the apocalypse, that occurs before a new cycle, a New Age, can be manifest.

Astrological themes in the *Prophecies* may refer to the planetary patterns that will occur towards the end of the millennium, and there are several other implications and images in the verses that might be applied to our age. The manifestations, be they stellar, environmental or personal, are forms taken by the unweaving, transitions through which the power passes. We need, upon the Way of Merlin, to be willing to meet this power, the Unweaving, within ourselves. We need also to be aware of it in the land, in the worlds.

Merlin is set upon the spiralling path of liberation and realization by destructive forces. Let us not doubt or hesitate over this, the taking power of the Goddess, the catabolic forces inherent within our being, our holism of consciousness/matter. If they are denied, they will manifest in increasingly exterior forms. The visions of Merlin are classic examples of this breaking-down process, this purifying but terrifying force at work. Let us summarize them briefly:

1. The child prophet is inflamed and inspired by the power of the Red and White Dragons, arising from within the depths of the land. The presence of a corrupt king, determined to sacrifice innocence to greed for power, is the catalyst and circumstance for this arousal of Dragon power. The resulting vision reaches to the end of time. The destruction of Vortigern (the image of The Blasted Tower in the Tarot) is merely one manifestation, one fragment of the holism in which an improper relationship between king and land is broken down prior to the coming of a rightful king. Even the ideal king, Arthur, however, is not fully realized, and is subject to the forces of breaking-down. But that is another story.

2. In Merlin's visions, the Land of Britain, as a real but simultaneous idealized or model environment, is purified. Three springs are transformed by the power of a maiden (see Appendix 3). She is, in herself, transformed through the process. It is a vision of purification, of maturity, and of the forces that flow through the environment and their cycle of potential changes.

3. At the close of the prophetic visions the same process that began with the dragons and the imbalanced king, then manifested environmentally with the Goddess of the Land, is

now revealed upon a stellar scale. At first it seems a chaotic apocalypse, as the signs of order and stability, the planets and houses of the idealized zodiac, begin to move out of their regular order, but as this disruptive and disturbing vision progresses, it passes into increasingly primal states. Beyond the planets, houses and signs, we find the universal Doorkeeper, Janus, the last image of polarity, of turning, of interchange. This entity and power serves the goddess Ariadne.

Ariadne is the Weaver, the Unweaver, who spans the Void. Finally the gate is closed, and existence as we know it ceases to be. Thus Merlin begins his life with a mortal mother and an otherworld father, but his visions reach to the conclusion of all life within the universal parent.

CHAPTER
3

Madness and Holism

A central feature of the Merlin tradition, and of many primal spiritual traditions world-wide, is that of disorientation, of madness. This does not sound too promising to the modern mind – today so much emphasis is laid upon integration, balance and seeking wholeness through a wide range of techniques, therapies and affirmations. And yet we seek such positive ends in the midst of a culture that is, by any definition, self-destructively insane.

The affirmation of a balanced psyche, of spiritual illumination, seems a proper counter-balance to the materialist depravity that we have created in modern civilization. Why do certain primal wisdom traditions, therefore, lay such a strong emphasis upon divine, spirit-inspired and human madness? Ought we not simply to turn away from the inherent madness in our society and find sanity through peaceful meditation and increasing self-knowledge? Is the madness of the shamanistic techniques or of the ancient traditions embodied within such techniques something atavistic, to be avoided, truly unsuitable for the modern man or woman?

The relationship between madness and wholeness, and more specifically between madness and the holism of the land, the planet, and all living beings, is at the very heart of the Way of Merlin. There is an interwoven or harmonically related set of realizations concerning individuality, holism, madness and inner balance amply shown in the Merlin legends.

It is significant that our modern stereotypes of Merlin, as the wise elder, the cosmic brother who channels meaningful messages and so forth, ignore that central theme of Merlin's madness entirely. The stereotypical wise elder is an image of wishful thinking in many ways, for it is the product of our insecurity and longing to revert to dependence upon an outside source for wisdom and strength, rather than experiencing the pain of seeking truth within ourselves.

To approach the harmonic set of realizations described, we might consider them within the context of the Merlin legends, though several other legends, tales and traditional themes could be quoted from widespread traditions.

Briefly, we are told (in the *Vita* and in Welsh and Scottish legends and folklore, with many similar tales found in Irish and Breton sources) that Merlin suffered what might today be called a 'mental breakdown'. Yet it is a breakdown of a very specific sort. We may need to be aware of the difference between such breakdowns as part of spiritual development, and as a phenomenon of a divisive antagonistic culture in which the individual is stressed beyond endurance.

I say 'may' rather than 'must', for almost any breakdown of rigid patterns of consciousness, of life, of personality, has the potential within it for spiritual realization and growth. The Merlin tradition, however, employs some specific methods and images leading to a type of disorientation, of madness, which is a stage upon the way towards a new quality of consciousness. This quality is particularly related to the holism of the land, the planet and all living beings.

From the very outset, Merlin's madness is concerned with the pain of separation and antagonism. His healing and realization eventually come from true unification, understanding of and direct involvement within – rather then intellectual assessment of – the holism of the land, planet, and Four Elements or Universal Powers.

This wisdom teaching is summarized in Figure 3, though it should be emphasized that the illustration is only a set of indications, a key to a pattern that must come alive within our consciousness rather than be looked at upon the printed page.

The madness theme is found in legends of many heroes, holy men, saints, wise women, prophets and magicians. It is also found

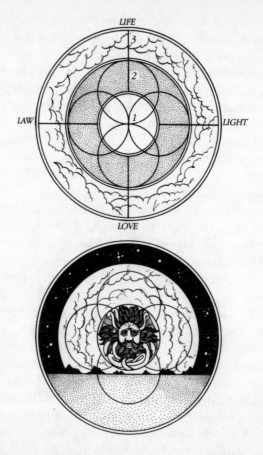

Figure 3: The Creation Vision

The original Four Powers (Life, Light, Love, Law) are uttered from the Void and unified by a Fifth, Being or Spirit. The cycle of energies is expressed as the Four Elements: Air, Fire, Water and Earth. This relative cycle of forces and forms is the Web woven and unwoven by the Goddess Ariadne.

The pattern is reflected through the Three Worlds of the Stars or the Universe, the Sun or Solar System and Planets, and the Moon or Lunar and Sub-lunar World. It finally manifests as the planet Earth, with Four Directions or Zones, Four Winds, Four Rivers and Four Oceans, all unified by a Fifth. The planet is a reflection of the universe, and contains the universe within it.

In the centre of the temperate or harmonizing Zone of Earth is the Gateway to the Otherworld or Underworld, found through entering sacred springs. According to the Merlin tradition (as retold in *The History of the British Kings* and the *Vita Merlini*) this central location is the island of Britain, with the hot springs of Aquae Sulis, Bath, England, presided over by the druidic god-king Bladud. It is also the energetic or spiritual centre of any land or chosen location, any dedicated Sacred Space.

in many folk-tales concerning ordinary men and women led by otherworldly sources or beings towards an altered state of consciousness, often as a physical entry into another dimension or world. The physical nature of the translation into other worlds is important; we tend too frequently nowadays to assume that it is 'all in the imagination'. Yes, it *is* all in the imagination, the imagination that includes your body and can move it physically into other dimensions.

There are several variant forms of inspired or spiritual madness, but it stems essentially from the collapse of our conditioned delusion of separateness. In this sense the primal traditions of the West share certain fundamental ideas with Buddhism, particularly those of Tibetan Buddhism, which merged with the magical or chthonic traditions of Tibet that preceded Buddhism as the main religion of that culture. There is no suggestion here, by the way, that the Merlin tradition is somehow derived from Tibet, only that certain fundamentals concerning transformation are found in the primal traditions of both East and West, as they all refer to the human soul and spirit.

Merlin is first driven mad by grief and compassion. This theme of compassion and sharing of the suffering of others is perhaps the main cause of his entire cycle of transformations that lead towards unity, towards wholeness. It is not a madness derived from intolerable self-centred situations in life, or from forced reduction and degradation of the self. In other words the madness arises from extending awareness beyond oneself, and truly experiencing the suffering of others. It is, in fact, the first step out of the isolated and protected selfdom of the personality into the sea of greater relationship, of potential holism, with other beings.

The individual becomes mad because he or she admits the existence of forces and shares feelings that were previously excluded for self-protection. The removal of self-protection brings inevitable confusion, pain, sorrow and loss of centrality. This initial breakdown is found in most religions and magical traditions through meditation upon the pain and suffering inherent within our world.

This is not to suggest that anyone is obliged to take this path towards transformation. There are other paths. But spiritual truths are found, if we choose to look, reflected in the culture that we have made. We wilfully ignore the essential truth of holism, of the unity of energy and life, suddenly to discover that we are destroying the planet, destroying ourselves. This is as true of one human as it is of a society, or a land, or of the entire Earth.

People entering the transformative traditions, be they spiritual or magical arts, frequently complain that they want to help others, improve the world, change bad situations, and yet are not given the means and power to do so. In the East we find a clear definition of paths that lead toward transformation or enlightenment, one of which is the way of good works, while within the Merlin tradition, we find not only the idea of taking into oneself the pain and suffering of others, but of absorbing the corruption of the land, and through taking it in, transforming it. This is not a spiritual way for those of us who seek to avoid pain at all costs. Many people will be averse to such a way, in which the individual body and soul is a proving ground and crucible for the pain and corruption of the world. Yet this is clearly the outset of the Way of Merlin, consisting of disorientation and madness through grief at the suffering of others.

There is a great difference between outlining this idea as an interpretation of legend, as an intellectual proposition, and experiencing it through altered consciousness. It cannot be overemphasized that the disorientation in the roots of the Tree of Transformation (Figure 2, page 21) is a real, although temporary, imbalance, a breakdown that must come before any new strength, understanding, energy or holistic world-view can grow within us.

The value of a tradition, of any sort, is that it gives us some framework within which to interpret events that happen during the stages of psychic transformation. Without the tradition, without the guiding story, parable or poem, we may lose sight of the way, and linger for far longer than we need in any one stage or state of consciousness. In times of extreme difficulty it is possible to use the tradition and its emblems, its tales, its rhythms, as a life-line. A typical example might be the use of aphorisms or wisdom sayings, such as are well known from the East, and it is interesting to find that the Merlin texts of Geoffrey of Monmouth, particularly the *Vita*, include a range of spiritual aphorisms.

THE TREE OF TRANSFORMATION

The transformations of consciousness defined in the *Vita Merlini* give a clear indication of what might be expected upon the Way of Merlin. In Figure 2 (page 21) we see them shown as a tree, giving an initial guide to our inner changes. This guide also shows stages of willed transformation; in other words, it indicates disciplines and arts that we might use to make specific changes.

Initially these changes are within ourselves, but any stage or art of consciousness-energy can flow to an outer sacred location, just as it can flow inwards through the sacred location within ourselves. The end of the Way is to merge inner and outer states and places inseparably, an end quite different from seeking to escape into paradise or withdrawing from the world. Although the elder Merlin of the *Vita* withdraws into spiritual contemplation, he does not entirely abandon the material world to do so. Indeed, we know from various Merlin legends that he becomes one with the land.

When we first approach the Tree of Transformation, it shows the apparently linear progression of Merlin's life experiences. We might take this sequence of powerful changes, as epitomized in the Merlin legend, and consider it as a model of the stages of transformation leading to enlightenment. Apparently linear models of consciousness should be approached with an open mind, however, if not with caution, for consciousness cannot be a set of rigid hierarchies.

Let us explore this further, for the holism of our own lives is never a rigid progression. Any model of spiritual arts or changes of consciousness cannot be confined to a linear hierarchy or set of graded changes or levels. If it were so confined it could not apply to human life, as it would be contrived or artificial, fitting an intellectual obsession rather than representing living energies.

Our lifespan, or perhaps we should say 'life-spin', is often represented as a straight line from cradle to grave. We talk about our 'progress through life', as if the human being is somehow separate from life itself yet still living an isolated antagonistic existence. This linear (Cartesian) approach to being is inherent in the materialism that is destroying our planet . . . destroying ourselves.

The Merlin legends show a life of deep change and often of turmoil, progressing around the Wheel of the Seasons (Figure 1, page 18). This Wheel is also the compass of Sacred Space, with the Four Planetary Directions (East, South, West, North), the stars Above, the depths Below and living being Within. Our life spins around the mysterious centre of being Within in a sequence of circles or spirals. Awareness is a sphere of relative perceptions.

The straight line or vertical graph is merely a convenient ploy to show a limited version of the life-spin upon the printed page. When we think of a tree, we tend to concentrate upon its vertical appearance above the earth, only occasionally remembering that it has roots below. And there is more still, for the seed upon its branch tips is, both literally and paradoxically, the source of its crown, trunk and roots. The tree is a circular being.

We might next consider that the cycle of the seasons is a rotation of energy within the tree, presenting its shape, colour, vibrancy or dormancy according to the phases of the cycle. This cycle of energies of the tree is stimulated by and harmonized within the turning cycle of the planet as it rotates the tree towards and away from the sun. The planet itself is also rotating in orbit around the sun, which in turn is moving around the galactic centre. Thus the life of a tree is a sphere of interwoven energies and movement. So is the life of a man or woman.

Upon the tree of Merlin's life, we see at first a simple progression from grief or guilt in the roots towards enlightenment through spiritual contemplation at the crown. Many powerful changes occur on the way, all of which are well described by episodes in Merlin's own life. A teaching regarding changes of consciousness and energy was embodied in the legend of Merlin's own development: a model life.

We must remember that a life, be it a tree, a human, a planet or a star, is an interweaving of energies in a relative sphere. The traditional way of coming to understand this seemingly difficult concept is simply to consider your own awareness. Where is it, and to where does it extend? Awareness extends to infinity in a spherical field about us. Think of your body, and the potential of awareness and perception in all directions around and about you . . . the result is a sphere with no concrete limits. Eyesight has a variable limit, depending upon circumstances as does hearing, and both have a general ultimate range for humanity. Touch and smell have smaller fields of limitation, but are often more powerful in their immediate effect upon the organism. Yet the imagination and the potential of thought have no definable limits.

Between the ultimate unlimited force of imagination and the receptive sense of touch we have a holism of energies and senses. Some are more subtle or dormant then others. The Way of Merlin defines the zones of this holism as a Fivefold Pattern, found in the universe, the solar system, the planet, the land, and the human being. (See Figure 3, page 54.)

Upon the Tree of Transformation the changes have a harmonic relationship as well as a superficially linear one. In the centre of the tree, half-way between roots and crown, we find two zones connected to prophecy. These are defined as prevision and cosmic vision. The two are interchangeable. We also find this harmonic pattern of interrelationship between the other zones of transformation:

1. Prevision/Cosmic Vision
2. Curative Transformation/Sexual Liberation
3. Liberation from Inner Powers/Disorientation
4. Spiritual Contemplation/Compassion
5. Grief and Guilt/Enlightenment.

CHAPTER
4

My Own Meeting
with Merlin

We are now approaching the second part of *The Way of Merlin* in which basic history of sources and theory gives place to practice. To mark this threshold, I should describe my own encounter with Merlin, which came as a complete surprise, and with no preparation or seeking or need on my part.

Before giving any details, I should say most of my encounters of this sort have been spontaneous and generally reluctant. I am not one of the increasing number of people who seek inner or spirit contact, and have never sought connection with glamorous or so-called 'famous' figures from the past, from myth or from legend.

In an age when there are many people claiming to have met Merlin and other beings, out of a range of various known and unknown metaphysical or spiritual contacts, when there are humans only too willing to receive messages or even commands from them, I regard anything of this sort with caution and skepticism. My own experiences are not exempt from this attitude of skepticism, and I do not revel in channelling, innerworld contact, spirit guides and the like.

As a rule, such popularized communications are fraught with nonsense and trivia, and the current craze for channelling is little better than an excuse for relinquishing responsibility. If a statement is 'channelled' it cannot be challenged, and the medium or channel cannot be held to account if it is wrong or simply stupid. There are always good exceptions to this rule, of course. I would not wish churlishly to dismiss all mediumistic or channelled communications, but merely to suggest that more common sense be applied to them.

I have come to accept only inevitable and, for me, inarguable contacts, and those only after years of careful thought and regular effort at discrimination. I feel that this is the most sound attitude to take to the protean mass of innerworld contact that can arise from natural sensitivity or specialized techniques. After all, this is how we screen our contacts in outer life, where we do not simply accept anyone, anything and everything that we bump into. Why should the inner world of consciousness or the realms of ancestors, spirits, or gods and goddesses be treated any differently? At the 1990 Merlin Conference in England someone told me a delightful American catch-phrase: 'Just because they're dead don't mean that they're smart!'

As I have mentioned elsewhere, most of the modern material that claims to relate to Merlin seems connected to the Merlin of Walt Disney rather than to any initiatory or prophetic tradition from northwestern Europe. It seems obvious that whatever we absorb into our imagination tends to regenerate itself as clothing, so to speak, for inner realization and communications. This is precisely why magical arts demand the expenditure of so much time and effort on detailed visualization of specific images. Eventually the images come alive and work for us as aids towards changes of consciousness.

None of this image building, as far as I can see, is identical to the specific contacts that are found at ancient sites. Contacts made in sacred places and through tapping into long established traditions can come alive even when their traditions have been disrupted or partly forgotten.

In my own experience of contacts from enduring traditions or at sacred sites, I have frequently found that the contact does not appear according to one's conditioning . . . and can sometimes be very far removed from it. This individuality of appearance or presence is important, for it shows that something is occurring that is not entirely confined to the imaginative stock of the seer or recipient.

While I tend to reject grave elders in pointed hats covered with stars as stereotypes, as false images of a patriarchal unhistorical non-existent Merlin, it could be argued that I would find inner contacts, whether Merlin or others, in a familiar guise more suited to my own studies. Merlin might appear as a bard or Druid, for example, or in a Celtic guise from the Dark Ages. He might appear as Lord of the Animals (shown as The Guardian in *The Merlin Tarot*), or as The Hermit. He might also appear as the boy Merlin who uttered the *Prophecies* to King Vortigern.

When I contacted a being claiming to be Merlin, none of these or similar forms presented themselves to my faculties. Indeed, the person that appeared to me was so unlike any of the images I might have romantically or academically chosen that I was rather taken aback. Perhaps the best modern image of Merlin that I have seen in a work of art is 'Merlin in his Shamanistic Guise' by Alan Lee, the original drawn in pencil on vellum. But my own Merlin contact did not look like this image either.

My initial encounter with Merlin was in 1982 as a result of a trip to Dinas Emrys, an isolated hilltop site in north Wales. Before this visit I had read *The Prophecies of Merlin* in the modern Penguin translation by Lewis Thorpe, but had not yet read the *Vita Merlini*. Indeed, I was deliberately averse to anything to do with Merlin because of the patriarchal male-superior stereotypes so frequently attached to his name, although around the time of my trip to Dinas Emrys I had begun to realize that much more lay behind the Merlin tradition than any modern stereotype. I had begun to seek a context and meaning for those parts of *The History of Kings of Britain* that contained mention of Merlin, and of course, for the separate text of the *Prophecies* embedded within the larger book.

I knew that the figure of Merlin had played an important role in certain inner contacts for Western esotericists or magicians of an earlier generation, including members of Dion Fortune's group, but I had no idea what form that contact took. My own teacher, from whom I had parted company some 10 years before my trip to north Wales, never mentioned Merlin as far as I remember, and was not involved in this type of tradition.

So there was little background, instruction, imagery, or even expectation for me to draw upon. I agreed to join the trip as it was part of a series of casual visits to isolated sites with a group of acquaintances who had realized that it was easier, and less expensive, to rent a van together than to go separately. We made several journeys of this sort in Wales and southwest England at this time.

My impressions of Dinas Emrys were surprising, as I had not expected much. I knew that it was the site that local legend and traditional history associated with King Vortigern's tower, and that there was a ruined structure on the summit, with earlier signs of settlement dating to the Dark Ages. [12] The name of the site means Merlin's Hill, Emrys being a contraction, perhaps, of the Latin name Ambrosius often attached to Merlin.

After a long tiring journey the group left the van, and began to climb Dinas Emrys. The first thing I noticed was that we were climbing a long spine of white quartz-bearing rock, with crystalline areas showing clearly through the undergrowth; it felt as if I were climbing the spine of an animal. When we reached the summit there was a clear view over the surrounding country, which must have played a part in the use of the site as a Dark Age settlement. It also provided the location for the military Norman-period tower that folklore wrongly attributes to King Vortigern.

The flat area at the top of the hill was wet and marshy, reinforcing the legend that the tower had fallen nightly because of the pool and cave hidden below it in the hill, a pool in which two dragons dwelt. The wet area is, according to archaeologists, the remains of a water collection cistern. Just beyond this marsh a large thorn tree grows, of the kind traditionally associated with Merlin and with the Dark Goddess. It seemed to me that the water seeped from a tiny spring or springs beneath this tree.

Our small group spread out to examine various areas of the hill, and after pausing to meditate briefly, just as I was about to leave the marsh and thorn tree, I had the powerful feeling of being watched by someone hiding behind the tree. I went around the tree, but there was no one there. As I was about to follow my friends to the further side of the hill, a man stepped out of the tree. There is no other way to describe this – it was not a faint impression or a spiritual vision, not a meditational intimation, but a man stepping out of the tree to stand before me.

He was short and broad, with a bald head and rounded face, aged perhaps 50 years or so, with unshaven cheeks and chin, but no full beard. He wore a plain brown robe tied with a dirty rope, and though he did not have a tonsure, looked at first glance rather like a scruffy monk. His build was very powerful, with wide short hands and thick forearms; his manner was demanding and stern.

He looked at me and said, without any preamble, 'I am Merlin. You will be my pupil.' This was a flat statement that seemed to declare an inevitable established fact; it was not an introduction or a suggestion.

I was astonished, and also resentful of what I took to be his domineering attitude. My opinion on this subject was to change, however, when I later grasped that he had no 'attitude' towards me. I replied that I would definitely not be his pupil. He said again, 'I am Merlin. You will be my pupil,' and again I rejected this forceful statement. It did not occur to me at the time that this was not a potential command, but a realized prophecy.

It was as if no one else was present, and though there must have been other people close to hand, I could see only this odd demanding man standing directly before me with such intense physical presence. A third time he stated I was to be his pupil, and on my third denial I added, 'Those ways are not suitable to our times. I cannot be an accepting pupil, that is not the way for me.'

His response suddenly changed and he almost smiled, looking at me as if seeing me for the first time. 'Very well,' he replied 'Perhaps we can co-operate on something.' And he vanished. It was as if something had snapped, and I returned to the same hilltop and tree, but back with my group of friends. As we went back down the hill I found a small piece of quartz rock lying on the spine of the ridge, and took it with me.

I wrote a detailed personal diary account of the event, which I have since lost. Some time passed, and my immediate memory of this strange experience faded. But within a year I was working on *The Prophecies of Merlin* for my edition now published by Penguin Arkana, and whenever I worked on the old text I felt the presence of this Welsh Merlin contact. The following year I worked on *The Mystic Life of Merlin*, also published by Penguin Arkana, which interprets the medieval *Vita Merlini* of Geoffrey of Monmouth. And by 1986 I had designed the cards and written the book for *The Merlin Tarot*, again with a great range of innerworld contact and elucidation. So perhaps we did co-operate on something.

My understanding or interpretation of this curious sequence of events is that my meeting was with *a* Merlin, and that no one has ever met *the* Merlin.

The name 'Merlin' was a generic title applied to a certain type of wild prophet or seer, inspired by the power of the Goddess of the Land (known in Ireland as 'Sovereignty'), by the Goddess of Poetic Inspiration (known as Brigid or Minerva) and by the Great Weaver Goddess (known as Ariadne). I have discussed already the rather obvious fact that this type of seer could equally well have been a seeress, though some of the inner energies, images and polarities would have differed. They would differ today between men and women, as these polarities are fundamental and not cultural. The material handed down to us, patriarchal as it may seem, is still descended from a Goddess culture, and from a holistic view of the universe in which a Goddess and not a God is the true divine manifestation. So in this brief summary of who or what Merlin was, and the three levels or modes of awareness relating to three goddesses, I do not hesitate to use the traditional male example.

I would suggest (without so-called hard evidence) that there is a deep level of transpersonal relationship between men and women implicit in the perennial traditions of the West. It is not reported fully in the ancestral texts, merely hinted at or obscured beyond mere intellectual recovery. The means of recovery of this further level are in meditation, visualization and spiritual intuition concerning the deeper energy exchanges within a holism, an environment, an interaction between life forms, man and woman, human and divine.

In the first level of inspiration as described above, the seer is driven mad and reverts to an existence attuned to nature, to the animals, taking on the form of the Lord of the Animals (Cernunnos or Pan), a form in which he appears at the height of his frenzy. In the second level of inspiration the seer gains an insight into the workings of the Wheel of Life and the Four Elements, and becomes aware of goddess-inspiration and the Otherworld. He is given the means and vehicle of reconstruction by an inspiring and enabling goddess. In the third level the seer attunes to universal consciousness, to the stellar tides and patterns, and uses the poetic holistic tradition that he has absorbed in his second level of awareness to embody and report what he experiences. The three goddesses interact and enable through the three levels or modes, yet they are one.

Considering Merlin as set out by Geoffrey of Monmouth, we find the traditional prophecies uttered by a boy or youth, the mad wild man occurring in adulthood, and the initiatory or holistic tradition defined in old age. These are the three ages or phases of a life-cycle, corresponding to the three octaves or major serials of the Wheel, and to the Three Worlds: Lunar, Solar and Stellar. (Such harmonic reflections are shown in several of our Figures here.)

So as Merlin is a title and not the proper name of a specific individual, there may have been more than one Merlin. In fact there is an interesting historical argument that seems to prove the existence of two men with the title Merlin during the Dark Ages. Thus there is an important difference between an *actual* Merlin, by which we mean a seer with a human origin, and an *archetypical* Merlin, who is an image embodying certain modes of consciousness and patterns of energy. This archetypical Merlin is closely related to a god, being the British equivalent of Apollo.

In either case, human or archetypical, the true Merlin tradition is different in many ways from the literary stereotype of Merlin as popularly understood today. The major differences are not merely of age or attitude, but of relationship to the feminine, to the Goddess. The original Merlin, boy, man, or elder, served the Triple Goddess; the propagandized image of Merlin has little or nothing to do with Her, and is supposedly deluded into witlessness by a conniving young woman.

So who or what did I meet upon the top of Dinas Emrys? I made a contact, across time, or more accurately in a state of timelessness, with a Merlin, perhaps the one associated with Dinas Emrys in Welsh tradition. He, also in a state of timelessness, met me (in his so-called 'future') and established a link between us . . . This is how prophetic traditions work.

I do not think, for example, that I was conversing with a phantom or an echo. The conversation was with a living person, although one of intense energy and a mental attitude very different to my own. It was not an encounter with an image, an archetype, in the sense that such images are used in visualization. Yet I know from experience that such archetypes, god and goddess forms, often overlay or indwell actual humans. It is possible to make a working distinction between the contact I had on Dinas

Emrys and the visualization or metaphysical presence of Merlin in other circumstances, such as the ceremony in Chapter 11 or the visualization in Chapter 10.

In the second part of this book we will work with several ways of making inner contacts, in the form of people, animals and plants. These are an essential aspect of the Mystery of Merlin. Before we do so, however, we must affirm a Sacred Space within which these entities and ourselves can interact.

PART 2
Techniques and Examples

The Gift

I sit upon a high place
On hard rock.
I look upon a land,
Hear ring of broken bells
Song of flown bird,
Anger of dead place,
Murmur of lost people.

No mere love can ease them,
No drug appease their pain,
No sleep heal such wounds.

Not I with my sight
Or harp of hands,
Not plucking strings
Not singing back daylight,
Nor I in the broken tree
The empty nut
Star-clouded
On the drawing waiting height.

Nor you, a single child,
Nor any child of blood
Can open terror's eye,
Pluck forth the root,
Then stem the deep-born giant of the flood.
Up stone and under reach
In earth the warm veins leach
Out dark gold from waiting suns
Into web-ways for your gift:

Friend's hand alone shall shape
The drowsy stone,
Becoming joy to heal.
Distant is the time of which I speak,

Open is the heart on that wild day
To all pain, all voices of the weak,
All victims of the Wheel.

Yet distant is come close
Upon this hilltop chair;
There is no moment of unwoven space
I may not touch,
No measure of unspiralled time
You may not share.

R.J. Stewart, 29 September 1983.

CHAPTER
5
Sacred Space

Sacred Space is space enlivened by consciousness. Let us be in no doubt that all space is sacred, all being. Yet if humans dedicate and define a zone, a location, something remarkable happens within that defined sphere of consciousness and energy. The space talks back. Eventually we have a dialogue with the Sacred Space: the seer and seeress communing with the land. This is the Earth and Lunar World of the Three Worlds shown in Figure 4.

Two octaves or transformations of this communion and communication are accessible, that of the Solar World, and that of the Stellar World. The Way of Merlin passes directly from the Earth to the Stellar World, from the sacred land to the vision and awareness of the Weaver Goddess. This is not a rigid transition, nor one that we are all likely to experience. The Way is flexible, variable, and works according to your own intuitions and needs. The simple basics are offered by the tradition, and it is up to us to redefine and energize such patterns for ourselves in a modern context.

The Way of Merlin is essentially a tradition in which a human being, or a group of humans, enables the land to talk to and through themselves. The land – any immediate locality enlivened by consciousness and energy flowing out from within ourselves – is attuned to the Six Directions. These are East, South, West and North, Above and Below.

The Seventh Direction is Within: within ourselves. This is the one Direction that cannot be conscious in the land, for within each human being is the ultimate spiritual seed that brings the land to full consciousness.

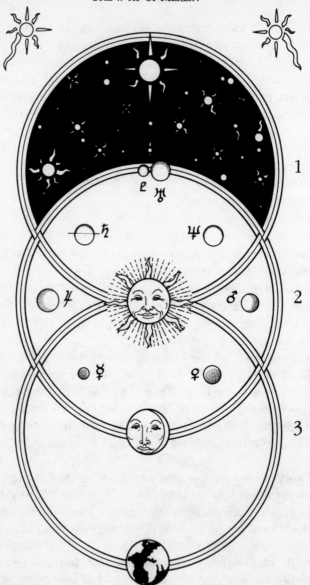

Figure 4: The Three Worlds

The Three Worlds of Stars, Sun, and Moon (including the planet Earth) are octaves of creation and consciousness. They may be understood as rising out of one another, or as three concentric spheres. The transformative process and potentially prophetic vision of Merlin is inspired in any man or woman through relating to Earth-energies, for the power of the stars is inherent within the depths of the Earth.

The protean awareness of the land becomes individualized, so to speak, through a conscious seeding of human energy, human awareness. This was a great spiritual and magical mystery known to the ancient world and now almost lost to us. The distinct characters, gods and goddesses, of localities, lands, continents and finally the planet, all make up the entity of Mother Earth. Within the heart of the planet are found the stars – an inversion of our usual linear consciousness that suggests that the stellar universe is 'out there'.

At any turning of the spiral around the Wheel of Life, a human can instantaneously pass through all forms within the holism of the world or worlds. Any location, any being, plant, animal, tree, deity or human can lead to unified awareness. This unification is represented by the Stellar World that encompasses all others, the web of Ariadne, the Weaver Goddess.

The Merlin tradition is frequently concerned with the alignment and purification of a corrupted land, and some powerful visions in the *Prophecies* define this process for us. (These are quoted in Appendix 3.)

In the *Vita* we find the equivalent purification and transformation working through the human mind and soul, the psyche of Merlin. He is the Fool or Dancer, The Hanged Man of Tarot imagery, who eventually cuts across the cycle of the Wheel of Life, and is both liberated and returned or reflected through the Three Worlds of the Moon, Sun and Stars.

The most obvious Sacred Space is your own body, the manifestation of all that you are. When this is aligned and attuned to a dedicated zone or physical location, the attuned entities (yourself and the Sacred Space) can interact.

This may sounds horribly complex in theory, but is simple, even simplistic in practice. It derives from the fact that we stand upright upon the surface of the land. Our heads point to the stars, while our feet touch the Earth. This is shown in Figure 5.

The Wheel of Life (Figure 1, page 18) includes the Four Elements, Four Seasons, Four Directions, and four life phases of Birth, Adulthood, Maturity and Age. It is a pattern of relativity, showing connections, holism, inherent within entities and qualities that are seemingly separated by our materialist

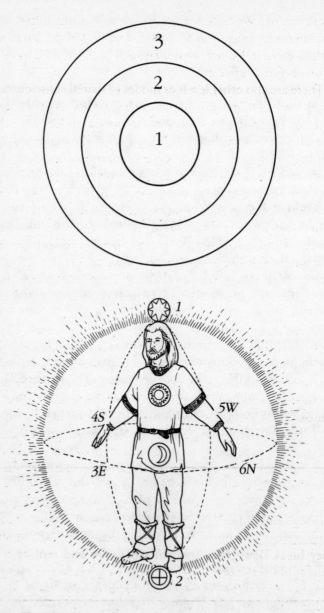

Figure 5: The Directions
Sacred Space is defined by the relationship between our body, our consciousness, and the land. Traditionally the Directions are mirrored in any location, land, human body, in the planetary body, and in the movement of the stars and planets.

conditioning. We have within us, however, a vast inheritance of consciousness from our ancestors, reaching right back to the earliest dawn of human awareness, and back before that to other dawns before humanity.

There are also other levels or modes of shared consciousness by which we should understand exchanges of energy between entities. Organic and inorganic life-forms of many kinds can interact consciously with us. Many beings in primal magic and spiritual disciplines are not of physical dimensions, and the old world-view made no separation between material and immaterial, physical and non-physical beings. Many living creatures, organic and inorganic, exist in more than one dimension, in more than one of the Three Worlds. Each of the Three Worlds has within itself many dimensions, many reflections. The Creation Vision (see Appendix 2 and Figure 3, page 54) is a description of resonance, interaction and connection through the worlds and dimensions of universal Sacred Space.

The collective level of human consciousness, represented by the presence of our ancestors in the Underworld, is deeply attuned to the flow of seasons, stars, land and planet energies. We are separated from this today, yet it still lives within us. We may, if we choose, make an intentional bridge between this ancestral consciousness and the individual and modern materialist consciousness. This should only be done if we fully understand our reasons for doing so; the Merlin tradition advises that humanity and the planet are one, that the planet and the solar system are one, that the solar system and the stars are one. Within the Way of Merlin this unity is our 'reason' for inner realignment.

Bridge-building, transforming, realignment, shape-changing, ferrying, regeneration – these are key ideas in the Way of Merlin. They break down false inflated separation and replace it with painful but ultimately perfect unity. The decision to make such bridges, transitions, changes of shape is your own, and the tradition merely offers pointers upon the Way.

If we work with the definition of Sacred Space and the Four Quarters, all of which are well described in the Creation Vision, we change and define our own vital energies, empowering and clarifying the Four Elements within ourselves. Usually the

Elements are active in conditioned and habitual patterns within us – some Elements may be highly active, while others are quiescent, or even blocked or inaccessible. By working with the Four Quarters in meditation and visualization, we can bring about a balance of the Elements within us. This awakening and empowering is greatly helped by defining and dedicating a Sacred Space.

EXAMPLES OF SACRED SPACE

Churches and temples are good examples of special structures, Sacred Space made materially evident for all to see, tapping into both physical and metaphysical energies. Indeed, the model of the Four Quarters, Above and Below, is epitomized in the great abbeys of the Christian era, aligned to Elemental, solar and planetary directions. Ancient temples were also aligned to certain stars, the rising and setting sun, and the energies of the sacred land.

The Way of Merlin is not a tradition that uses great religious buildings, and essentially it focuses upon small localized areas and upon individuals or small groups. Throughout the old Merlin sources we find a continuing criticism of dogma, political religion and worldly or materialist concerns, and to balance this a devotion to nature, to the sacred land, and to the feminine forces of the universe. So although temples and churches are classic examples of Sacred Space, they may not be suitable for something as primal as the Mystery of Merlin and Ariadne. The judgement or intuition in this matter is essentially your own. It will come from experiment and with practice. The Way of Merlin is often a solitary way, though many non-human companions are found upon it.

There is a good rule that helps us through early work with this definition of Sacred Space: 'Make it simple.'

The only essentials are the Four Directions of East, South, West and North. Use a pocket compass to find out where they are, for they relate to the planetary magnetic fields, and to the relative positions of the moon, sun, stars and the Earth. If East is before you, all other directions are set out accordingly. If you are working in the southern hemisphere you will probably need to reverse or exchange attributes to suit your planetary position.

In a primal world-view we find East, Spring, Air, before us; South, Summer, Fire, to our right; West, Autumn, Water, behind us; and North, Winter, Earth, to our left. Above are the stars (including the sun and planets) and Below is the Earth, containing the Underworld or Otherworld. Figure 5 shows this in relationship to the Three Worlds or octaves of consciousness, and the human body which mirrors these within itself.

BRINGING SACRED SPACE TO LIFE

To bring this simple model to life is not as difficult as might be thought, for it is inherent in our very nature, our structure, our consciousness, our humanity, our land, our planet, our solar system. It is about relativity, a relativity unified and temporally defined (i.e. through the spirals of time) by consciousness. When this realization comes to Merlin, he is cured of madness, a cure that is both stimulated and confirmed by his drinking from a pure spring that rises out of the land.

Let us consider the basics of a training programme that can be worked regularly and rhythmically to attune the Directions both in ourselves and in a chosen location. The key idea here is rhythm, a regular fourfold pattern-making around the Circle. The rhythmic fourfold cycle is unified by the meditations on Above, Below and Within.

1. Begin with Silence (see the exercise on page 127).

2. Out of Silence be aware of your essential Being. This is the directionless Direction of Within.

3. Be aware of the East. It is before you. It is filled with the energies of Spring, of morning. It ushers in the vital power of the Element of Air, clean, fresh, renewing, invigorating, healing and enlivening. All beginnings, all rapid potential energizing forces commence in this Direction. It is the Direction where the sun rises over the horizon.

This type of meditation and visualization is often helped by imagining a door in the Direction that you are working. You may open and close the door at will. When you open it the energies associated with that Direction pour through it; when you close the door they reduce in level, but may remain present. Once a space has been defined it retains a raised level of energy; this is the 'atmosphere' felt in meditation rooms, temples, churches and sacred sites the world over. Once Sacred Space and the Elements have been aligned within ourselves, the same raised energy remains, even when our inner doors are formally closed and we seem absorbed by outer activity.

Eventually we may be conscious and active with the Quarters fully open in ourselves, but this is a rare state to be in, and in any mystical or transformative work, it is essential to be self-critical. The Way of Merlin is very strict in this respect, for it repeatedly breaks down the ego, the false self that aggrandizes and declares itself to be the owner of power, the enlightened and wonderful, the stereotype king, queen, wise man or woman.

4. Next we work with the South. This should be on the day following the East if you use a daily cycle. Wherever you sit or stand is the centre of Sacred Space, of the circle or sphere of the Universe. You begin by briefly opening the East as before, then turn to face South. The opening process is repeated for this Quarter, using the attributes shown in Figure 1 (page 18).

5. Next we work with the West, briefly opening East and South first, then turning to face West and opening that Direction.

6. Then we work with the North as before. It is helpful briefly to open every Quarter, whatever your main intention for a Direction. The Elemental cycle takes four days, one for each Quarter.

7. After opening each Quarter as before, meditate upon the divine stars Above and the planet Earth Below. This should be the fifth day of the cycle. Conclude by attuning to your essential Being, which is within you. If you wish, a separate day can be devoted to the communion with the divine Being within. This is done through Silence.

So now we have a very simple working pattern, turning around a circle of the Directions, defining and realizing the energy associated with each Direction. You may alternate between working this pattern in yourself, which is to say feeling the energies in your own energy field, and defining Sacred Space, which is to say using a room or a chosen location.

In the Way of Merlin the finding of a sacred spring or tree is another essential task, a powerful communion. These aspects are dealt with shortly. It does not matter which order you work in; you might work with the Cycle of Directions for some time before you decide to find a spring or tree, or you might prefer to find these entities immediately. It is essentially a matter for your own intuition.

The Creation Vision is a powerful holistic image, and after some work with the cycle of the Directions and Elements, the implications and energy of Figures such as 1, 3 and 5 (pages 18, 54 and 76) will change for you. At first it may all seem an assembly, a retrospective recreation of the Creation Vision old text quoted in the Appendix, but after some meditation and visualization, it will come alive. Once you have worked with the Images and People, using visualizations or dramatic enactment as suggested in our later chapters, the flat pattern on the paper page will become a merest shadow of the reality. Such patterns, glyphs or mandalas should never be restricted. They are not merely 'symbols', but are living representations of a reality that we have within us. The glyph does not simply map the reality, it changes our perception of it.

see p. 192

DANCING THE MYSTERY

The Mystery of Merlin is full of movement. We may interpret this movement in two possible ways: it might be the compulsion of a soul travelling around the Wheel of Life, unable to pause, rest, or find centrality, find peace; or it might be the essence of universal motion, the dance of the Four Elements that rotate and cause the Wheel, defining Sacred Space. If we learn how to use our compulsive movement creatively, it becomes attuned to the flow of the Elements. Key passages for this sense of relationship, from the natural world to the supernatural, are found in the *Prophecies* and *Vita*. Gaelic seers were still perpetuating a teaching of this sort, which we would nowadays call holistic, in the seventeenth century, as reported by the Reverend Robert Kirk in his *Secret Commonwealth*.[13]

In the medieval Merlin legends we find that the prophet is constantly moving, travelling between city and wilderness, love and isolation, pain and joy, around and around the Wheel of the Seasons. He runs with the wild herds, and climbs to the highest hilltops to view the stars. Many parallel legends of saints and holy men involve the image of incessant motion. Celtic saints, for example, were renowned for leaping. This is not an eccentricity, but a traditional way of describing the spiritual essence of movement. Sacred dance is hardly known today in the West, though, having been ruthlessly suppressed.

The Merlin tradition gives some clear indications of a specific pattern of movement within nature, enhanced within Sacred Space. This pattern can be directly enacted as dance or ceremony. It initially involves the cycle of the Elements, but after this cycle is energized and realized, it changes. The change of direction generates a profound change of energy.

This dance pattern is not confined to the Mystery of Merlin, and is more truly an aspect of the energies inherent in the power of Ariadne, the Weaver Goddess. In the Way of Merlin it is given form as the Threefold Death, the 'Z' sign (see Figure 6). The key image for the Threefold Death is The Hanged Man of the Tarot, who, when he is reversed, becomes The Dancer. The description of The Hanged Man connected to Merlin comes from the twelfth-century *Vita*, which predates the earliest known Renaissance Tarot cards by at least 300 years.

Let us explore this pattern further, and examine some ways in which it might be brought out as actual movement, dance, in group or individual work. The most direct summary follows:

Sacred Space is dedicated and defined by the Six Directions (East, South, West, North, Above, Below) and energized by the Four Elements (Air, Fire, Water, Earth). The Elements and all associated attributes (see Figure 1) are set into motion by rotating sun-wise, from East to South to West to North and back to East. This rotation is the primal cycle of the Wheel.

The simplest way of doing this is to circle the dedicated physical space, recognizing or declaring each Quarter as you pass through it. This simple movement is a conscious mirroring or recreation of the primal World. By attuning Space in this way we bring the Elemental energies that underpin all creation into a conscious

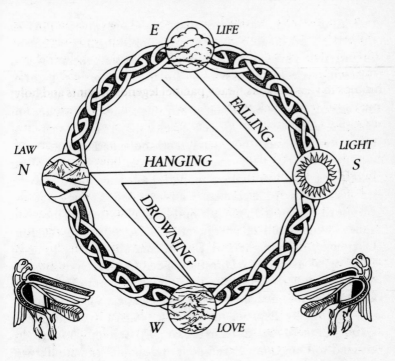

Figure 6: The 'Z' Sign or Lightning Flash
The serpentine or 'Z' sign is an energy pattern that cuts across the cycle of the Four Elements, suspending all turning of the Wheel of Life and Change. In the Merlin tradition it is associated with the Threefold Death, a theme which originated the Tarot image of The Hanged Man.

relationship with ourselves and, more subtly, energize the physical environment by acknowledging its inherent living powers. The inherent view of the Way of Merlin is that consciousness and energy are one: you and the land are one Being.

In practical work, if we define Sacred Space and the Directions, and work within that Space in acceptance and response to its inherent consciousness and energy, then remarkable results arise. The consciousness/energy process is one of mutual resonance: we benefit from its effect, as does the environment. We discover that the environment has octaves, and the sacred land becomes the Sacred Being, the universe. A cycling pattern of movement around the Circle is a powerful way of building this relationship.

Once the cycle of energy is well established and generating

increasing power, variations may be made in the circular movement. Such variations act, in a simple manner, as energy circuits that cut across or through the basic generating and dissolving cycle. Religious symbols and mandalas or glyphs are not merely subjects for meditation, they are ground plans for sacred movement. This is a 'hidden' truth in the structure of ancient temples and worship places: their shape is a shape of energy/consciousness, not merely a symbolic declaration.

Christian churches are aligned according to the Four Directions, usually with the altar in the East. This cruciform shape was used in sacred architecture and dance long before it was employed in Christian church building. Nevertheless the great abbeys were vessels of energy, attuned according to the Four Directions, the Height and Depth, and the central locus or Crossing, where the Four Directions meet. In pagan and Christian worship, the sacred centre was the original altar position. In early Christianity four archangels were located at each Quarter of the church (usually Raphael in the East, Michael in the South, Gabriel in the West, Auriel in the North). Certain saints are also attuned to Directions. Pagan gods and goddesses were likewise associated, in the older religions, with Directions, Seasons, and Elements.

The key pattern inherent in the Mystery of Merlin is that of the 'Z' sign of Threefold Death (Figure 6). The Threefold Death is the ritual associated with sacrificial kings, saviours and self sacrifice generally. If you would find yourself, lose yourself in the Threefold Death, dissolve yourself in the perfect dance. The Threefold Death consists of Falling, Hanging and Drowning (see Appendix 4). This pattern contains within it the following mystical concepts:

(a) Free falling as spiritual Life through Air or originative Being with no intent, temporary identity, or motive.

(b) Hanging upside-down in perfect Balance between the polarities of Light and Law, Fire and Earth, incandescent energy and materialized energy. The inversion is that of spirit and matter.

(c) Drowning in the Water of perfect Love.

These are deep concepts for meditation and contemplation, spiritual powers that transform the soul. Yet we may approach them directly through the body, for the inversion of spirit and matter enables the awakening of spiritual force within form, through the direct experience that they are one, and that separation is a delusion. This delusion is generated by our acceptance of the Wheel as a rigid or unopened circle, when it is, in truth, an open spiral.

In a very simple but powerful dance pattern, we may turn around the circle, building the rhythm and pattern of the Four Elements. When this rotation is well established, the dancers suddenly move East, South, North, West. From this 'Z' movement or Lightning Flash or Serpentine figure, we may return to circling, or we may pause for inner stillness in response to the altered energy pattern. The place of power is the West, within the power of Water and universal Love.

This much is the basic pattern, which can be enacted by one individual, or by a group. The physical movement is essential, and the transformative power does not awaken fully without it. It may be done as a dance to drumming and music, or as a simple processional movement. Traditionally it is accompanied by spinning and leaping. Many ritual dances from folk tradition, particularly those preserving death and resurrection symbolism, use this type of pattern.

The same Mystery is found in the 'Hymn of Jesus', a primal Christian dance ceremony that is reputed to be handed down from the source, the direct oral teachings of Jesus to his group of followers. (This is quoted in Appendix 5.)

In the Way of Merlin several variations are possible upon the central theme of movement, and may be developed after the basic pattern has been practised. An empowering way of working with this dance is for group members to take it in turns to embody and mediate the energies of each Quarter (Figure 1, page 18) and, after working with the Quarters, of the People (Figure 7, page 113). In a small working group, a dance cycle might involve pattern-making as described above. This would be followed by a cycle in which four members mediated the Quarters while others made the circle and 'Z' sign movements. Once everyone in the group has worked through this cycle, as mediators of the Quarters and as the dancers, the cycle is repeated. In this further phase the People are mediated, and not the Quarters. The dancer or dancers then become both Fool and Merlin, encounter the People and experience the Triple Transformation of Falling, Hanging and Drowning in universal Being.

If the group has sufficient members, it is possible to work with the Quarters and the People. For this the group needs to have 12 participants. The thirteenth presence is the spiritual Being that manifests in the centre of Sacred Space, and inspires a corresponding spiritual power from within ourselves.

CHAPTER 6

Spring and Tree

The locations of the Merlin tradition are variable – they suddenly change from a small region to the entire land, or leap into a universal vision. This fluctuation is a matter of octaves: according to the law of octaves your backyard is the universe; the universe is one stone in a small cave in Wales.

Merlin, and other seers and seeresses within what we are broadly calling the Mystery of Merlin and Ariadne, spent time at trees and at springs. To work the Way of Merlin as we are gradually developing it in this book, we need to relate to such locations. This is a physical relationship first and foremost, and not a theoretical or symbolic one.

Why is this contact necessary? Because we are one with the land, and trees, springs and caves are power points that tap into the energies of the land, and then reach into other dimensions altogether. Our unity may seem abstract or idealistic to the modern mentality, but it is simply a matter of energy. If our own energy is exchanged through specific locations and companion beings, remarkable changes can occur.

Does this seem far-fetched? What about the cells of our bodies, each one a living being, a commonwealth that makes up the organs that appear as a physical human . . . ? Just as our bodies are composed of countless living beings, separated yet united, so are we part of other bodies, and the interaction is found in many dimensions, not just that of the organic world. The human body and consciousness are one entity, and through the transformative methods found in the Mystery of Merlin, we can begin to realize our unity within the greater environment of the land, the planet, the solar system, the stars. They are all our body and consciousness.

FINDING THE SACRED SPRING

A real problem with modern visualization and integration techniques is hardly ever voiced, perhaps because people are only now becoming aware of it. Most modern techniques seem to emphasize what the old seers might have considered an obviously artificial confinement: everything is done upon an inner level.

This emphasis upon purely psychological or inner levels was essential during the earlier years of this century, when Western consciousness was morbidly fixated upon materialistic and compulsive action, and needed desperately to be loosened by turning within. Towards the close of the twentieth century, however, we are rediscovering the intimate relationship between our inner and outer worlds. So it is not sufficient merely to visualize an inner spring in yourself, powerful as this type of work may be. The visualization must also attune to an actual outer spring, well or water source. The Way of Merlin is rooted firmly in the sacred land, and cannot be cut away from it and continue to flourish.

So how do we set about finding a sacred spring? Is it not an impossible task for the city-dweller? In the old days a seeker after truth found a spring and lived close to it, but this seems unlikely in the extreme for us today. Let us examine the possibilities and find within them a creative way that will work in modern circumstances.

Finding a Spring

Wherever you live, whatever your life-pattern, you can find a sacred spring, a physical sacred spring, and not something upon imaginal levels of perception. Firstly there are acknowledged sacred springs, found through studying history, old tradition or ethnic beliefs. In Europe there are thousands of hallowed springs, many with a tradition of magic and worship dating back into the pagan and prehistoric periods. Some have been absorbed as

Christian shrines, others may be found as wells in city, town or village locations, while yet others are at isolated sites which may be discovered through exploration or by research. If you live in an urban environment in Europe you may be surprised at the number of old wells and springs that can be found by patient research, particularly if your location has a history as a settlement. If you live in a rural environment, this task may be easier. If you live in a new city, with little or no historical background to it, you may have to go into the country to find a sacred spring. In America, Canada, Australia, or any 'new' territory, the ethnic traditions of the original people of the land will reveal sacred springs, wells or water sources. Some of these are becoming better known, while others remain hidden.

In the most obvious sense, you may be able to make a pilgrimage to a sacred site, or to several sites, and encounter a sacred spring. You may find a holy well or spring close to your own home, and not necessarily a famous one. The choice of spring is intuitive, and not always dependent upon fame, size or location.

Beyond this first level of finding a sacred spring that has a tradition of power associated with it is another, equally possible, equally powerful. That is to find a spring solely by intuition. You can aid your intuition if necessary by using a large-scale map of your locality, upon which most springs and water sources will be shown. Modern interest in dowsing may be helpful in this context, as there are many books on finding water and energy sources using rods and pendulums. The process should not become obsessive or demanding, however, and the main aim of this aspect of the Way of Merlin is to find a sacred spring, not necessarily to become a dowser!

Apart from venerable sacred sites, each of which has a power and a personality of its own, the most powerful springs are those that arise in caves or clefts of rock, and from within the roots of trees. If you can find a natural spring of this sort, you should spend time in meditation and develop an intuitive relationship with it. If you cannot find a natural spring close to your home, then you should definitely make a dedicated journey to a known sacred site with a powerful spring. The physical movement, and the time spent with the spring, are essential, and cannot be by-passed in favour of sitting at home and visualizing.

Visualization

Visiting a site is not necessarily enough, and visualizing an abstract or idealized spring is definitely insufficient – the inner and outer journeys and contacts must be fused. So, having visited a spring, or found an unknown spring or well or water source through intuition, and formed a relationship with it, however brief or long, we can then work upon this contact in visualization.

If you have made a visit to a great sacred site with a spring or water source, then it may be unlikely that you can visit it regularly. But once you have made the physical contact, you can return to the site in meditation, through the visualizing ability of your imagination. This may be aided at first by use of photographs if absolutely necessary, though these should be abandoned as soon as possible in favour of your own visualizing power. (Incidentally, the use of videos or films of sacred sites is not recommended other than for general education. Television causes your imagination to atrophy, to weaken, and to rot. Do not take my word for it, but if you regularly watch television, try spending three weeks or more without, and discover how your imaginative and visualizing abilities gradually restore themselves.)

If you have located a small unknown spring, and your own intuition has declared it to be sacred, then you may be able to visit it regularly. If so, then you should meditate there as often as possible. In either case, through physical presence or through distance contact, you may work through several stages.

1. Actual contact with your sacred spring, either direct or distant. This consists of being at the site (either physically or in imagination), and attuning to its individual feeling, flow, energy, rhythms. Having spent time on this, you may then work with specific visualizations such as our examples in later chapters, which use springs in various ways. It is essential that you develop your own entry visualizations, encounter visualizations, and dialogues with a sacred spring.

    Keep notes after each meditation or visualization; you will be surprised at what they contain and reveal. In a later stage you will probably abandon note-taking altogether, but it is a valuable aid for the first year or two of inner work, or during the first year of working within a specific attuned tradition, regardless of experience or lack of experience in inner disciplines.

2. Specific visualizations – these may use the spring as a gateway, and as a boost, a source of energy and clarification. This is best done at the site itself, but if you have visited a sacred spring and established some contact with it, it is possible to draw upon its energies despite distance.

3. Ritual drinking or washing. The most important water traditions world-wide are those of drinking and washing in a sacred spring or river. If you can do this regularly you are fortunate, but for most of us it will be a rare or even one-off experience. A working compromise, which, it must be emphasized, is valueless unless you have been to a sacred site and drunk of the waters, is to build the contact as described above, and then dedicate some pure water to be the waters of your sacred spring. Strange as it may seem at first, filtered tap water is best for this, as it is not from any specific spring or well.

If you are working the Way of Merlin, you may need to keep your contact attuned to a land and environment suited to this path. This becomes more difficult if you attempt to tune to sacred springs that have other spiritual or magical traditions firmly established within them. There are many important decisions inherent in this process, including that most fundamental one of how you relate to the land in which you live.

Working with a sacred spring will clarify such decisions – Merlin was finally cured of fits of madness by drinking the wholesome waters of a spring that suddenly rose from beneath the earth, where none had been before.

FINDING A SACRED TREE

This task is similar to that of finding a sacred spring, with the obvious exception that there are few, if any, trees left today that were once, or are still, considered sacred. Do not let this discourage you, for a tree today carries within it the inheritableness of its ancestors, just as humans do. The tradition of sacred trees was once widespread, and has been preserved in folk culture well into the modern period. While there may not be numbers of obviously sacred trees around, unlike ancient, historically sacred sites, there are many potentially sacred trees which have inherited the magic of their ancestors. All trees, all planets, all living beings are sacred.

Each land or region has trees sacred to it, trees of particular character, energy, qualities. We have a mass of information on this subject handed down to us from various sources. As a rule you should work with trees that are within the spiritual or magical traditions of the land in which you live. You may also work with trees and plants that are defined by an existing tradition. Ideally the two, land and tradition, should share much in common. If you find that they do not, you may use an open technique of finding a tree and acknowledging it as sacred. We will return to this simple technique shortly.

In the Way of Merlin the traditional sacred trees are the oak, the thorn or blackthorn, and the apple.

The oak is associated with long life-span and wisdom, and is often regarded as a 'male' tree, though this is nonsense in biological terms. It is, however, associated with male aspects of the sacrificial Mysteries. The oak is the tree of kingship, and was originally the soul-vessel of the sacrificial king. While sacred kings often died upon stones, they spoke out of, and returned to birth from, trees. The oak is also associated with lightning and gods of lightning, such as Zeus or Jupiter, and the Celtic wheel and thunder god Taranis. Oracular oaks are sometimes linked to Apollo or to Zeus in classical tradition. Druids held oaks in especial reverence, and the mystery of the sacred mistletoe is associated with both the oak and the apple.

The thorn covers a family of trees, some of which are winter flowering. Thorn trees bear fruit and spines, and are sacred to the goddess of taking. In the initiatory traditions of the Celts, the thorn tree was associated with seership and the second sight, and marked the entrance to the Otherworld or fairy realm. There are, of course, protean mythic traditions concerning thorns and sacrifice, including those of Christianity, grafted onto earlier sacrificial myths and rituals.

The apple is usually thought of as the tree of the goddess of giving, but in tradition we sometimes find a more complex picture. The fruit may be poisonous or maddening if stolen, eaten at the wrong time, or unhallowed by the blessing of the Goddess or Fairy Queen. The apple tree is found in the Fortunate Isles or the Underworld.

Another connective within the Merlin tradition is that of the heroic task of recovering golden apples, well represented in classical myth. These grow upon a tree on a distant island, guarded by a dragon. Curiously when a hero gains the sacred apples and gives them to a goddess as originally commanded, she simply puts them back on the tree again.

Occasionally we also find the ash within the Way of Merlin, a tree associated with Odin, and the World Tree Yggdrasil in Norse tradition. The ash is traditionally the tree of spears, of staves.

Before selecting a sacred tree, you should have contacted and had some experience of the oak, thorn and apple. There are variants of these trees around the world. As with sacred springs and companion creatures, the physical contact is essential. It does not have to be perpetual, daily, or even regular, though regular contact is good; but it must have been established properly. Vision alone is not enough, and reading about trees, tree-lore, and legend is almost valueless. Most if not all true magical, mystical and spiritual traditions rely upon touch: you must touch a sacred tree, touch the earth, touch the Goddess within a stone, a spring, a land.

Tree Contact

In magic wisdom and spiritual traditions, meditation is often recommended in contact with trees. Sitting under a tree, leaning with your back against it, is a different meditational experience to working at home.

There are many possible 'explanations' for this tradition and its effect. In Western magic and mysticism, the tree links the worlds: it has its roots in the Underworld, grows through the Earth world, and reaches its crown to the Sky world of sun and stars.

The mystery of a tree is that a major part of its being is within the Earth. When we relate to a tree we meet this part of it. This in turn opens our own awareness of our being within the Earth, and in other dimensions from which we normally exclude ourselves.

The purpose of working with trees, springs and animals might be defined as 'interaction': through interaction with these orders of being we come alive in areas and states of energy and consciousness that we have forgotten or lost. This is a somewhat reduced definition, however, for the true purpose is to enable unity – humanity, the land, and all living beings within and upon it, are one.

In the primal traditions we try to attune to the tree itself, to enter its nature, its individuality, its collective awareness, its energy.

The oak, thorn and apple produce quite different effects in meditation and visualization. Each tree will communicate a stream of images and sensations, and enable specific innerworld or ancestral contacts. You need to try this steadily for yourself, and not predetermine anything that might happen.

The oak often tells of long periods of time, many thousands of years, and of great movements of trees through seeding and growth across the continents. It also attunes to the long cycle of sacrificial kingship, dedicated births, lives and deaths in service of the land and the people. Innerworld contacts at oak trees tend to be priests or sacred kings. This means anyone who has mediated spiritual power, or anyone who has made an act of self-sacrifice. Do not expect kings and priests to come to you waving banners and wearing crowns, for many are quite ordinary and unpretentious. Some come to the inner vision in working clothes.

The thorn often tells of ancestral lore, frequently relating tales of pain and suffering. The thorn also balances this stream of consciousness with its early blossoms, showing that beauty is reborn out of harsh winter, that petals and thorns are part of one tree. It also links to the Underworld and the Dark Goddess, and may bring contact with priests and priestesses or mediators of this type of energy. Fairy contacts are frequently made through thorn trees, and gifts of seership and encounters with the Fairy Queen begin under such trees.

The apple is a friendly, fruitful tree. The giving powers of the Goddess are inherent in the apple, with the caution that her fruitfulness and blessing should never be abused. The apple brings an energy of fertility and sustenance, and often generates contact with innerworld beings who are concerned for the relationship between humanity and agriculture. Interestingly, the apple is connected to the development of culture, and has attuned to the changes and cycles of human culture and civilization through many centuries. The apple is also a gateway to the Fortunate Isles.

Finding a Tree

Many other trees than these will work upon the Way of Merlin, and one of your tasks is to find a tree that relates to you in some way. This can be done very simply, by taking a walk in an area where there are trees, and trying to feel if you have an affinity with any particular one. This need not be an overt technique or show of contact; it can work just as well in a park or garden as it can in the wild. Touching the tree, remembering its feeling, you can establish some contact in meditation from wherever you may be.

You may also collect seeds, such as acorns, and try germinating them. The seed of a tree, even grown in a pot, is part of the original tree. I have a sacred oak tree, planted over 20 years ago in a pot. It was grown from an acorn from an oak upon an ancient site in Britain, associated with sacrificial kingship. This is not the only tree I work with, but it retains its living contact with the ancestral primal oak tree wherever it may be. This tree has moved location several times since it sprouted in its original pot in the early 1970s.

Trees are used as entrances to the Otherworld, both in visualization and through physical contact, and if you make contact with a tree it will feature in your dreams, just as the other contacts do. If you have a garden, plant sacred trees. Those trees that self-seed and grow spontaneously are often especially helpful upon the Way of Merlin: there is no such thing as disconnected growth, no presence that is not wholly through the Three Worlds.

In Celtic tradition, for example, the rowan tree was planted near to doors as a bearer of luck, and a particularly powerful tree was said to be the rowan that self-seeded by your door. This power would be in any tree that grows by any door: trees are doors, doorposts, and doorkeepers. These may seem, to the materialist intellect, to be idle superstitions, but when worked with upon deeper levels they reveal remarkable power at work. It is the level of consciousness in ourselves that defines ignorance or wisdom, not any particular belief or tradition, religion or science.

Pairs of trees are often used as gateways into the Otherworld: passing between them in either direction can change your consciousness and energy patterns. This may be done with contacts or specific innerworld locations in mind. You may also, of course, step through randomly.

CHAPTER 7

Companions, Allies and Dreams

COMPANION AND INHERENT CREATURES

For clarity of definition and practical work, I have divided spiritual creatures or allies into two major categories, although there are others. These are 'companion creatures', which relate to us but are not necessarily within us, and 'inherent creatures', which may or may not be companions or allies, but which we have within ourselves. These working definitions, which will be developed and expanded shortly, are helpful in interpretation, and clarify our relationship to the creatures concerned, both inwardly and outwardly.

The use of companion and inherent creatures has attracted enormous attention in recent years, both in psychology and in revivals of primal or shamanistic magical arts. Popularly called 'totem animals', such creatures are found in every spiritual and magical tradition world-wide. Even Christianity associates certain saints, Evangelists and archangels with specific creatures. The Evangelists Matthew, Mark, Luke and John (eagle, lion, man and bull) and archangels Raphael, Michael, Gabriel and Auriel are also associated with the Four Directions (East, South, West and North), for they are the keys to Sacred Space within a Christian spiritual tradition. The archangels were retained in Catholicism from the gnostic traditions, and are still invoked at the Quarters in some variants of Western ritual magic today.

It is perhaps significant that these archangels are not found in the Creation Vision of Merlin (Appendix 2), though the primal pattern of the Creator uttering Four Powers or relative zones and worlds is clear. The vision is not orthodox, and fuses druidic and primal or mystical Christian elements. It also develops into a long list of companion creatures.

Most companion and inherent creatures are naturalistic, though there are a range of beings that are not. We shall return to this difference shortly.

Modern revivals of shamanism seem to have completely overlooked the native European use of spiritual animals or companion creatures, despite a staggering amount of evidence ranging from early myths and legends to later published alchemical and mystical texts. The Merlin tradition may be proven to derive from a Celtic culture, with many hints of pre-Celtic tradition, though there is no hard proof in a scientific sense of such older deeper strata. Inevitably, though, we find that companion creatures play a major role. Modern psychology has also rediscovered certain aspects of such creatures, but tends to limit them to fit materialist theories of the psyche. No such limitations are found in the spiritual traditions.

We find that Merlin is associated directly with specific creatures: the wolf, the deer, the pig and, by both direct and indirect association, the hound. These are not the only creatures, however, and we should not fall into the trap of making definitive lists. Merlin is sometimes linked with the raven or crow, and this creature is found both in Celtic tradition as the bird of the warrior and death goddess Morrigan, and in Norse tradition as the bird of Odin. There are strong similarities between the Merlin tradition and that of Odin, but also many important differences. A detailed comparison would not be appropriate for this book, and remains to be explored thoroughly by a scholar and poet immersed in both Norse and Celtic tradition . . . who, of course, has met both Odin and Merlin!

Beyond the personal companion creatures of wolf, deer and pig (to which we will return shortly), we find long lists of creatures, both naturalistic and fabulous, in both the *Prophecies* and the *Vita*. Animal transformation and attributes are also very well developed in other areas of Celtic tradition, myth, legend and folklore. [14] What does this mean for us today; how might we work with such ideas, with such creatures?

The basic methods of working are similar in any tradition: the seer or seeress, magician or meditator, whatever term or style of work is employed, relates to and works with creatures *from different orders of life*. This particularly refers to those creatures that are inherent within or natural to the land in which the initiate lives. Some inherent creatures of the land are no longer found in our environment, but a simple working rule is that companion creatures should be natural to your land and should be living species. There are, however, as always, some exceptions to this rule – these might typically be the companionship of land-inherent creatures that are no longer found in the modern environment, or are extremely rare; or supernatural creatures.

Companion creatures may be animals, birds, fish – any type of living creature whatsoever. Insects seem more rarely found than other orders of life, but are well known as tribal and companion creatures. The grasshopper, sacred to Apollo, is a typical example, and of course, the spider, sacred creature of Ariadne. Flies and flying insects are often found in myth and folklore as messengers and agents of conception (either of ideas or of life), while bees are sacred to the goddess of fertility and fruitfulness. These are merely a few examples of insects within mythic and initiatory traditions, and part of the task before you upon the Way of Merlin is find such connections for yourself. This task of discovering connections applies to any type of companion creature, though human-inherent creatures work in a slightly different way.

The Creation Vision gives a holistic, ever-expanding list of powers, zones and inherent life-forms, balancing this expanding universe by simultaneously contracting into the Otherworlds, reducing its vision to the entrance of sacred springs, and then opening out again in another dimension.

In the *Vita*, Geoffrey of Monmouth borrows his long lists of creatures of land, sea and air in part from other writers (such as Isidore of Seville) working within a hallowed literary tradition. The oral context, however, is one of bardic poetry and lists of creatures from Celtic tradition, to which Geoffrey also had access.

Unlike the *Vita*, the *Prophecies* do not often relate creatures to one another holistically, but animals, both natural and supernatural, do appear in profusion. Many are merely loose disguises for figures in medieval politics, but others are clearly mythic. Some, as I have suggested in *The Prophetic Vision of Merlin*, may be truly prophetic in the sense that we can apply them to persons and situations that occurred long after the text was written out in the twelfth century.

Let us now leave sources and comparisons, and move to practical work with such creatures.

Companion Creatures

Companion creatures are living beings that are inherent within, and found living in, the land. The land itself is a living entity, in which all life-forms are interconnected. We know this today from a materialist viewpoint, almost too late, as it seems. This interconnection was an undisputed truth, though, to the seers and seeresses within the Way of Merlin, the prophetic tradition of the land, the Goddess, and inspiration.

To work with companion creatures we need to be clear in our intentions, and to throw off a few typical modern misconceptions concerning 'totem animals'.

Companion creatures are not symbols; they are not effigies or representations of something else. Nor are they simply inherited tribal attributes from a more primitive life-style. This type of interpretive thinking is usually derived from Christian conditioning, implying that all non-human creatures are somehow lesser. In this divisive, essentially antagonistic world-view, only humans are of any potential value to the Creator. Modern Christianity assumes, and still asserts as dogma, that other creatures have no souls.

But living creatures are our companions upon and within the land and the planet; they travel with us, we cannot avoid relating to one another. Their life is our life. The shamanistic traditions know this very well, and such truths were retained for centuries in the West in folklore, esoteric tradition, and, more formally, in mystical and alchemical texts or techniques. Materialist sciences, however, merely see other living creatures as potential subjects for experiment, never for conscious relationship.

When we work with the intent of relating to other creatures consciously in a spiritual or magical way, something very unusual happens. One or more creatures come and reveal themselves to us.

Note that they choose you, you do not choose them. The idea of choosing a creature because it has attributes that you feel represent your ideals, or that you would like to attain, is quite alien to the power-traditions of direct work and conscious association with living creatures. The idea of affirming yourself through choosing an animal is sometimes found as a product of modern psychology. However we find it in practice today, it is certainly the result of the unnatural rift between humanity and other orders of life that has been created by orthodox religion and materialism.

Upon the Way of Merlin a creature (or creatures) will choose you and reveal itself as your companion. The visualizations in this book give some typical imaginative scenarios that help this process. Often the creature is not what you would expect. Some people resist the creature that chooses them, because its presence pushes them towards a realization that they have previously avoided, while others will welcome their companion creatures as long-lost friends. The range of reactions is great, just as the range of creatures is great. Do not make the mistake of over-interpreting – the creatures must be met, and related to, in their own right. Very often our response to a companion creature defies interpretation.

Wherever possible you must come into physical contact with your companion creature, however difficult this may be. You should try to dissolve the barriers that our society has raised between ourselves and other life forms: very few people have ever come into close contact with an animal other than a domestic pet, and very few of us truly identify meat with living creatures.

This does not mean that we have to go to opposite extremes, however. Our chances of encountering a wolf, the companion creature of Merlin, for example, are limited. But as a meagre adventure we can at least visit a zoo or, better still, a wild-life preserve where such creatures live in their natural habitat or in relatively free conditions.

This brings us to an important point: in any Mystery there are a few specific creatures, and in the Mystery of Merlin we find the wolf, deer and pig singled out as Merlin's companions, so therefore you will need to establish contact with these animals if you work upon the Way of Merlin. You may find it necessary to stop eating the flesh of the pig or deer, at least until you have worked with these animals inwardly and gained a fresh perspective. They are not merely symbols of energies, but living creatures that embody and transfer and enable these energies. They do not merely represent the wild side of humanity (as is frequently assumed); they are the living wild forces that interweave between humanity, the land and the Otherworld.

Companion or spiritual animals can go into dimensions generally unknown to humanity, and can lead us in and out safely. This is one of their major companion roles. You might ask: 'Why do they do it?' The answer is inherent in the Creation Vision: we are all part of one another. There is no deal between us and the animals, just as there is no deal between humanity and divinity. If we think in terms of deals and self-interest in the context of spiritual traditions, we inevitably fail to transform ourselves, and so build increasingly isolated false self-images. This is amply defined in the Merlin legends by the story of King Vortigern and his collapsing stronghold, shown in the Tarot as the catabolic trump of The Blasted Tower.

Between humans and the companion creatures energies are exchanged . . . and this applies to those creatures that are supernatural just as much as it does to the natural ones. Such exchanges are natural interactions, not bargains of self-interest.

Inherent Creatures

There is a difference, often difficult to detect, but important to us, between companion and inherent creatures. Your companion creatures may or may not be inherent. What is an inherent creature? It is that animal, bird, fish or insect that is most apt for certain of your energy patterns.

We all have creatures inherent with us; astrology world-wide employs images of creatures, for instance, and we frequently mirror or express the creature that is associated with our birthdate or other patterns within the natal chart. In a popular and superficial sense, in Western astrology, we find that people with the sun in Leo have leonine characteristics, sun in Capricorn goat-like tendencies, and so forth. This type of inherent creature is related to the Elemental energies of the sign.

There is a great truth here, for all living creatures of any kind embody Elemental powers and patterns. This is one of the keys to the fact that our companion spiritual creatures, by which we mean real animals, birds, fish and insects, can enter other worlds. Their Elemental pattern is different to ours, and they can act as guides and protectors, enablers and guardians. Our *companion* creatures interact with the land and other dimensions as well as ourselves. Our *inherent* creatures are characteristics, embodiments, mediating paths and forms for power from deeper levels within ourselves. We relate to companion creatures, but can transform into inherent creatures. Be cautious with this potential of transformation.

To find how companion animals relate through various worlds, we can take a typical example. Think of the dog, who guards his human's home faithfully, yet is also the god Anubis, guardian of the gate of life and death. In the Merlin tradition, the hound and wolf represent the polarities of the dog. Hunting hounds pursue the deer in the ritual of the Threefold Death, and the Wild Hunt of both Celtic and Norse myth and religion ushers the souls of the dead in and out of other worlds. The hounds are not mere representations of qualities, they are powerful living creatures in more than one world.

Inherent creatures, however, may be taken as emblems of the psyche, in a materialist sense, and as indicators of energy and behaviour patterns – the mystic Pisces in popular astrology, the aggressive Aries, the stubborn Taurus, and so forth. Trite but truthful instant summaries of a subtle complex art, the art of defining a person's inherent creatures. These are seldom limited to the sun sign, and may also be defined by other means than by astrology, though astrology is very helpful indeed, even in its modern abstract Western version.

A seer or seeress who has worked with companion and inherent creatures can feel the inherent creatures in others, and trained and gifted seers can intuit or discern or see the companion creatures of others, though this is more likely to have surprise elements to it, as the creatures always choose you, and may manifest quite suddenly or unexpectedly.

Family, Clan or Tribal Creatures

A further group of inherent creatures are those of your family or clan. If you know what your ethnic and family origins are, you may be able to find a clan animal. Certainly people of Scottish descent are able to do so, due to the popularizing of Scottish clan traditions in the Victorian era. It may be valid for you to have a family name researched and to meditate upon any heraldic creature that is suggested by the research. Do not take this too seriously, as most heraldic research is very superficial. Nevertheless, it may be an avenue that yields interesting results.

You may encounter your ancestral creatures in meditation and visualization, perhaps without knowing their ancestral connections. You may also be spiritually admitted to a clan or family through the agency of a companion creature. This is quite a frequent occurrence during work with such creatures.

If you work with the wolf, deer, pig and hound, you are, effectively, seeking admission to the Mystery of Merlin, and to the related Mystery of the Wounded King. Both Mysteries are united by the theme of the Threefold Death, and the foundation within awareness of the Goddess.

WHAT IS A MERLIN?

The other creature that seems important in the Merlin tradition is, of course, the hawk. Literary commentators have suggested that 'Merlin' is a variation of the Welsh *Merddyn*, which is certainly true. But this does not make any difference to the inherent hawk presence in some aspects of the tradition. Let us examine these briefly, for if you enter the family of Merlin, within the web of Ariadne, then the hawk will be a likely encounter, with the spider, wolf, deer, pig and hound.

The hawk is associated in Celtic tradition with the month of May, the turning point of the Pleiades. This transition marked the entry into summer (rather than the position of the sun itself), just as November, with setting of the Pleiades, marked the turning into winter. The Pleiades are an important stellar group in magical and religious traditions world-wide, featured in the *Prophecies*, and are still of significance in primal cultures today.

We also find that the hawk has a hidden connection in Britain to a primal deity of light, where the English St George, warrior, patriotic figure and native variant of the Archangel Michael, replaces several Celtic figures that might be termed light-heroes. [15] These are defined as either deities or the semi-divine sons of deities in Celtic mythology. As Merlin is a prophet and not a hero figure, this may not seem a promising connection, but let us follow it further.

George seems to have originated as a Christian saint in Palestine. The ancient basilica of St George at Lydda in Palestine incorporate a shrine to the earlier hawk-headed saint Mena. Within its foundations is a temple of Horus.

Horus is the Egyptian divine child of light, who is also involved in the concept and rituals of sacrificial death. The conflict between Horus and Set, a dualistic theme that is not given emphasis in the Merlin tradition, was enfolded within the later imagery of Archangel Michael and Satan, or St George and the Dragon.

The dragon is the primal creature of the Mystery of Merlin, representing the polarized fire within the Earth, the power of the land, and the fire within ourselves, the rising flame of prophecy. In a simple sense the Red and White Dragons reveal not only our inherent vital energies, but also the energies of the land. We need not confuse the propagandist images of a conquered dragon and 'evil' with the primal mystery of humanity and geomantic and vital forces. It was the deliberate practice of early Christianity to take the themes and images of the pagan mythology and culture and subtly corrupt them.

The ancients repeatedly identified Horus with Apollo, and there is a connection, as we have already described, between the child Merlin, the Celtic divine child Mabon, and the primal Apollo.

The Greeks asserted that Apollo was a Hyperborean god, from the land at the back of the north wind. A classical description asserts that Apollo returned to a triangular island in the North every 18 years to be worshipped in a circular temple of stone and praised with the music of the harp or lyre. His mother was supposed to have come from this triangular island, off the coast of Gaul (Europe). If you have followed the Merlin legend closely (which is a basic requirement if you are to work within this tradition), you will see some similarities in the flow of images. The triangular island may be identified with Britain, the sacred enclosure of Merlin.

To return to the hawk, the bird of the seer or seeress, there is also a poetic and inspirational force at work: it flies up into the light, yet looks down and sees the smallest movement upon the earth; it strikes with great speed and surprise, falling like a stone or thunderbolt, as fast as lightning. The hawk is one of the Sky-world birds of prophecy and clear-vision, seeing in the light of the sun, just as the owl is the Underworld bird of prophecy and divination, seeing under the light of the moon. There are many more connectives of this sort to follow once you enter the weaving of companion creatures between the worlds.

FINDING YOUR COMPANION CREATURES

Most of the thematic visualizations in this book involve companion creatures, and if you work with these you will find that certain creatures come to you during the visualizations. These will be *your* companion creatures. As the visions are determined by the traditional scenarios that they recreate, they may not reveal your entire range of companion creatures, but will establish contact with the main ones that relate to the Mystery of Merlin.

There are also some shorter general exercises that can put you into contact with creatures, without a complete inner journey or complex visualizing experience.

The classic sequence from Celtic legend is found in *The Mabinogion*, and is quoted in Appendix 6. This may, in itself, be worked as a visualization, and I would recommend developing an inner familiarity with this traditional vision. Simply follow the story as translated from the ancient Welsh, but leave a silent pause for meditation and visualization. During this pause a creature will come to you. (If you wish a more formally developed visualization, there is 'The Cry of Merlin' in Chapter 12.)

Simple exercises aimed at companion creature contact might be as follows:

1. Go to your sacred spring or tree.
   a) As you travel, what creatures do you see upon your journey? Write them down if necessary, and meditate upon each one.
   b) Meditate at the site: does a creature come near you, or do you hear or see any creature while you are there?

c) In your meditation at the sacred spring or tree, seek to make an inner contact with a companion creature. This may flash before you suddenly and withdraw (a common occurrence) or may remain as a contact and steady presence. Immediately after your meditation write some brief notes, as the memory may fade.

2. If your work is done in a room that you have attuned to a sacred spring, follow (c) above. Some alternative methods are as follows:

a) Using *The Merlin Tarot*, shuffle the entire deck thoroughly. Spread the deck out face down upon a flat surface, and run your fingers along the back of the cards. Select three cards this way, and meditate upon the creatures that are shown. You may repeat this selection of three creatures until you have done it three times. By this stage you should have a clear indication of at least one companion creature.

b) If you have a clan family or tribal creature, meditate upon this and try to establish a relationship with it inwardly. This may or may not work, and if you feel it is not productive, do not spend too much energy upon it. Tribal creatures will often be present in your group of companions, even if you are not consciously aware of their connection.

3. Use the dream contact techniques described in the next section. These can be very effective in establishing and building contact with companion creatures.

DREAMING ENCOUNTERS

In your work with Sacred Space, the Elements, and the entities of the Mystery of Merlin, dreaming plays an important part. The dreaming process of magical or spiritual traditions is different in several significant ways, however, to that of modern psychology. This is primarily because the dreams arise from contact with other beings, and are not limited to reflections or representation of your own psyche.

Magical or empowered dreams can be induced either by coincidence, occurring unwittingly, or through intent. Let us examine some of the simple techniques for dreaming with intent.

These will be helpful in discovering your companion creatures and in meeting and relating to the People on the Way. The People themselves are discussed in the next chapter.

Dreaming with Intent
One of the simplest and most effective ways of entering dream contact is through a brief meditation before sleeping. You should enter Silence (page 127) and briefly define Sacred Space (page 78). If you seek a contact that is found in a specific Direction, you should meditate facing that Direction. If you do not know of an appropriate Direction, simply sit in the centre of the Sacred Space facing East, or in the Direction that you have already been working with on that day.

Do not, however, go into a detailed visualization to build an image of whatever you wish to dream about; leave this for conscious waking sessions. Simply face the appropriate direction, if you know what this is, and know or calmly affirm that you will meet your contact during sleep. Then return to Silence, and so to sleep. It helps not to be distracted after this dedication, and to be asleep as soon as possible.

Keep a notebook, and write down your dreams if you awake in the night, or, more usually, first thing in the morning. With practice you will be able to remember dreams with increasing ease. If you are accustomed to writing down dreams as a result of therapy or psychology or other systems of working with the psyche, you should be careful not to try to fit your dreams into these frameworks.

Dreaming encounters are specific meetings with actual beings, and are not merely a series of emblems and scenes arising in the dreaming consciousness. With some practice you will be able to distinguish contact dreams from other types of dream, and to be aware of their difference.

Using Specific Images
You can also help the dreaming process by working briefly with ready-made images. Tarot cards are particularly useful for this, though you could use images that you have found in other visual sources, or even draw your own.

Using *The Merlin Tarot*, select a trump or other image that matches your choice of inner contact. There are correspondences between the trumps and the People on the Wheel. Simply study the card briefly in your meditation, and affirm that you seek to meet this person or creature during sleep. Some people like to place the card under their pillow, but this is not necessary. I prefer leaving it in the centre of the Sacred Space, which acts to place the image in the centre of your own field of awareness and energy.

You should work around the Circle in the relationship patterns shown in Figures 1 and 7 (pages 18 and 113), always seeking a balance. There will always be certain images and contacts that you do not like, or that you feel are hard work, or even that are, seemingly, hostile to you, while others will be more friendly and desirable, even alluring.

Always aim for balance, and make notes of your reactions to the trumps during this cycle of dream work. You will find your reaction to the image while awake is sometimes different to that which occurs during the dream. Comparing the two may give insights into further areas of inner discipline, energy and contact.

Using Random Images
This follows the same procedure as 2 above, except that you draw a card at random from the trumps. You will find this method particularly fruitful after you have done some basic work around the Wheel. You can use *The Merlin Tarot* in this way for inner contact with people and with companion animals. Every card in the deck has one or more companion creatures of some sort upon it, except for some of the higher trumps that have human or divine figures only, and one lesser trump that has no companion creatures in it because they have refused to be in it: I leave you to discover this for yourself if you work with the deck.

How Do the Dreams Work?

Dream contact is essentially a meeting between yourself and another being. There may also be scenes, symbols, changes and a host of associations and feelings inherent in dreams. The foundation is one of contact, however, and the beings are real entities and not merely artificial images.

Through working with the pattern of any Mystery, we attune to it. If you travel on the Way of Merlin, you will meet people and creatures that are within that way, that are part of the sacred land, inherent within the universal vision. We simply use a tradition with its pattern and people as a guiding system, never as a rigid dogma or a religion. When you meet these entities, there is an interaction. The legends of Merlin reveal this transformative process in his own life story.

Sometimes the entities will appear in a form identical to or similar to the image that you commenced with, such as a trump or an illustration, although this is not the only form that they can take. Contact dreams often work with a variety of shapes; the same contact can take several different forms, yet you will know that it is the same contact because certain themes, feeling and energies run through the dreams.

During early stages of contact dreaming you may find that a being hides behind or within another. This is quite a common experience, and if you question a contact in a dream, the first person or creature will often reveal another. A similar transformation or masking occurs in waking visualization and spontaneous seership. You need to use your intuition upon this subject, and with practice you will get to know certain regular contacts and images, and to detect those that are embedded or masked in preliminary forms.

Dream encounters will often result in teaching – the contact will teach you matters inherent in the Way of Merlin and Ariadne. Contacts will also test you . . . Remember they are not simply constructs of your own psyche, and will often challenge, test and demand. You do not have to consent to any suggestions though – this is an enervating habit that we see all too often in modern 'channelling'.

Some of the encounters will only open out if you challenge the people that you meet in the dream. This need not be an aggressive challenge, but one of questioning, declaration of intent. There is always a balance to find between learning and questioning that which is shown or taught.

Many inner contacts have a humorous side, and certain beings will seek to make fun of you or to send you on wild goose chases. A wild goose chase may lead to a companion animal, or even to another world, providing you are not misled. This is an aspect of the contacts' instructional experiential energy, and is not spiteful or malicious. Remember, your own spiritual intuition and common sense are always the best guides.

Spiritual creatures, such as companion animals, are also met in dreams, and they act as guides into other worlds. This type of dream can be powerful and disturbing in the early stages, and predefined sequences such as the sample visualizations in this book can help to familiarize you with the experience. There is no easy way of working through such encounters – just as there is no easy way of drifting through life, growing up, or any other transformative experience.

Chapter
8

Working with
the Images

The Mystery of Merlin has a coherent set of images: these appear as People (personae) who often cross the boundaries between humanity and divinity. They appear primarily as humans in the legendary progress of Merlin around the Wheel of Life, but through their personalities we find god and goddess powers at work. Sometimes they are openly described as deities, while at others they are masked. In a few cases a brief reference masks a powerful god or goddess image. This brevity is found in the powerful apocalyptic vision of Ariadne in the *Prophecies* (Appendix 1), in addition to earlier descriptions of powerful beings within the chaotic framework of prophetic verses.

The relationship between the various characters in the *Vita*, and therefore the energies that they embody and mediate, is shown in Figure 7 (page 113). Just as Merlin moves around the Wheel of Life, so he meets certain people during that movement. Each person mediates and represents the powers of the Quarters in which they tend to appear, though they may also move from one Quarter to another, and are not rigidly locked into any one location.

This fluid mobile relationship is revealed in the transforming role of Merlin: he is the Child or Fool, the adult Madman, the mature Elder. The Child is the pure centre of the Circle, but the Adult develops by moving from this centre outwards into the cycle of the Wheel. The Elder has traversed the cycles and eventually become liberated from them: thus the Elder and the Child are unified. This triple pattern applies ideally to us all, male or female; Child, Adult, Elder (see Figures 8 and 9, pages 114 and 115).

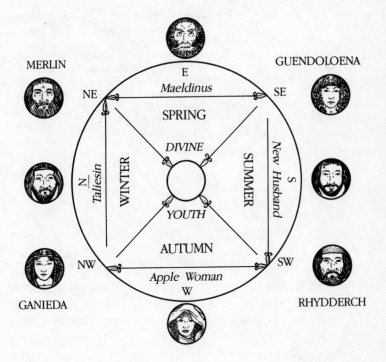

Figure 7: People on the Wheel

In the Mystery of Merlin specific powers and People are located in Sacred Space, upon the Wheel of Life and Change. Merlin encounters these People in various ways leading to transformation. The pattern can be used in meditation and visualization, or in ritual movement and dance. The names are those found in the *Vita Merlini*, but the qualities and energies are both human, archetypical, and, in some examples, divine.

NORTH-EAST: Merlin at the point of transition from one cycle to another, from winter to spring, death to birth.

EAST: (Spring) Maeldinus, Wild Man of the Woods/Cernunnos, Lord of the Animals. Merlin driven mad by grief and compassion and living in the wildwood.

SOUTH-EAST: Guendoloena, wife or lover of Merlin/Lady of Flowers embodying the goddess of spring and sexuality. Elements of Air and Fire.

SOUTH: (Summer) The new husband of Guendoloena, representing the continuing cycle of sexual love.

SOUTH-EAST: Rhydderch, the perfect king of summer, beneficial lord of the material world. Forms a polar reflection or opposite to Merlin. Elements of Fire and Water.

WEST: (Autumn) Apple-woman guardian of sacred or poisoned apples. Once lover of Merlin. Embodies forces of breaking-down and purification, masking a Celtic goddess of life and death and the Fairy Queen of Gaelic tradition.

NORTH-WEST: Ganieda, sister of Merlin, wife of Rhydderch. Embodies the enabling powers of the Goddess, equated with Minerva, classical goddess of cultural development. Helps to bring Merlin from madness into balance. Elements of Water and Earth.

NORTH (Winter) Taliesin the bard of wisdom. The classic Celtic figure of instruction, wisdom and poetry. Instructs Merlin in the holism of the universe by declaring the Creation Vision. Elements of Earth and Air.

CENTRE: The Divine Child or Original Being, at the centre of all existence and all beings.

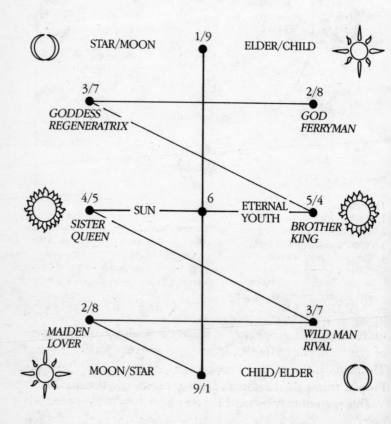

Figure 8: The Lightning Flash and the People Within

The encounters in the Mystery of Merlin are also potential and psychic patterns within ourselves. The flow of changes in polarity and function may be read in either direction.

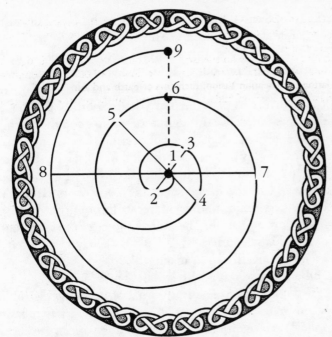

Figure 9: The Spiralling Path

The spiralling path from primal Child to Elder to primal Child.

1. Child/Elder
2. Maiden/Lover/Rival-Self
3. Wild Man/Lover/Rival-Self
4. Brother King
5. Sister Queen
6. Androgyne Eternal Youth
7. Goddess
8. God
9. Elder/Child

It is, initially, the resonant effect of the Seasons and Elements upon the developing individual that causes the life-cycle of movement. This should ideally be in tune with the greater cycles of the land, the planet and the solar system. Usually it is not. Through this spiralling movement the individual meets the People, whose interaction and power causes transformation.

This pattern may be used in several levels or working models, or we may choose to develop simple phases and extracts from it. An excellent modern development would be to use the pattern for empowered movement, in dance. The dance of the Elements, of the spirit, becomes our dance, mirrored through the movement of the body. While dancing the Mysteries is a powerful method of working (see Chapter 5), it may require some preliminary experience of Sacred Space, the Elements, and especially of the People before it comes into full effect.

We may also work with this holistic pattern in visualization, not as an escapist exercise, but to bring the energies through more fully into ourselves. In primal and early cultures and in the oral traditions, there was probably no 'visualization' in the modern sense. Images came alive through stories, songs and the rhythmic year of the seasons, gods and goddesses. There is no doubt, though, that highly trained visualization was and is carried out in magical and spiritual arts, in monastic orders, in shamanistic workings, and in the deeper oral traditions of initiation. The foundation of visualization, whatever its form or content, is the power of our imagination. The inherent force of the imagination is not individual, but universal. Whatever we may imagine has the potential to be realized . . . made real.

Techniques of working with specific sets of images have been used for thousands of years in spiritual or initiatory disciplines, and when we use our imagination in a dedicated way today, we may follow such traditions. This is not a dogmatic or archaic way of working, for the images in the mythic traditions of our world are, depending upon culture, collective and highly energized. We may start with an apparently archaic image, such as that of Merlin or the Goddess Ariadne, but the transformative effect produced is out of all proportion to any intellectual reasoning or historical argument. In other words, we do not work with these images in visualization because they are old, or even because they have a collective value or history, but because they are potent.

Visualization is an inherently natural and simple act, which we develop as children but tend to overlay with conditioned responses as we grow older. If we recover the simple skills of visualizing, the images act as interfaces or vessels for energies that we might not be able to tap into otherwise.

The technique of dancing the patterns will also allow us to tap into transformative energies, provided the dance is a dedicated movement and not an alternative entertainment. Two great sacred powers have been devalued in our culture: that of images and that of dance. So we have to work to recover their sacred quality within ourselves – but the effort is always worthwhile.

Much of the Way of Merlin is about interaction, about meeting either energies or entities. The interchange between ourselves and these other beings under heightened energized circumstances, when our minds and emotions are not following a customary round, leads to deep inner transformation. Many people ask what is the point of spending hours in meditation and visualization to meet innerworld beings – but this is, perhaps, the wrong question. The encounters are not ends in themselves, merely a half-way situation, for they are the means toward inner change. It is not necessary for the innerworld beings of any tradition, be they orthodox deities or more obscure entities, to *do* anything. There is a popular misconception that in magic, or even in religion, one builds up to a meeting with an otherworldly being, a deity, or even God, and that this being willingly 'does something' to you. This sometimes occurs, but the more usual situation is simple and natural. By actually coming into the presence of an innerworld being, god, goddess, powerful image or whatever, changes are triggered within us. Our energies are realigned, often into their proper alignments, removing blockages and sluggish patterns that we have accumulated during a lifetime, or even over many lifetimes.

If we seek to change ourselves, there is a range of techniques and traditions available, and the Way of Merlin is simply one powerful old tradition that works. Like many others it involves a legendary cycle of encounters, with each encounter triggering changes within ourselves. It is a concentrated and rapid way, not necessarily easy or relaxing. But the changes that are triggered are our own inherent natural changes; they are not imposed upon us by the personae, deities or innerworld contacts.

To put this more simply, we can bring it out and compare it to encounters in the human world. When we meet people day by day, some have little effect upon us. Others, however, have a radical transformative effect – merely by meeting a person and spending time in his or her company we are changed. And the more intense the energy level is between ourselves and others, the more effect the encounters have upon us.

Human emotion is the most obvious example of this – being in love changes our lives. Upon an inner level, the holistic traditions use powerful personae (such as gods, goddess, heroes and the like) to give form to levels of energy that we do not usually reach. These images have a counterpart within our own psyche, but are not limited to it or totally contained within it. They also represent real, living, conscious, independent beings. When we meet such beings in a state of heightened awareness, the encounter and exchange triggers what might be called our latent changes. These encounters of the transformative or magical traditions are identical in many ways to the experiences of human life and relationships, but are impersonal and highly energized. The impersonality is essential – in time, with energy, in attuned or sacred space, it leads us towards transpersonality.

If you work with the cycle of People, the personae found in the Way of Merlin, you will change inwardly. Most of the People are images or archetypes rather than historical persons. Merlin is unusual in that he is human and historical, an image, an archetype, and also masks an ancient god form. Most of the others, however, do not have the human element. When you meet these others they will appear as real presences, and not as vague idealized or rarefied fantasy beings. Because of their absence of humanity they can be very intensely focused upon specific functions, though in each case the first image will mask further images and powers. Thus we may pass through the personae and images towards primal gods and goddess forms. (See Figures 8 and 9 for these connectives.)

PEOPLE, PLACES AND POWERS

The fact that images come from a perennial world-view is not of great value in itself, and there is no point in trying to escape into mental constructs that have no relationship to modern civilization. The contents of a Mystery, however (people, places, powers and transformations) may be brought alive within ourselves. This is not through intense unnatural effort or repeated conditioning, but through germinating the seeds of their inherent presence within us. Any mythic pattern, any set of related images, will work, although the resonance and transformative potential of a Mystery rooted in our own land is often greater than one grafted from elsewhere. All such ways eventually merge, yet the environmental and collective ancestral powers may differ from land to land. Some of the most powerful vital ways of transformation are those that recognize the harmonic or holistic relationship between ourselves and the land, the planet, and the universe . . . or universes.

So if we choose to work in the Way of Merlin, we are working with images and energies, People and powers, that attune to sacred places in the land, and are inherent in ancestral or collective consciousness. Thus if we relate to the land and awaken the power within ourselves that these images embody, we can draw upon an amplified or energized means of personal and transpersonal growth, change, transformation.

Paradoxically, as a Mystery is a holism, it may also be activated anywhere on the planet, though it is at its most potent in those environments best suited to it. This harmonic zoning of the planet is described in the Creation Vision of the *Vita*, and still holds today.

Examples of unsuitable religious or cultural impositions are, sadly, easy to find. We need only think of the disaster of Christianity, derived from a minor patriarchal desert religion and grafted by force of arms upon the people of a temperate environment. In this instance aggression and destruction of the religions of other lands, other cultures, was perpetuated for centuries.

On a mythic level, however, the world's traditions tend to merge, sharing much in common, and transcending the dogmatic antagonism of formal cults or religions. The transformative magic of primal traditions is important to us today, and is now beginning to receive the revival of attention that it deserves.

To realize the potential transformations inherent in the Way of Merlin, we can work through the images and energies that it defines harmonically. The journey from Divine Child to wise elder is our own journey; Merlin merely represents a highly energized life, attuned to the land, and, through this attuning, to the greater environment of the universe. The transformations and polarizations of the Way are found equally in women and men. There is no reason why Merlin should not be female; the journey of the soul or spirit towards wisdom is not gender-defined, but polarity-enabled.

When we meditate upon or visualize encounters with the People, we are giving imaginative form to energies within ourselves, energies that might otherwise be blocked or dormant. The harmonic sequence of adventures upon the Way reveals a deepening and increasingly potent liberation of energies. These are represented by the People, who also represent the inversion or guarding and restricting aspects of the energies.

This initial analysis is not too far removed from materialist psychology, but the images and energies in a mythic magical and spiritual tradition involve many more levels of power than those in a materialist one.

All of the People may be found upon a human level, upon an inner or personal psychic level, upon a natural or environmental level, and as divine or transpersonal, even universal forces. Thus they are inherent within us, but resonate to energies that are, until we truly change, effectively outside ourselves.

This process of unification is not simply one of psychic integration, for it involves unity with the sacred land, relationship to other orders of life, identity with planetary forces, and growing into a universal or stellar consciousness.

People upon the Way

Who or what are the People in the Mystery of Merlin? In the following working set I have concentrated upon the 'major' People or personae. This is not because one person is ultimately of more value to us than another, but because they fall into harmonically related types. These tend to polarize as pairs, then as triads, then as fourfold or squared relationships. To simplify this pattern of relationship we may work through the 'major' People in encounters, a process that we will return to shortly.

People in Pairs

These People in the Mystery emerge from and return to Original Being, Universal Spirit, or God:

1. Spiritual Child (equally male and female): Potential Being.
2. Lord of Animals/Lady of Plants: Openers and Guardians.
3. Youth of Three Disguises: Polarizing Phases (bisexual).
4. Enabling Sister/Enabling Brother (Ganieda and Rhydderch): Enablers and Disablers.
5. Morgen (Priestess or Goddess of Transformation) and

II SUN

VII FOOL

XIII HANGED MAN

X GUARDIAN

XIX EMPRESS

VI JUDGEMENT

Figure 10: Trumps from the Merlin Tarot

The Sun: The Divine Child
The Fool: The Youth of Three
   Disguises
The Hanged Man: Threefold Death

The Guardian: The Wild Lord of the
   Forest
The Empress: The Lady of Flowers
Judgement: Ariadne

Barinthus (Ferryman or Carrier of Consciousness and Spirit):
Transformers.

6. Ariadne (The Weaver and Unweaver of Creation): Being into
Non-Being.

Ariadne is very important as she is the Great Goddess weaving in
out of the Void, the power that polarizes Being and Unbeing.
Thus Ariadne and 'God' are the ultimate polarizations that our
awareness may imagine or encounter.

The Seventh Pair

Another pair described in the Merlin legend are Bladud and
Aileron, two winged mythic beings who preside over sacred
springs. Their physical location is Aquae Sulis, the hot springs and
ancient temple at Bath, England.[16] These beings are the most
ambiguous, yet as they are guardians of energy, and of the gateway
between the inner and outer worlds, they are of great value and
significance.

Bladud is closely related to the bardic god of inspiration,
learning and regeneration, and in Geoffrey's various references is
described as the patron of the druidic arts of shape changing,
flight, ancestral magic and the like. Aileron ('Wings') is his
feminine counterpart, maintaining the polarity theme that runs
throughout the legend, imagery and prophetic traditions
associated with Merlin. Bladud's very name is comprised of two
elements meaning 'bright' and 'dark' (Bel and Dud).

We find this cyclic energy again in the mysterious figure of
Janus, keeper of doorways and thresholds (see Appendix 1). Janus
is associated with the apocalypse of Ariadne, being the last
doorkeeper before her sanctuary and the unweaving of time and
space. He is mentioned again in Geoffrey of Monmouth's *The
History of the Kings of Britain* as presiding over a temple under
the river Soar in Leicestershire in which skilled craftsmen made
offerings every new year.

The tradition of mythic People, rewritten by Geoffrey, preserves
a cycle of polarity. It reveals male and female deities or persons,
but also suggests a cyclic and ultimately bisexual power within the
individual, with ourselves. This theme of bisexuality is defined in
the context of the Fool or Merlin or the Youth of Three Disguises,

who ultimately undergoes the Threefold Death (see Appendix 4). Bisexuality in this context may mean either the joint potential of male and female in us all, regardless of gender, or an ideal or realized hermaphroditic balance; it does not necessarily refer to sexual habits.

THE VISUALIZATIONS

In any myth or legend we find a merging of the natural and supernatural, the human and the otherworldly. There is a strong tendency for certain patterns to emerge, such as the fourfold Elemental cycle, the Wheel of Life, the Three Worlds or octaves of the primal cycle, and so forth. Such patterns and harmonics are properties of consciousness, they are fundamental shapes or cycles by which we respond to all levels of existence. Spiritual traditions remind us that the patterns are fundamental to our consciousness because they are images of ultimate Being: we reflect a relative pattern that runs through all existence.

Our separation of the worlds, however, is purely a conditioned mental product. They are not as distinct as we might pretend. In the Merlin tradition we find seership, prophecy, and human and non-human beings inextricably connected. We leap from one world to another with no warning, and find People who are simultaneously human and divine.

This may be interpreted intellectually as the rag-bag inheritance of Celtic tradition and mythology, worked up into medieval literature or preserved as folklore. Yet the interconnection of the mysterious and the mundane (in modern terms) is an integral part of spiritual tradition. All myths, all magical and spiritual paths, are concerned with the fusion of the worlds.

In some traditions there is a deliberate effort to recover a lost awareness of spiritual reality, and we find this expressed in the Merlin tradition in terms of the purification and redemption of a corrupted land. This theme is aptly prophetic and amply realized and manifested in the twentieth century.

In orthodox religion we find the concept of a dual pattern, heaven and hell, good and evil, dark and light. Such rigid dualism is unnatural: in nature there is no rigid dualism, only rhythmic interaction. If we are to recover ourselves and our world, we need to be liberated from antagonistic separation. One of the inherent values of the Goddess traditions, such as the Way of Merlin, is that they reveal a unified rhythmic vision of reality to us, a vision that corresponds to patterns deep within us. Most of our personal transformation and liberation is from material overlaid upon the primal patterns: only at a later stage do we find liberation from the primal patterns themselves. This is found in the octave of consciousness/energy defined as the Stellar World (Figure 4, page 74).

In most mythic sequences, however, the worlds interact freely, with people passing to and fro and transforming without any suggestion of dualism or separation. This holistic awareness is our proper condition: separation and dualism are merely relative states, not spiritual truths.

To recover this quality of awareness, in which separation between the worlds or energies is variable, there are many techniques. Visualization is effective in charging, energizing, and opening out the collective images. These images resonate with energies in ourselves, and cause changes to occur. This all sounds methodical and intellectualized, but the secret is to do it and not think about it. Visualization is an extension of story-telling and primal image-making. It is not a specialist art or superior technique.

In our examples of visualization there are a number of different ways into the Otherworld, and the process of transition is intentionally kept fluid. There are innumerable combinations of images and routes towards transformation, and the sole value of a tradition (be it religious, magical or psychological) is to give a general framework.

Primal traditions have a paradoxical power of providing very well defined impersonal frameworks which immediately begin to transform and liberate their initiates once they are brought into use. The tradition is eventually transcended and outlived, and dissolves itself through our use of it. Yet without direct personal definition of a tradition, of its people, places, energies, encounters and so forth, it cannot truly come alive. We bring it alive within ourselves. The tradition is a living way, not merely a list of stops along a route.

Once you are familiar with the basic attuning of Sacred Space, and the working with images and energies within that space, many potential encounters and variations are possible. After some experience of this type of work, you will find that the energy and effect of a visualized sequence varies according to the methods of entry.

In the basic examples in this book, as already mentioned, the Otherworld is entered in a variety of ways. There is no dogmatic demand that you follow any one of them, but they all work because they are within the general framework of a powerful tradition. The framework supports us, energizes us, gives shape and direction; without it we may drift or merely stagnate. The intent, however, is entirely our own, and has to come from within ourselves.

To suggest how flexible the process of visualization within a tradition may be, we can look at actual examples. If we use the visualization 'Morgen in the Fortunate Isles' in Chapter 14 we find that it does not involve Barinthus the Ferryman as a direct image, yet the energetic process of transformation and transition which he mediates is still at work. Barinthus is encountered in a separate visualization (also Chapter 14), in which our arrival in the Otherworld is left to free meditation and inner contemplation. This is likely to give results that are different from the defined encounter in the Morgen visualization.

There is no rigid predefined step-by-step system, despite the apparent detail and complexity of the tradition, its people, places, powers, and events. Because of this fluidity and flexibility, it is possible to use the images freely or in structured scenarios. Most important is the concept of leaving silent spaces, in which the deep energies will work directly, and in which visionary developments of the theme may take place.

As another example of working within a tradition but using it in a modern context, we might consider the traditional vision of Ariadne in the *Prophecies* (Appendix 1). This is apocalyptic and disturbing – not in any sense of 'evil', but because it describes universal transformations that are painful if not impossible for the human personality to relate to. In our visualization of Ariadne (Chapter 9), the disruptive imagery is modulated through a number of intermediary images and patterns. Also, the other

People and encounters in the Mystery of Merlin all mediate the power of Ariadne in varying patterns. But in our visualization of Ariadne the apocalyptic power is still present, for it cannot be reduced or circumvented, although it may be approached gradually. This is the reverse of what we hear of Merlin, for he had the full apocalyptic vision while he was still a youth. The choice is ours.

This variety and potential of patterns in visualization is often seductive. It can become, at its worst, a kind of psychic television. At its best it is used as a protean and inspiring means of arousing energies through the imagination.

Now, before we work with the guided visualizations themselves, it is worth outlining the basics of a visualization technique. Even if you are familiar with visualization, you may benefit from working through this short outline, as it suggests the integration of imagination and Sacred Space, and has been proven through experience to work powerfully with the Merlin tradition and related themes.

The Visualization Technique

The basics of entering into visualization are as follows:

1. Work in a location that will not be disturbed in any way.
2. Dedicate the Sacred Space, beginning with the centre, then the Four Directions: East, South, West, North. Complete with Above and Below (as in Figures 1 and 5, pages 18 and 76).
3. Sit as seems best – chair, floor, cushion. The aim is to be relaxed and balanced.
4. Enter into Silence. This is an essential part of the working, and without it visualizations will be less effective. An exercise for entering Silence is outlined below.
5. Out of the Silence the Directions may be reaffirmed, bringing in their attributes as in Figure 1. This may be as brief or as long and full as you require.
6. After a short pause with eyes closed, focusing upon your spiritual centre, the narrative is commenced.

The visualization may be read from a text, such as the examples that follow, or it may be worked from a prerecorded tape.[17] But best of all it should be learned by heart and told aloud, in the manner of direct story-telling.

Once a group or individual has developed some visualizing skill, and has familiarity with a set of mythic images (in this case the images of the Way of Merlin), a significant degree of improvisation and inspiration can arise. The preliminary methods and the essential absorption of the mythic structure and images are usually necessary, though, before the spontaneous level truly comes alive.

Entering Silence

There are a number of techniques for approaching and entering Silence used in both Eastern and Western spiritual disciplines or inner training. We shall concentrate upon one closely associated with the Western arts of transforming consciousness. This is twofold reflective Silence, in which we begin by defining a Sacred Space, such as a room or undisturbed location.

The Silence begins with seeking outer Silence, the traditional and hallowed technique of withdrawal from the noise and bustle of the consensual world. We find this withdrawal heavily emphasized in the Mystery of Merlin, for he is described in the *Vita* as driven into the wildwood by grief and suffering at the loss of his people in a senseless battle. This withdrawal into nature is still found today, when deeply shocked war veterans hide in the wilderness and refuse to relate to regular society. On a personal level it is the choosing of a silent location, an act which in itself begins to sanctify and enliven that location, by the very nature of being there and meditating in it. The reflective level of Silence is, of course, within ourselves. The outer and inner Silence eventually merges together.

The method for seeking outer Silence is simple, and is based upon the concept of universal and individual spheres or fields of consciousness/energy/entity, and the Directions of East or Before, South or Right, West or Behind, North or Left, Above and Below. Your centre of being is the Seventh Direction, which is Within. We may work through this method stage by stage as follows:

1. Sit in a relaxed upright position (upon a chair or upon the floor if you are indoors). For this exercise the hands are usually laid

in the lap, palm up, with the thumb-tips touching . . . some experimentation will find a comfortable balanced location for the hands using this finger position, either with the back of the left hand over the right, or vice versa. The feet may be lightly crossed at the ankles (again right over left or left over right is found through your own intuition and preference, as it varies from individual to individual).

If you use a ground-contact posture (such as a simple cross-legged position), your hand position may remain unchanged, but the legs are usually crossed in the meditators' or hunters' squatting posture, known around the world since ancient times. The Lord of the Animals, Cernunnos, is frequently shown in this position in Romano-Celtic carvings. So we might feel that it is particularly apt for meditation in the Way of Merlin, as one of the primal god-forms in the Mystery was once represented in this posture.

The mystical insight and magical or energetic tradition concerning this position is that it makes maximum earth contact. Energies are drawn into and out of the earth by the contact between the legs, thighs, genitals and buttocks in such postures. It places the Earth and lunar energy centres directly into touch with the sacred land, and therefore with the Underworld.

Another traditional posture is one in which the head is placed between the legs, with the body curved into a circle. This is the position of prophecy used by seers the world over, including Biblical prophets. It works through the flow of energy between the head, or stellar centre of energy, and the genital or lunar centre of energy. This second position need not be used in early work, but is effective after some practice in meditation, energy realization and the other techniques suggested in this book.

2. After a period of steady, calming breathing, with eyes closed, a brief visualization and definition of the Six Directions is made, as already described, and as shown in Figure 5. This results in a generally attuned or orientated sphere or field of entity and energy: our self located within the room, the land, the planet, the universe, aligned according to the Directions and as balanced as possible.

3. We now seek to still customary inner activity (having already stilled outer activity). This is undertaken by inwardly reducing your sense of time, space and energy:

   a) seek to suspend your sense of the passage of time
   b) seek to suspend your sense of space
   c) seek to still all energies within yourself.

   This technique acts upon your entire entity, and makes no separation between inner and outer conditions. The method is one of drawing inwards towards Silence. As time is stilled, as space is withdrawn, and as energy ceases to interact, we pass deeper and deeper within towards our source of Being. All that remains is quiet, steady breathing, the breath of life itself.

4. Emerging from Silence involves drawing in a deep breath and exhaling it. This First Breath of air may then be uttered as Four Vowels, realigning the stilled sphere of being.[18] We may also go no further than drawing the breath and returning to outer consciousness. With practice it is possible to reach through the three phases of timelessness, spacelessness and poise (stilled energy) very rapidly.

To begin with, entering Silence requires patience and repeated simple practice. Strenuous effort will produce the opposite results to those required, and will trick the mind into many side alleys of trivial interaction. The secret is to approach the stillness, the Silence, that is already within you, deep at the centre of your being. That Silence is the state of un-being upon which our being is founded.

The approach to Silence creates relative conditions of stillness, peace and poise. If we truly reached Silence we would pass into a state of existence that cannot be apprehended, for we would reach universal poise, perfect stillness. This condition, if such a word may be used, is found in various definitions in the world's mystical and religious teachings. It is the undifferentiated, unconditioned indefinable, the Void out of which Ariadne weaves and unweaves the universe. In the Mystery of Merlin this is a reflection, a return to that state described in the Creation Vision which says that in the beginning the Creator caused Four Powers to emerge out of Nothing.

The Vision

Time flows back now forward
to an end enveiled.
End beginning where I see
a woman drawing in a thread.
In open dragon-glee she smiles
full knowledge,
Sitting weaving on a throne of lead.

Beyond gate-watching silver head
my vision seeks.
The void breathes in all stars
and blows out night,
flows soundlessly where one,
poised for passing to and fro,
sits waiting on a throne of light.

R.J. Stewart, 1987

CHAPTER 9

The Vision of Ariadne

There was an old woman tossed up in a basket
Seventeen times as high as the Moon,
And where she was going I could not but ask it,
For in her hand she carried a broom.
'Old Woman, Old Woman, Old Woman,' said I
'Where are going to, up so high?'
'To sweep the cobwebs out of the sky!'
'Shall I come with you?'
'Yes, by and by.'

Old English Nursery Rhyme

ARIADNE

We might think that Merlin is the most important figure in the
Mystery of Merlin, but he is not. Or, paradoxically, we might say
that he is the most important central figure, but also the most
disposable. Throughout this reassessment of the Way of Merlin we
have discovered Merlin to be the flexible protean centre, the spirit
in the process of transformation from beginning to end to
beginning: Child, Adult, Elder, Child. When we rebuild this
pattern as a Mystery, as a formal method of working, Merlin is
yourself, myself, everyone.

The key figure and ultimate power in the Mystery of Merlin is
not Merlin, but Ariadne. Historically Ariadne is elusive, referred
to in several myths and legends as a figure connected to threads,
weaving and labyrinths. She is also involved in the growth or

realization of a hero, as in the classical legend of Theseus and the Minotaur. In the Merlin texts and in Celtic legends such as *The Mabinogion* we find her as the Goddess of the Wheel, Arianrhod (Silver Wheel). It is clear from the *Prophecies* that Ariadne is a universal goddess, a stellar power, who opens and closes the gates of creation. Merlin's ultimate vision is of her unweaving the manifest universe, shown in terms of the zodiac, its houses and planets.

So Ariadne is the Weaver Goddess, the Great Goddess of the ancient cultures, and, most important for us as modern people, a powerful mode of consciousness and energy. Whether we see the universe as a random collection of exploded matter or the product of a patriarch Creator, such conceptual models steer our own reality, tending to both mould and limit our understanding and self-expression. If we approach the universe as Ariadne, the Weaver of the Void, we are opened in response to her. Her power is that of Becoming – whatever we may become, whatever becomes, is of Ariadne. And her power is also of Unbecoming, for whatever is made is simultaneously unmade. She is the Gate of the Void through which infinite potential and infinite dissolution flow. The threads of her weaving are the stars moving through space and time . . . three main strands of energy, time and space, co-existent.

In the *Prophecies* Ariadne is attended by Janus, a two-headed image, god of thresholds and transitions. Our month of January, at the turning of the year, is named after this classical deity. He is shown as a figure with two faces, one of a child, one of an old man. Thus Janus is the living polarity, beginning and ending, that is woven by the Goddess. In the Way of Merlin he is the Child and Elder Merlin unified.

Ariadne is the most terrifying power we will ever encounter, yet she is also the most loving and enduring. If we choose to seek the centre of her web we find the Void, yet we also find the Light that issues from that Void, and the peace that dwells beyond our innermost centre of Being. To reach this centre we must experience her power of dissolution, which is described in powerful imagery in the *Prophecies*. Thus the Transformations of Merlin (Figure 2, page 21), are really octaves or links between outer form and inner force, between the personality and the source, between the powers of the land and the universe, between Merlin and Ariadne. The earlier stages of dissolution and re-creation are concerned with personality, with sexuality and fertility, and the union between humanity and the sacred land. The subsequent stages are concerned with the spirit and its relationship to universal Being. Ariadne is finally met between and beyond beginning and end; she is the ultimate dissolution and creation.

Let us now proceed to the visualization in which we meet Ariadne, the Weaver Goddess.

ENCOUNTERING ARIADNE

After a period of Silence, Sacred Space is opened and enlivened.

We begin by seeing a hearth, with a gentle fire burning. This is the home hearth, the eternal light of companionship, family, friendship, love. We feel the warmth of this fire upon our faces, and as we do so, build the image of the fireplace. It is of rough stones, with a thick wooden lintel, and a wide dark chimney. The logs in the fire are of aromatic wood, and we smell the scent of pine, cedar and other tree resins. Tiny sparks shoot from the logs and rise to vanish into the darkness of the deep chimney. We sit, and breathe deeply, and experience rest and peace. *A pause for silent meditation here.*

Now the flames have died down into a calm red glow, and the room is filled with shadow. We look upon the embers and seek vision within them, in the way of the ancestors. Here are all tales, all songs, all visions found, beyond the threshold of the fire. As we look upon the embers, we see fleeting images of hearth fires, of travellers' fires in the wilderness, of beacons blazing on hilltops, and of the perpetual fires in small shrines and great temples. These rise and fall, rise and fall, until we focus upon the tiny glow of one last remaining ember in the dark hearth. It sheds a clear ray of light into the shadow at the back of the fireplace, and in those shadows we see a movement, a tiny flash of colour.

Looking closely at this moving, glittering colour, we see that it is a strand appearing out of the shadow and returning to it . . . a strand lit by the last ember, yet out of reach of the heat. Into the dim light comes a tiny spider, weaving her web. Upon her back is a clear mark, which lightens and fades as it catches the glow of the soft ember light. We look upon this mark as she weaves her web in and out of our vision, and gradually our perception narrows until we see only the glow of light, the growing web, and the jewel-like mark upon the spider's back. *Pause for meditation here.*

As our eyes grow accustomed to the shadow, we see that behind the web is a tiny cleft in the stones, and instantly our attention is fixed upon this. We see the web enlarge and billow out from the shadows towards us . . . It is filled with silver light, and flows out and around us, enlarging until we pass through its strands untouched, and fall towards the cleft within the darkness before us.

We fall through silence and shadow, stillness and calm. We forget the room and the hearth, and know only stillness, silence, gentle falling into peace. Now we come to rest in an unknown unseen place of stillness. We breathe deeply, and wait. *Pause for breathing and Silence here.*

Out of the shadow before us we see a shape forming. It is a Gateway with two uprights and a lintel. We look upon this dim shape and see one upright is silver and one black, while the lintel above is of a clear crystalline material flecked with fragments of different colour. Gradually we rise and walk towards this Gate. Our feet are upon a dark surface that we cannot see, but which we feel as we walk forward; the Gate slowly comes into view and we realize that it is of immense size, standing in the soft darkness, leading from the shadow to the shadow. As we approach the Gate, we see that there are no doors between the uprights. Slowly we arrive at this huge portal, and look first at the black pillar, then at the silver pillar. Now we look up at the crystalline pillar far above us, and in its depths we see flickers of light and movement.

As we look up, we seem to grow, or the Gate seems to shrink. The crystal lintel is now level with our eyes, and we suddenly realize that to pass through we must leap immediately into the unknown shadows beyond. Without a further thought, we jump through.

As we jump a series of images seems to meet us: flickering patterns of old memories, faces, places, some that had almost been forgotten, others that we remember well. Through this host of images we hear a deep sibilant sound, a pervasive hissing underpinned by a deep resonant flowing tone. For an instant a babble of voices rises through this sound, then falls still. The host of images fades to be replaced by a single clear object. We see that it is a face, one half in darkness, the other half in light. One half is that of a child, the other half is old. We look upon this face, young and old, dark and light flowing together. *Pause for silent meditation.*

Slowly the head begins to rotate, and as it turns a light appears and passes across the darkness. The head begins to move rapidly until its features blur together, and as it spins it slowly reduces in size until it vanishes. The light that spreads through the darkness is starlight, and we find that we are in the centre of a vast wheel of stars, rising and falling all around us. The stars rise above and fall below us, and their movement is the cause of the sound . . . the hissing and resonant tones that we hear are the voices of the stars as they turn and flow through the Void.

As we realize that the stars flow through the Void, we are aware of a dim figure before us. It seems close and of human size, yet also vast beyond measure. We see a woman sitting upon a throne; her face is covered by a deep hood. In her hand she holds a distaff, a long pole with a triple thread falling from it. This thread leads to a spindle that spins in at out of our sight, forming endless patterns about us, weaving in and out of the flow of stars.

This is the Goddess Ariadne, Weaver of Being and Unbeing. As we look upon her, her deep hood slowly unfolds and falls back . . . At first we see a face, beautiful and terrible, then through that face we enter the Void. *Silent pause here.*

Out of the Silence a sound emerges . . . It is the sound of breath. We become aware of a breathing in and out, and realize that this breathing is our breath and yet the breath of all Being. We breathe, Being breathes. Slowly we feel form assemble from the breathing, and realize that we have a body which is the body of all Being. The stars are within us, we are formed of the Weaving.

Gradually we become aware of a tiny red glow in the shadows, and find that we are sitting before a hearth fire. Behind and above the embers is a spider's web, barely lit by the fire. As we look, the ember slowly dims, until it is the smallest spark, the seed of flame that remains through the long night. We know that we may draw fire from this seed at will, and use it to bring light out into the world beyond. We realize that the seed of fire is within us, in our hearts, and meditate upon our true will and perfect Being. *Pause for meditation here.*

Now we slowly return to outer consciousness. The fireplace and glowing ember gradually dissolve, to be replaced by a familiar room. We are sitting in the dedicated space that focuses our energies. Let us now return to our outer world to bring with us the realization and the power and the peace that we have found within the presence of Ariadne.

CHAPTER
10

The Mystery of Merlin

This visualization uses images taken from the traditional life story of Merlin. The method is to use a cycle or sequence of encapsulated tales, generating brief key images from the Mystery but not expounding them in full. Some of the People and themes are developed in the visualizations which follow, others you will want to work with and build for yourself, once you have worked through our key examples.

Rather than intense visualization upon a single theme, the story cycle, a method well established in oral tradition, particularly in the highly concentrated ballads and similar narrative epics found world-wide, gives short bright sequences of images within an overall tale. Any one of these images may be a further tale in its own right, and in the almost lost art of true oral story-telling, many digressive patterns and harmonic changes were commonplace. In oral tradition, the images may become rationalized or confused, though many magical ballads found in European and American tradition are remarkably coherent and powerful; but in magical practice we can employ the sequential process to create a total change of consciousness.

Although the story-telling style may seem initially to be less intense than our other visualizations upon major themes, it is in many ways more demanding to undertake, for it involves several fairly rapid changes of imaginal scenery and locations, and a very wide range of energies.

Rather than agonise over the technicalities of such a method, we allow the tradition or Mystery to work for us, for it has been tested through long periods of time, and has powerful innerworld connections.

The images are part of a mystical or magical tradition of story-telling containing both psychological and cosmological exposition. The visualization does not extract these as academic texts, but employs the primary images found in the texts within an overall story in which we meet Merlin, who then reveals to us glimpses of the cycle of his Mystery, which is also in part his biography.

The origins of this story cycle are organic, they derive from a collective relationship between humans and the land stretching back into the most primal prehistoric times. In its shortest format, the story tells of the First and Last Being: his or her journey from divine childhood at the moment of creation of the worlds to ultimate old age and wisdom at the end of all things. This cycle is found in the Tarot, with the development of The Fool into The Hermit. It is also found in the Merlin literature, for in the *Prophecies* (preceded by some biographical matter in the *History*) the child Merlin sees right to the end of time, often in remarkable detail in the context of British future history, but with a deeper cosmological vision of the powers of creation and destruction controlled by a Weaver Goddess called Ariadne. In the *Vita Merlini* the mature Merlin experiences many transformative events and encounters, and finally retires to a stellar observatory with a small group of companions, having reached immense age and wisdom.

The same is found in the major myth cycle of *Mabon* from Celtic tradition, though much of this cycle is now lost. Here the imprisoned child Mabon is only discovered through the assistance of the oldest creature of all – a salmon, magical or companion creature of wisdom, who has heard him cry. Thus the Mabon cycle, in which a marvellous child is stolen away from his mother at birth, kept prisoner in a mysterious place and is the subject of many heroic rescue ventures, is found inherent within the Merlin cycle, sharing many of the major characteristics. Both sets of tales include a strong emphasis upon the orders of creation – Mabon is found only with the assistance of many wise animals, while the *Vita* has not only many companion animals in direct connection to Merlin, but also an encyclopedic expansion of natural history, added to the original oral theme by the prolific Geoffrey of Monmouth, who drew upon the classical sources known in his day. As the details of both the Merlin and Mabon Mysteries and their close connections have been discussed elsewhere, we do not need to take the comparison any further here. But there are some valuable teachings inherent in the theme that are used for advanced magical arts, particularly the motif of *imprisonment*.

Following this motif, the Merlin cycle reveals the child Merlin, born of human and non-human parents, imprisoned by the traitor Vortigern, who intends to sacrifice him in a corrupt magical ceremony to bolster up his own power. The prisoner is liberated through his prophetic revelations, which he makes in a cave beneath Vortigern's stronghold. In the *Vita* the mature Merlin, in a state of madness, is imprisoned by King Rhydderch, chained to a post at the gates of the city. Their exchange of views is a typical argument between spiritual inspiration and worldly power.

The Mabon cycle reveals the mysterious child, stolen away from his mother at birth, and imprisoned for an immense period of time in a fortress, but with many creatures and heroes attempting to set him free. Similar imprisonment motifs are found in the Welsh *Triads* involving heroes, youths, and even King Arthur. [19] This theme of Arthur and imprisonment is also found in the important ancient Welsh poem 'Preiddeu Annwn' in which Arthur and a band of heroes enter the Underworld.

The theme recurs in a very widespread ballad, found in many variants in Europe and America, known in its English variants as 'Lord Bateman' or 'Young Beichan'. In this version, the hero is chained to a tree or post by a Saracen king, but is eventually liberated by the king's daughter who exchanges vows with the prisoner. Upon his departure, she seeks him out in a magical boat, an important recurring theme in Celtic legend, and eventually true love wins through. Many further instances could be cited relating to imprisonment with a magical or mythical significance.

It is generally assumed that the prisoner is in the Underworld or Otherworld – many variants of the theme state this expressly and it is reiterated in the early Christian motif of Christ descending into the lower worlds to liberate the souls trapped therein. [20]

Here we find a paradox, for Christ also descended to the human world, and it seems likely that this world is the 'hell' from which some early Christian sects sought liberation. Gnostic tradition made no doubt about this teaching. However, we should seek the primal foundation of any myth, no matter what tradition we employ in actual practice.

From the various known traditions, we can presume that the original tale concerned a Divine Child, Perfect Being, taken from his Mother, The Goddess, and imprisoned within, and through the creation of, the outer or expressed worlds. The vast cycle of time and adventures leading to his ultimate liberation comprises the story of the cycle of the worlds. When the Child is released, the worlds come to an end. But there is also the implication that the process is mirrored upon a human level, for the divine spirit is inherent within humanity: when the motif is attached to a human being, he or she undergoes a harmonic or parallel imprisonment, and not merely that of physical incarnation, for incarnation is taught, significantly, in many spiritual traditions world-wide to be the route to liberation. The imprisonment is within the Underworld, the region of direct power that underpins material dimensions, and yet paradoxically contains the highest or originative spiritual reality. Thus a hero or otherwise sanctified person stands in for or reflects the Divine Child in an experience which *mirrors* the primal myth. The true meaning of the enduring tradition of sacred kingship is found in this Mystery, far removed from the crude rationalizations of victimization for the health of crops or any other superficial reductionist explanation.

Having said this much, there is no suggestion that *all* ritual sacrifices were undertaken with a profound purpose, for there is ignorance, viciousness and folly in all human activities at all times. We are referring here to the deepest spiritual levels of the sacrificial motif, levels which have been claimed as the sole property of Christianity, but which are undoubtedly known in non-Christian and pre-Christian religions and metaphysical traditions.

A third resonance is found when the Divine Child, the Son of Light, incarnates within the human world. This is a reflection of the original imprisonment which occurred at the beginning of all worlds, but the Son of Light willingly imprisoned in the human world (a motif reflected yet again in his trial and death found in the redeemer myths) is really present in these worlds to liberate humanity.

So we find that Merlin, who begins as a magical child, is imprisoned by Vortigern, but his liberation is gained through the arousal of the Red and White Dragons, and he foresees to the very end of creation in his sequence of prophetic visions. The content of his prophetic vision contains keys to liberation, not only through prediction or foreknowledge, but through the cosmological and magical visions within the text, which may be used as methods of transmuting consciousness.

The sacrificial element in the Merlin stories is found in the central motif of Threefold Death, which in the *Vita* is centred upon a youth, though in other variants is undergone by the prophet himself. To conclude the *Vita*, Merlin lives to a great old age after many profound experiences, and withdraws to spiritual contemplation, but in magical traditions he is still present in a dimension close to our own, and intimately linked to the land of Britain. We should remember, however, that Merlin may be contacted without being in Britain, and that there are many related images of innerworld teachers which will attune to the Mystery of Merlin, or to related Mysteries within any specific land or location.

THE MERLIN VISUALIZATION

Silence is entered, Sacred Space is opened and enlivened. The visualization is begun with a Crossing Formula:

> In the Name of the Star Father *Height/Above*
> The Earth Mother *Depth/Below*
> The True Taker *Right Hand*
> And the Great Giver, *Left Hand*
> One Being of Light *Totality/Circle*.

A small candle or night-light is lit in the North, the Direction of Merlin.

We begin by building in our inner vision the clear image of a narrow winding track. This track leads up a steep hillside between leaning trees and bushes; it is stony and rutted, and many wild plants grow around its steep banks. The trees curve over the track, almost joining above to create a tunnel. We enter this living archway, and begin to climb up the hill. As we pass along the steep track, we can sense a presence in the bushes, watching us, following, sometimes moving ahead with faint rustling sounds. We can see nothing, yet we know that this presence, filled with curiosity, accompanies us on our journey.

The overgrown tunnel of trees ends at the top of the hill; we emerge onto a small flat summit, and before us we see an immense view stretching away to the horizon. The other side of the hill leads down steeply to a wide flat plain, lit by a deeper red sunset. The land is filled with long shadows and low light, and far to the West there is a glimmer of the sea. There are low rounded hills upon the plain, like islands, and as we watch the sun set, tiny fires are lit on the summits, as the watchers make ready for night. A bright star rises over the horizon, radiating colour as she climbs into the dark blue sky.

At the very edge of the tree line behind us is a ruined tower, close to where we emerged from the steep path. The stones are crumbling and black and green with age; long creepers and ivy grow all over this tower, and its shape is softened by decay and foliage. As we turn towards the tower, a light springs up in the single window near the top, as if someone stands unseen within the chamber, and holds a lantern up for us.

We take one last look at the sunset lands far below, and turn to enter the tower. There is a plain wooden door, charred with fire and blackened with soot. We push upon it, but despite its damaged appearance it holds firm and does not open. Through the tangle of ivy high above our heads, a dim light streams out of the slit window, but although we push on the door and knock loudly with our fists, no one comes to greet us. We pause for a few moments to consider our situation. *A short silent meditation here.*

Out of the silence of the night, we hear many tiny sounds: the rustle of wind in leaves, the distant calling of an owl, and the faint lowing of a cow far across the dark plain. Suddenly a shrill sound pierces the night from the window above us – three high-pitched whistling calls. From the bushes in the darkness we hear a scurrying scuffling sound and the snapping of twigs as something rushes towards us. For an instant we feel that a vast creature is about to hurtle itself into our midst, but to our surprise it is a small black and brown pig. It trots right up to the door. The pig ignores us, and nudges at the foot of the door with his snout, grunting and squealing in excitement. We hear a loud click as if a lock has opened, and the pig pushes the door open and runs inside. We hear him scrabbling up the stairs, grunting happily. The door is open, and we hasten to follow the pig.

The stairs are of crumbling, deeply worn stone, also blackened by fire, and they curve steeply around the tower, leading to a single chamber at the summit. We reach the entrance, which is covered by a fine woven cloth with many faint patterns upon it; the chamber within is perfectly round, and lit by a small dim lamp hanging from the centre of the ceiling. A peat fire glows redly in the fireplace, and the floor of the chamber seems covered with feathers. At first the room appears to be empty, except for the pig, who is eating noisily from a bowl by the fireside. Then we see a dim figure by the tiny slit window; he sits upon a three-legged chair, and has a hood drawn over his face. As we realize he is present, he sits up and takes notice of us, throwing back his dark hood. His face is lined and aged, his hair is long and silver-grey, he has a black and grey beard. His eyes are bright and penetrating, filled with compassion and understanding. He raises one hand and beckons to us slightly. We draw near and sit at his feet among the feathers on the floor. We know that this is Merlin, the Prophet and Master of the Western Mysteries. *A silent pause for meditation here.*

Merlin reaches into the shadows behind his three-legged chair, and as he turns we see that the chair legs each have a different colour, red, white and black, and are inscribed with minute curving, swirling patterns. His black robe flows over the seat of the chair onto the floor of the room. It has ragged edges, like crow feathers, and we can see the glimmer of other colours revealed and then concealed, as if all the feathers of every bird in the land are woven into another garment beneath. He turns back towards us, holding a large battered, well-worn book, which he faces towards us for us to see clearly. It has a scuffed torn leather cover with many stains, and is bound with blackened metal clasps and corners, which might be of silver. We can see faint words and decorations tooled into the aged leather, but the meaning is unclear. When he is sure that our full attention is upon the book, Merlin opens it and turns the pages, seeking for a certain place. As the pages turn we hear faint sounds of voices, music, chanting, animals running and calling, birds flying and the distant faint surging of waves upon the sea-shore. Merlin holds the pages flat, and the noises cease. He suddenly holds the great book up, with the pages open towards us, revealing what he has chosen.

We see black curving script in neat lines, and a tiny illuminated picture in bright red, blue and gold marking the topmost left hand corner of the page. It shows a walled turreted city, and just outside the city gates, two boys are playing with a ball. As we look at this tiny image, it expands and fills with sunlight: we seem to fall into the scene, and suddenly find ourselves standing before the tall white towers and the wide open gates in the hot summer sunlight. We see that one boy is a child of almost ethereal grace and beauty, and know that this is the young Merlin. His companion is dark and haughty, and while the young Merlin wears a plain woollen tunic, faded and patched, his companion wears a rich black and gold tunic and green trews. They throw the ball to one another and bounce it against the wall, but there is a tension in the game, as if they have just argued.

From the open gates a troop of soldiers strides. They are tall mercenaries in battered helmets, carrying an odd assortment of weapons. They are dressed in dull blue and grey tunics and trousers, with strips of brightly coloured rag and feathers in their long greasy hair and on their scarred arms. They suddenly surround the boy Merlin and march off with him, down the road, away from the city. His companion stands aside, and bounces the ball, uncertain what is happening. As the troop of mercenaries and the young Merlin pass down the long road, the light seems to fade, and darkness falls. We see Merlin's companion run into the city, and the gates are pulled shut. Then we feel sorrow, for we know that young Merlin is to be imprisoned, and that someone intends for him a terrible death.

In the darkness we hear the rustle of pages turning, and remember that we sit before the aged Merlin in his tower. He is leafing through his large leather-bound book, and somewhere in the chamber we can hear the pig snoring. Merlin selects a page and again holds it up for us to see. In the dim lamplight we see an illuminated picture of a hill. The side of the hill is cut away, in the manner of old pictures, to let us see within. Two tiny figures sit by the side of a pool deep within the hill. As we look at this scene, the image fills with light and expands. We somersault into the picture and find ourselves upon our feet behind a mound of fallen rock littered with shovels, picks and buckets.

On the other side of the rocks is the pool, and we look over the mound to see the young Merlin sitting cross-legged by the pool-side. His eyes are closed, and he does not move. A faint light seems to radiate from him. Close by, sitting upon an ornate throne resting precariously in the mud and rocks, is a thin brooding man with long red hair and a wispy beard. He tugs at his lower lip with one hand, his fingers heavy with rings, many amulets and inscribed bands upon his arm. We realize that this is Vortigern, the great king. He stares at the waters of pool, his heavy-lidded eyes occasionally turning to look at the boy. As they sit in silence, the waters of the pool begin to move and seethe; steam rises, and two shapes float to the surface, thrashing together in violent movement. The boy Merlin opens his eyes, and points triumphantly at the pool. We feel a sudden surge of joy and exaltation. There is an explosion of light so brilliant that our eyes close and fill with tears, and vivid coloured shapes flash against our eyelids. Darkness falls, with tiny faint lights echoing and exploding within it.

In the silence that follows we know that the child has been released from his imprisonment. We hear the turning of pages, and open our eyes to see the dim circular chamber lit by the central lamp. The fire glows and emits the distinctive smell of burning peat; the little pig sleeps before the hearth grunting softly. The aged Merlin pauses for a moment as he turns the pages, and smiles gently at an image that we cannot see. The air is filled momentarily with the rich scent of summer flowers, and for a moment he lingers over the page as if lost in memory. But he turns another page, and another more rapidly. Faint sounds blur through the rustle of the turning pages, the galloping of horses, the clash of arms, the screaming of wounded men. Finally Merlin pauses in his turning, and once again holds the great book up with the pages for us to see. There is no written text, no tiny formal illuminated figures, but a deep window fills the double page, looking onto a dark purple stormy sea. We are drawn through this window, and fall upon a cold sandy beach. The salt smell of seaweed is around us, and we hear the waves biting and lashing at the shore. A cold rain falls, and the wind swirls and screams.

Through the storms we hear the sound of wheels scraping through the wet sand and rocks. We see two figures, huddled against the weather, pushing a small cart. One wears a long dark cloak and a broad-brimmed hat; the other is dressed in a green and yellow chequered cloak, stained with rain. His long flowing hair is bound by a silver circlet around his head, and across his back a small harp is slung in an ornate red and gold leather case. We realize that this is the bard Taliesin, Silver Brow, and that his companion is the mature Merlin. They trudge past us wheeling the cart, and we see upon it the body of a tall man wrapped in a bloodstained purple cloak. They pass very close to us, yet do not look at us; their faces are drawn, exhausted, sad.

By the shore they lower the shafts of the cart, and Merlin walks to the very edge of the sea. He faces into the storm, and raises his arms in supplication. His hat blows away in the rising wind, and we hear snatches of a deep resonant chant in a language that we do not know. The storm builds, and the clouds lower slowly down upon the beach, issuing an endless flood of heavy rain. As we look at Merlin by the sea's edge, the waves washing over his legs, we realize that a dark shape is slowly approaching the shore. At first we think it is a tall-necked creature from the deep sea, then we realize that it is the prow of a boat. Standing in the stern is a huge figure wrapped in undulating sea mist. We try to see more of this mysterious vessel and ferryman, but now the bard Taliesin comes before us, and spreading out his tartan cloak, flings it over our heads. In the total blackness of that cloak we see no more.

The sound of pages turning, and the dim red glow of a fire brings us back to the tower. Now Merlin shows us a series of tiny images, rapidly turning the pages of the book with its face towards us. We see men building a circular stone structure with many doors and windows; a tall queen stands and directs their work, while just upon the edge of each picture as it ripples past, we see a naked man capering madly. He is wrapped in ivy garlands and ropes of flowers, a set of antlers sprouting from his hairy head. The building is finished, and a sudden spiral of stars appears over it.

Merlin spreads the book upon his lap, where we cannot see its content, and turns to the last page. He pauses for a moment, and slowly holds it up for us. We see the image of the Weaver with her distaff, turning the Spindle of the Worlds in the depths of space and time. We see an aged man and a tiny child – somehow both are Merlin, yet sometimes becoming female, now young, now old. We see ourselves there briefly, then the image fades into a spiralling of stars, which slowly turns and vanishes.

Merlin closes the book with a loud snap that jolts us wide awake, and lets it fall heavily upon the floor, throwing up a cloud of feathers. As the feathers fall we see a spiralling pattern upon the back cover, embossed deeply into the leather and coloured with many faded tints. It is a picture of an old man with a tall staff walking along a spiralling road, leading to the centre of the image where a tower is shown. The very top of the tower is set with a rough white crystal. Merlin bends and places both his hands over this crystal for a moment, and we hear a muted resonance. He draws back and the crystal begins to shine. We look within it and the embossed picture upon the page turns black, until all we see is the crystal and the images within it. *A period of silent meditation here.*

Now the image of the crystal fades slowly, and we look about to find that we are in an empty chamber, with dawn rising through a narrow window before us. The three-legged chair is unoccupied, and we see that it is not coloured, as we had thought, but of crude unpolished wood. The fire has gone out, and the lamp is missing, but in the dusty feathers upon the floor is a distinctive shape, as if a large book has lain there for some time. The chamber has a faint odour of peat smoke, and of pig.

We stand, and make our way down the spiralling stair that seems very short, barely three turns, and beyond the door, which stands wide open, falling from its hinges with age. The forest has grown right up around the tower. Indeed, this seems almost a different tower and a different forest to those that we entered, but a clear path leads away through the trees, sloping gently downhill. It is as if the land has sunk and the forest grown, and the tower crumbled into a tiny overgrown stone chamber.

We take the path, and the sound of many birds singing fills our hearts with joy. It is morning, and a new world comes awake with the rising sun. *Music here if possible and a pause for meditation and realization.*

Now our vision is drawing to an end. Let us still our awareness of the inner realms, and be wrapped in silence before returning to the outer world. Now we close the way in the words and by the power of the ancient Mystery: **Peace is a secret Unknown.**

The word 'Amen' is resonated by all, and a period of Silence observed. The visualization is now over, and those present depart in their own time. The central light may be left burning in the room.

Contents of the Visualization

The visualization is divided into 12 parts, and although these lead into one another within the overall frame of reference, they can be defined and briefly examined separately as follows:

1. The entry to the inner world, dedicating and enlivening Sacred Space. This is energized through the Crossing Formula and visualization. The first part concludes at the entrance to the tower, with the meditation period seeking admission.

2. The appearance of the companion creature (the pig) able to gain for us the admission which was previously barred.

3. The ascent of the tower and the vision of the aged Merlin, concluding with the meditation upon his presence.

4. The magical implements: the three-legged chair and book. These are the traditional implements of seership and prophecy. The ancient seeresses of classical Greek and Roman temples or oracular shrines sat upon tripods, and the triple symbol is preserved in legend and folklore, relating to the three aspects of the Great Goddess, or the three essential ingredients or magical compounds of blood, sweat or seed, and body or tears.

   In metaphysics these are the triple universal threads of time, space and energy, woven inseparably by the Weaver. The three strands or tripod legs are coloured red, white and black.

   The book may be regarded in several different ways: it is a formal presentation of the mirror or shield of the northern

Quarter, the reflecting and purifying Element of form, or Earth. North is the traditional direction associated with Merlin, and with prophecy.

It is also the archetypical book of all knowledge and wisdom, but in this particular case it is the book of the Mystery of Merlin. This is the inner or magical version of that 'great Book' which Geoffrey of Monmouth claimed to have used to copy his *History*; it is the volume of collective and ancestral memory and myth. It may only be activated, however, in very specific modes or levels, for a total activation might lead to madness and destruction.

5. Image (a): The young Merlin and his companion or twin (tanist) playing ball outside the city. Although this refers directly to the legend of Vortigern and Merlin and the Saxon mercenaries and invaders, there are some sub-textual elements worth commenting upon briefly. The two youths relate to the ancient pattern of sacred kingship, in which two brothers or polarized male candidates were frequently found. They become the Dark and Light Brother in myth or folklore, the Accuser and the Innocent. We find this in the Christian mythology of Jesus and Judas, but the motif is widespread in legend of a non-Christian origin or tradition. In the Mystery of Merlin they are Merlin and Dinabutius. Merlin is accused of having no proper father in a childish argument, but this reveals his double nature (born of virgin and daemon) to the messengers of King Vortigern. Finally Merlin is carried off to be sacrificed, in order that Vortigern's false tower might be upheld by innocent blood. Thus this earliest reference to the youthful Merlin (from the *History*) is an undoubted sub-story linked to the pagan system of sacrificial kingship. It ends with a feeling of sorrow, loss and imprisonment.

6. Image (b): Young Merlin and Vortigern at the underground pool. Merlin proves that two dragons exist, and their appearance leads him into a prophetic trance. The vision ends with a feeling of joy and liberation. We do not, however, enter into the prophetic sequence at this stage.

7. Merlin examines his personal life in the book, but does not

reveal it to us as a specific vision. We develop this theme in the visualization 'The Lady of Flowers' in Chapter 13, in which we meet one image or form of the Goddess-power associated with sexuality and fertility. In the Merlin legend, as in other Celtic myths, she is represented as a woman of flowers, an idealized lover.

8. Image (c): The carrying of the wounded king to the Otherworld. This is a major visualization in its own right, but here we only enter into part of it, and that part is shrouded in mystery and uncertainty.

   In this vision the bard Taliesin protects us from the presence upon the boat that Merlin has summoned. To see this Ferryman direct we must die. In visualizations he is usually given the form of the Celtic god Barinthus, a type of sea or navigating deity, as named by Geoffrey in the *Vita*. In the present vision, however, he is present in a higher or more direct form. We shall work with the image of Barinthus in a separate visualization in Chapter 14.

9. Image (d): A rapid series of pictures blurring together, showing the mad Merlin and his sister Ganieda, an archetypical human who embodies the goddess Briggidda/Minerva, building their stellar observatory.

10. Image (e): The Weaver (the trump of Judgement in *The Merlin Tarot*). This major image is the culmination of the sequence that we have seen. There are a number of implications concerning sacred kingship, wounding, imprisonment and liberation, and the synchronicity or spiritual astrology of such events through long spirals of outer time. This type of astrology is not identical with our modern Western astrology, though they have much in common.

11. The back of the book: This shows Merlin climbing to his tower or *esplumoir* to await our coming. The final paradox is in the crystal of vision set into the image of the tower on the back cover of the great book. It is at this point that we may receive visual impressions from other worlds and beings. These are not always conditioned by the imagery built up through the story sequence.

12. Conclusion: The transformation of the chair, the absence of the book and lamp. Merlin has departed, and the magical implements of book and three-legged chair plus the lamp (symbol of The Hermit in the Tarot) have vanished. The chair that remains has no magical qualities, and we are left to decide for ourselves the truth of the experience of meeting Merlin. The tower and landscape, however, have been transformed, as if a long period of time has passed, far longer than the one night implied by the sequence of vision and the rising dawn.

If Merlin has revealed the mythic past to us during the sequence of visions, we emerge in the final stage into the paradisal future. We meditate upon this transformative possibility, as we return to the present time and place.

Finally the sequence is closed by a period of silent meditation and the word of power 'Amen'. Sacred Space is closed with a final affirmation and return to Silence.

Chapter 11

Ritual Creation
of the World

To show how a group working with Sacred Space can be developed, I have chosen an example from an actual gathering at Hawkwood College, in Gloucestershire, England, in 1987. This was a weekend course or workshop, with approximately 50 people attending, and a strong emphasis upon practical work rather than theory. (Figures 1, 3, 5, 6 and 7 will be helpful in following and working with this material. A useful exercise is to draw out the ground-plan of the People, Directions, and movements.)

Two key events in the weekend were an improvised visualization, which appears in this book as 'The Cry of Merlin' (Chapter 12), and a ceremony, 'The Creation of the Worlds', which follows shortly. To give some indication of how the events worked in practice, I have included my own notes from 1987, with some brief additional comments in the context of this book. I have left the notes as they were, without trying to edit or expand them in any way. As suggested earlier, note-taking is often helpful after visualizing and working with Sacred Space, but it should never become obsessive.

THE CREATION OF THE WORLDS

The People at the Quarters:

Taliesin (East)   Instructor in the Mystery Tradition: Priest
Bladud (South)   Sacred King: Mediator of Ancestral Power
Morgen (West)   Regeneratrix: Priestess
Ariadne (North)   Queen: Goddess

The functions of each Quarter/Person:

East: Summons the Wind and powers of Purification (Purification)

South: Summons Fire and the Company of Blessed Ancestors in Light (Illumination)

West: Summons Water and the powers of Regeneration (Regeneration)

North: Summons the Earth/Stars and the powers of Transformation (Transformation)

The People at the Cross-Quarters:

Guendoloena (Southeast)   Mediates the power of Spring
Rhydderch (Southwest)   Mediates the power of Summer
Ganieda (Northwest)   Mediates the power of Autumn
Merlin (Northeast)   Mediates the power of Winter
and transition from the inner world. No representing Officer.

The Company: If there are more in the group than specified by the People at the Quarters, Cross-Quarters, and other locations, the Company affirms that the gathering represents all humanity, past, present, and future.

The Herald: Questions or challenges/invites as indicated below.

   A central light is lit.
   There is an opening reading from the Vita Merlini: *The Creation Vision (Appendix 2).*
Herald: Are there Four within this space to speak for the Four Powers?
   The Four Directions declare as follows:
East: 'I am named Taliesin; it was I who taught the patterns of the Creation of the Universe to the questing Merlin, according to the ancient and enduring tradition of the Mysteries of Life.'
South: 'I am named Bladud; it was I who opened the Gates to the Otherworld, when they were sought by the questing Merlin according to the Mysteries of Light.'
West: 'I am named Morgen; it was I who took the questing Merlin to the Fortunate Isles of the West for his regeneration through the Mysteries of Love.'

North: 'I am named Ariadne; it was I who gave the vision of eternity to the questing Merlin when his perceptions flew up to the stars through the Mysteries of Universal Law.'

Herald: 'How shall these Mysteries be made One today to recreate the World?'

East: 'By the power of Life in me I invoke the Element of Air that all corruption shall be purified and made clean.' *(Invokes)*

South: 'By the power of Light in me I invoke the Element of Fire and the Company of Illuminated and Blessed Kings and Heroes, that all seeds of new beginnings shall flourish and grow strong, by the fire of innermost power made manifest in the outer world.' *(Invokes)*

West: 'By the power of Love in me I invoke the Element of Water that nourishes and distils, enabling regeneration and rebirth.' *(Invokes)*

North: 'By the power of universal Law in me I invoke the perfect Element of Earth, that the wonder of the stars may be reflected within the regenerated world now and forever.' *(Invokes)*

Herald: 'How shall these great powers be made manifest?'

Ganieda: 'Through the fullness of the questing fruitful mind may a perfect kingdom be enabled.'

Guendoloena: 'Through the rising growing joy of balanced feelings shall that same perfect kingdom be enlivened.'

Rhydderch: 'Through honourable and immaculate deeds and works shall that perfect kingdom be made whole.'

Herald: 'In the Northeast stands a misty figure, waiting at the point of spiralling, the place of transition. No one person here may speak for him, for he is Merlin in the past, in the present, and in the future. His role is to fuse these powers as one, to make ready for the Blessed Son of Light within the centre of our circle of creation.'

East: 'Who stands for the ultimate Roots of the World?'

The Company: 'We all stand, then, now, and forever.'

East: 'Who stands for the Plants of the World?'

Company: 'We all stand, then, now, and forever.'

East: 'Who stands for the Creatures of the World?'

Company: 'We all stand, then, now, and forever.'
East: 'Who stands for the Men and Women of the World?'
Company: 'We all stand, then, now, and forever.'
South: ' Who will stand for the Earth?
Who will stand for the Moon?
Who will stand for the Sun?
Who will stand for the Stars?
Who will stand for the great primal Dragons?
Who will stand for the First and Last Breath of Being?'
North: 'In the pattern of the Weaving moves the Child of Light who may be male, female, or both, the spirit who spoke through Merlin, who hung upon the Tree of Triple Death, with hair spreading through the burning river of time, with hands extended in blessing and compassion upon all who suffer, all who live in ignorance and darkness.'
West: 'By the secret way across the Abyss of the Great Waters the Child of Light comes, tempering all powers into one harmonious choir; passing to and fro between the Worlds and the Void according to perfect will. This Being waits, now, only for our willing recognition . . .'
South: 'Let us pause now, and willingly recognize the Child of Light that has come among us.'
  Pause for contemplation.

South: 'Blessed is the Being of Light that comes among us, Blessed is the Light within us, and Blessed is our Being One in Light.'
All affirm: In the Name of the Star Father, The Deep Mother, The True Taker, and the Great Giver. Amen.

South: 'Now is the time of transition, carried by the figure of Merlin standing in the Northeast. He bids us take a new image of the World and send it forth according to the hallowed methods of our Mystery.'
East: 'Through this Eastern Gate the World is renewed . . .'
West: 'Through this Western Gate the World is renewed . . .'
North: 'Through this Northern Gate the World is renewed . . .'
South: 'Through this Southern Gate the World is renewed . . .'

Herald: 'Three Wheels are known in our Mysteries, the Wheel of

Fortune, the Wheel of Adjustment, and the Wheel of the Universal Judgement . . . Let the members of this Company pass forth into a new World, each according to the Wheel that he or she understands.'

East: 'Let there be peace between us and the East.'

South: 'Let there be peace between us and the South.'

West: 'Let there be peace between us and the West.'

North: 'Let there be peace between us and the North.'

All: 'In the heights and in the depths let there be peace now and forever.'

The Herald leaves the room, leaving the door open for others to follow. A silent meditation is optional before leaving.

The last person to leave extinguishes the central light, gently closing the Four Directions.

Notes: Merlin Weekend 'The Mystic Life of Merlin', Hawkwood College, 27 March, 1987

My recollection of this event is now one month late (29 April) due to pressure of work and repeated illness from a 'flu virus.

Very tired on arrival, still coughing and overheating from 'flu. The entire weekend was worked from improvization and key diagrams, no written text other than occasional readings from sections of the *Vita Merlini*. It was clear that an oral expansion of the lore was different in many ways from the written interpretation in my books; several people on the course commented to this effect during the weekend.

I feel certain further unprepared oral expansions of the material would be very rewarding; there is more material available to work with. *(Many of these expansions and developments are covered in this book, but the key to primal traditions is always in practical work.)*

As the *Vita* represents an active tradition rather than a mere textual collection or structure, much of the expansion during oral tuition comes from direct inspiration and inner contact; here is where the much abused and misunderstood concept (found in magical groups) of 'contact' comes into operation: one has to balance actual knowledge and discipline with the organic conceptual flow of inner contact. Too much of a movement to either extreme leads to fruitless effort.

Notes on the Visualization
(See 'The Cry of Merlin', Chapter 12, for a version of this visualization.)

The improvised visualization was worked with about 50 people. It centred upon the three aspects of Merlin in tradition: Bright Youth; Mad Prophet; Wise Elder. Curiously, during the improvised visualization they appeared in the order of Madman, Youth, Wise Elder. This visualization led rapidly via a naturalistic journey and companion creatures to a curious 'castle' or building upon an island in a large lake or sea inlet. We reached the island over a tidal causeway. The building had a firm structure of its own, and my use of the word 'castle' led to some confusion as people tried to adjust the image to a medieval type of structure. It was in fact quite different from such a building. Perhaps it is an innerworld variation of the Observatory described in the *Vita*; at any rate it is a building associated with the Mysteries of Merlin.

We progressed no further than the first small chamber or receiving hall, though I was aware that there are other chambers beyond this which may be entered in the future. This realization is interesting, as the castle is transtemporal and the other chambers correspond to phases of time – thus some are the past and others are the future.

In the centre of the chamber that we entered was a circular stone altar. It looked rather like a large truncated pillar or perfectly circular flat-topped standing stone. This supported a strange crystal sphere, which was itself made of many concentric interwoven spheres. These were complex and yet balanced in a very perfect ratio. Within the crystal spheres were the maps or archetypes of the worlds that are taught in such detail in the Mystery of Merlin.

Details of the visualization are now blurred in my memory, but at some point everyone was given a token. Each member of the group found a creature to ride upon (there and back between the turning of the tide), either horses, goats or stags. Several people mentioned that a creature chose them rather than vice-versa.

I did not have a creature to ride, but to my own surprise flew above the riders. This image, I think, refers to a very important and enduring hawk contact which I have had for about 16 years now, and obviously has some poetic ramifications in connection with Merlin and with a very primal fusion between certain kings/heroes and raptors. This feature was all the more striking to me as it was totally unexpected.

The Ceremony

Based upon a very simple short script, this ritual working was a 'Creation of the Worlds'. The entire event was very calm and powerful. It soon became apparent that there were wheels within wheels in this ritual, a feature that I have noticed repeatedly in group workings.

One odd feature of the event, for me, was that I was unable in any way to concentrate upon or visualize the image of Merlin for which a station had been allocated in the northeast corner; indeed, every time I looked (physically) towards this empty position, my eyes refused to see it and slid off to either side.

I have previously visualized, invoked and conversed with the image of Merlin with considerable success; whatever was happening during this particular ritual was something of a different order, though other members of the group found no problem in visualizing Merlin and sensing his presence. I have no explanation for this phenomenon, though I am aware that it represents some type of inner contact that is deeper than the usual level of imagery, probably to be grasped through contemplation and meditation rather than visual imagery or structured imagination.

If what I could not see was Merlin, it was Merlin upon a level that could not be approached outwardly or through standard images within the Mystery.

My memory of the event is slightly blurred, and I have no recollection of what happened during the meditational period, though I am aware that the ritual achieved its stated outer/inner purpose, plus a number of other ramifications or harmonics that we were unable to grasp at the time.

The closing of this working was very powerful and important, and several people mentioned to me that they had felt a surge of power right at the very end of the working. Once again it is difficult to define this phenomenon. After the hall had been emptied, I changed into regular clothes, and was strongly drawn to return, thinking that people would be sitting there in meditation.

To my surprise the hall was totally empty, but this physical emptiness was soon replaced by the feeling of a vast company on inner levels, seated in a circle about the central Flame. It was this gathering that I had picked up inwardly. As soon as I was aware of the company present, I was invited to sit and participate in their deliberations (these were the actual 'words' implied by the invitation). I did sit for a few minutes, but most of what was being deliberated was quite beyond my comprehension, and though I was urged to stay, I rose and left.

I was uncomfortable, as this seemed to be a gathering that affected in some way the fate of our planet, though to phrase it in this manner sounds pretentious. It was something to do with the First Wheel (Fortune) on a planetary level, with consciousness (i.e. entities/beings) from the level of the Second Wheel (Adjustment or Justice) acting upon the collective consciousness of the First Wheel to effect adjustment. In some manner which I do not grasp, our group working was a small harmonic of this process. There was no sense of gratification on being invited to attend this gathering – which I was told was constant but with changing membership – only unease and a feeling of inadequacy.

In retrospect it seems that certain rites, ceremonies or patterns of movement and energy, encapsulated in the Mysteries of Merlin, enable energies from that Assembly or Convocation to work more directly upon our outer world. Without the enabling patterns, the energies flow through the cycles or rotations of the outer wheels. I note all of this merely as the impression arising from the ceremony and the meditations; I do not hold it as a 'belief' and do not suggest it as 'truth' or dogmatic fact to anyone else. In all such realizations we must use our own intuition and common sense.

25 April, 1987: I seemed to glimpse briefly the figure of Merlin early in the morning in the abbey ruins. He darted immediately behind a column and passed from my sight. This fleeting contact reminded me that I had neglected to correlate my impressions and make notes from the Hawkwood weekend. More central was his reminder that I should begin some further work on projects in hand, which have been currently set aside due to pressure of commercial work composing and writing.

CHAPTER
12

The Cry of Merlin

Silence is entered, and Sacred Space is enlivened.

Let us build in our imagination a landscape: it arises before us, and we pass into it. It is a great primal forest, with towering trees and many deep shadows and pools of light. The light is green and gold, and we hear the wind shaking the high leaves and branches. We stand upon the forest edge, and at our feet is a tiny trail, leading off among the trees and through the thick undergrowth. As we stand at the threshold of the forest-edge, we hear among us the sounds of moving trees and calling birds, a faint distant laughter. Darting between the trees we catch fleeting glimpses of a figure in a ragged robe, with long flying hair. For a moment it seems about to turn and look back at us, then laughing again, runs away into the forest. We know that we must follow this wild man/woman, follow the cry in the wildwood.

As we cross into the forest and pass down the trail, we sense the presence of the great trees. Their vitality feels warm, and they seem to be aware of us as we pass among them. The trail is narrow, a deep slot made by passing animals among the thick carpet of fallen leaves, branches, and tiny forest plants and flowers.

Again we hear the wild laughter, coming from a tree close by, then the sound of footsteps scurrying off. Again we hasten to follow, running deep into the forest. Even as we move, we can hear many birds calling and flying, seeming to move with us, and hear many animals moving through the undergrowth. Yet we see nothing of them, they remain hidden from us.

A third time we hear the wild laughter, and suddenly we

emerge into a forest clearing. In the centre of this clearing is a tiny spring flowing from red rocks licked smooth by creatures seeking salt. Sitting upon the rocks is the wild man/woman, staring at us, laughing. As we enter the glade, he takes a small wooden flute from his robe, and begins to play a high haunting melody. As he plays a wind rises, and a shower of rain falls into the clearing. As the rain eases we hear a great beating of wings and a rushing sound, and in an instant the glade is filled with birds and beasts of all kinds. They stand around the edge of the clearing, looking upon us without fear, calm and ready.

To each of us a creature comes, and chooses us as a companion, and even as this choice is made, the wild man/woman leaps over the rocks, and onto the back of a huge stag. They race off at great speed into the forest, and we follow with the animal host, each of us travelling with our companion. As we rush headlong through the trees, the company of animals gradually draws away, until there is only our own group, each with a new companion animal or bird, and the wild man/woman riding the great stag leading us onwards.

Suddenly the trees thin, and we emerge upon the shore of a great lake. Beyond the lake are high snow-capped mountains, and in its centre is an island, with a dark building upon it. Our guiding creatures stop at the lake shore, and wait. The wild figure upon the stag rushes straight for a stone causeway that leads over the water to the island, and within a moment disappears from sight into a gateway of that dark castle.

We pause and look upon this island place. It is of dark smooth stone, with a central round tower, and two smaller towers flanking an arched gateway. We can see no windows, and the surface of the stone seems polished like glass. Beyond the central tower we can just see two further towers on the opposite side, balancing those of the gateway facing us. We know that we must enter this mysterious place of power.

Our companion animals quietly withdraw into the forest, after pausing to drink from the clear waters of the lake. We walk slowly over the stone causeway to the great arched gate, which we find to be closed. There is no sign of the wild man/woman of the woods and the great stag, and all is still and silent. We hear the waves of the lake lapping gently, and the lonely cry of shore birds. In the distance the sun shines, reflecting brightly from the snowy mountains. We wait, and try to find within ourselves our true reason for being at this gate. *A short pause is made here.*

As we seek and try to find that true reason, a small section of the gateway opens, a narrow door within one half of the great double-gate, just wide enough for one person to pass through at a time. From inside we hear faint echoing laughter, and one by one we pass into the chamber beyond. We find this to be a simple courtyard open to the sky, with three doors, one into each of the gate towers, and one into the great central tower. Even as we look the central gate opens slowly, and as it opens there is a gust of wind, and a shower of sharp rain scatters into our faces. Within that wind we hear the sound of many voices, and of people moving about us, as if the castle is filled with an invisible host. The wind and stinging rain cease, silence falls again, and we enter the central tower.

We come into a circular chamber, with a low domed roof and a floor that slopes gently to the centre, leading down to a deep well. Around the walls of this well chamber are many carvings of figures, animals, birds, humans, and other beings. First we look upon these figures. *A pause here.*

Now we turn to the central well, and slowly, one by one, make our way towards it. Lying flat upon the floor, we look into its depths. This is the well of transformation, and within it is all power, all potential. Let us look into the well in silence.

Here a longer pause for silent contemplation.

One by one we rise from the floor, and make our way around the well chamber towards the door, keeping in our minds and hearts whatever we have seen and felt rising up from the well. As we draw back, one of the carved figures on the wall comes to life. This figure approaches us one by one and gives to each of us a small gift. Look well upon the figure, remember who or what it is, and keep the gift safe.

We now leave the central tower, and as we do so we hear again the sound of that great host, this time with music and laughter, as if a huge celebration is going on invisibly all around us. *Joyful music may be played here.* In the courtyard our companion creatures wait for us, and we greet one another with pleasure, as old friends.

The great gateway out of the castle stands wide open, and ahead of us on the causeway we see the wild man/woman riding the huge stag, but now in the company of two other creatures that we look upon and remember. Suddenly our entire company picks up speed and rushes headlong over the causeway to the shore and forest beyond. As we move we hear the sound of many horns blowing in the castle behind us, and they echo back from the high distant mountains across the lake. Now we enter the shadow of the trees, and realize that the sun is beginning to set. Our companion creatures carry us rapidly to the forest edge, and we look out over a night landscape towards a distant land. We hear again the haunting laughter, and the sound of hooves moving lightly over the forest floor. Then one by one our companion animals depart, each looking fully upon us and giving us a final communication.

It is time to return to that outer world, that distant land in which we spend our lives. Let us step over the threshold of the forest, and even as we do so it begins to fade. We pause in silence, and gradually find that we are sitting in a familiar room. Let us return fully to our outer awareness, and quietly waken to the customary world. When we seek to return to the other world, we can draw upon our companions, and the contact and gifts given to us in the heart of the mysterious castle. Now it is time to fully return. In our future meditations and contacts with our spiritual animal or bird, we will know how to use the gift given to us in the castle.

The group takes notes, discusses if required, and disperses.

It is often useful, especially in the early stages of this type of work, to write out individual experiences immediately following the visualization. A simple checklist would be sufficient, though often more items will come to mind when we start to write. The list would include, as a minimum:

1. What animal or bird chose you as a companion?
2. What happened when you looked into the well?
3. What figure came alive from the wall of the chamber?
4. What gift was given to you by the figure?
5. What were the two new creatures attending the wild man/woman and the stag?

CHAPTER
13

The Queen of the Mound,
The King of the Forest

We now move on to visualizations in pairs. The first of these centres on the Lady of Flowers, also known as the Queen of the Mound, and her male counterpart the Lord of the Animals or King of the Forest.

In the next chapter we will be working with sequences that lead to Barinthus, the Ferryman of the Soul, and Morgen, the priestess of transformation and regeneration.

THE LADY OF FLOWERS

We begin by looking into a box. This box is made of wood, and has the shape of a bee carved upon its lid. As we look at the box, the lid slowly opens, and looking inside we see a frozen winter landscape. Cold grey light floods from the inside of the box, and we see frozen ground, flat and bare, with no sign of life.

Now the box expands, and we pass within, into the winter landscape. We stand upon hard earth with sparse frozen grasses in white clumps. A straight path leads away towards the horizon, lined with close-laid flat black stones. They are slippery with ice, and we realize that we are walking over a frozen marsh. The hard ground and tussocks of grass to either side of the path will melt in spring, and become soft marshland. We may choose to walk upon the icy path or to risk the frozen marsh, not knowing how strong the surface is.

Across the flat horizon is a faint grey line, stretching as far as we can see to both right and left. The black path leads straight towards it, and we set out, knowing only our intent: to find the Lady of Flowers. Here in this bare frozen marshland, there is no sign of warmth, no flower blooming, no living creature to be seen or heard. The cold wind rustles the frozen grasses, and the sound of its passage is like a flurry of sighs and moans.

Now the grey line upon the horizon is clear to see. It is a wall. Gradually we approach this wall, and discover that it is of great height. The cold wind seems to draw our heat from us, and we long to reach the shelter of that great wall. Drawing closer to it, we see that it is made of immense blocks of stone, laid into one another in a seemingly random manner.

The path leads straight up to the wall, and seems to run into it. There is no gate or opening; the path merely stops dead before a huge block of grey-green stone. The immense stones are fitted closely together, without mortar, and yet are of many shapes and sizes. Such work seems impossible, beyond the skill of human builders. We shelter beneath the wall, which protects us from the icy wind. Here we reaffirm our intent to meet the Lady of Flowers, and meditate in silence, waiting for the next stage of our journey to become apparent. *Brief pause here.*

As we meditate, we hear the faint sound of an insect, the first sign of life that we have found in this barren frozen waste. The humming sound grows louder, and looking between the great blocks of stone, we see a bee squeeze and struggle though a narrow gap. She rests for a moment upon the stone, then moves through the pattern of a strange dance, turning and twisting, vibrating her wings. We are drawn into the rhythm and pattern of the bee-dance, and watch in fascination. Each movement seems to tell us something that we have always known, something for which there are no words.

The bee suddenly stops dancing, and flies steadily off to the right. We know that we must follow. The bee moves quickly, and we are hard pressed to keep her in sight. We run between the high wall on our left, and the frozen marshland on our right, breathing deeply, exerting our full energy and strength to keep pace. Our breath gradually deepens as we find a second wind within us, and suddenly the pace is exhilarating and powerful, we feel that we can fly along with the bee for as long as we need. The great grey stones of the wall blur past us, and we feel a growing heat within, as a source of inner fire rises up.

As we feel this heat, we see the bee slow in her flight, and suddenly fly up and over the top of the wall. We stop to look up, then down, and discover that we are standing before a small wooden gate set low in the wall. A long black timber lintel supports the massive blocks above, with two wide stone uprights on either side. The gate is about half our height, and of dark wood. It is made of one solid plank, as if cut from a great tree long ago. We look upon this low gate, and see an image carved deeply into its wood. *Pause for meditation here.*

The gate slowly opens a small way, and as it does so the winter wind rises and howls around us. In the distance we hear the sound of horses galloping, and the faint baying of hounds carries in the rising wind. We bend and squeeze through the narrow gap, and find that we are in a low tunnel leading through the wall. Now the thunder of hooves draws close, with the braying of shrill hunting horns, and the roaring of a great pack of hounds. The icy wind screams through the gap in the door, which suddenly slams shut. We pause in the dim light of the tunnel, and hear the hunt pass by outside the gate, which vibrates with the sound of their passing.

The low tunnel leads towards brilliant light, and we have to bend almost double to travel along it. A faint scent fills the air, which grows warmer as we approach the light. We emerge into a wide garden, filled with a profusion of plants and flowers. Many bees and other insects fly back and forwards among the flowers, and the air is warm and filled with rich complex perfumes.

We see huge flowering trees of types unknown to us, growing alongside tiny familiar herbs and flowering plants. The entire garden is wild yet cultivated, a mingling of known and unknown trees, flowering bushes, and growing plants of innumerable varieties and colours. The perfumes are heady and strong, and we walk out onto rich grass studded with flowers, and see many winding avenues and narrow trails between the trees and bushes. The entire garden is a complex natural maze, with no seeming order, yet we feel that there is a guiding principle within it. Through this maze we seek the Lady of Flowers. *Pause for meditation here.*

Deep within the garden we hear the call of a cuckoo, and we set off down a path that seems to lead towards it. The path twists and spirals through huge banks of flowers blazing with colour. Some are the familiar flowers of home, while others are from a time and place unknown to us. Now we pass through an area filled with plants that seem to belong to another world, with leaves of darkest green and black shot through with red hues, and wide white and purple flowers with deep red hearts. Some huge close-shut black flower heads open out as we walk past them, and turn their open blooms to follow us. As we move away from them, we see them slowly close again. We realize that we should not touch any plant or pick any flower in this garden.

The cuckoo calls again, and after it we hear the voice of a song thrush. Following that song we take another branch of the many paths. Now the plants and flowers gradually change, and the strange growths are left behind, to be replaced by those which we know and recognize. We feel a sense of peace, of coming home.

A small stream runs by the side of the path, with shoals of little fish swimming in it. A grey heron stands upon a steep rock, and as we approach she spears a fish and flies off upstream, in the direction that we are travelling. Again the thrush calls and after her we hear the voice of a dove. We realize that many lines of bees are flying up and down this path, and feel that we are approaching a sacred place.

The path rises gently and leads towards a low grassy mound. From out of the mound, between two rocks, the clear stream emerges. We see the bees busily passing to and fro from a deep cleft above the spring. The low grassy mound is empty, yet we feel a strong sense of presence here. We climb up onto its wide top, and see the vast garden laid out around us. There are many meandering paths and zones of trees and plants, stretching away as far as we can see. We have lost our sense of direction passing down the maze of connecting paths, yet in whatever direction we look we cannot see the great wall through which we entered.

The humming of bees fills the air, and there is a strong scent of pollen and honey. The sense of presence intensifies, and a blurring of our vision occurs, as if a golden mist is hovering in the air. We sit upon the grassy mound, and commune with the One who comes among us. *Silent meditation here.*

Out of our silent communion we hear a haunting song, lilting and rising from the distant trees. It sings of joy, of love, of flowering, of fruitfulness. The Lady has passed from the hill and leads us back into the garden. We follow the sound of her singing down the side of the grassy mound, and into the trees beyond.

The singing voice leads us into a stand of trees and flowering bushes woven into a shelter, a bower. From out of the leaves and blooms a face looks at us, and seems to change its likeness. A gentle wind shakes the leaves, and the face changes again, sometimes becoming familiar, sometimes unknown.

As we look upon this changing face among the leaves and flowers, two strange creatures appear at the entrance to the bower. They are tall and slim, with a human-like shape, and long flowing green and white hair. They look upon us without interest, merely accepting our presence, as if we are rain or sunlight. They slowly part the bushes and reveal a gently-sloping stairway leading into the ground below. The song fades, and we realize that we must take this secret way out of the garden. The steps are made of wood, and the descending passageway is dimly lit by a faint golden light emanating from the earthen walls.

As we enter the passageway, the branches and leaves move back into place over the entrance. The descent is short, for only a little way ahead of us the passageway stops, opening out into a low circular chamber. There is a door set in the wall opposite us, a small wooden door with a symbol carved deeply upon it. We look closely at this symbol, and wait for the door to open. It opens onto a familiar room, and we pass through, to take our places sitting and focusing upon a small wooden box.

The box radiates a warm spring light, filled with blessing and promise. Slowly the lid closes, and the image dissolves. Now we return to our outer consciousness, bringing with us whatever the Lady of the Flowers chose to give.

THE LORD OF THE ANIMALS

We begin by looking upon a stone, building its image clearly in our imagination. It is a grey lump of rough stone with quartz veins and metallic colours running through it. We look upon this stone closely, and see many shapes and contours, subtle colours and patterns within it. We feel its substance, its nature, its essential being: stone.

As we become absorbed in this stone, the entire vision opens out and we discover that the stone is a high spur of rock rising over a wild forest land. We fall slowly towards this rock, and land upon a wide ledge. There are coarse grasses and tiny dwarf plants growing all round us. We find that we are in a mountainous land, with thick forest in the valleys below.

As we look down into the trees, we hear the sound of wild music from within a deep valley, the shrill notes of a reed pipe playing a strange undulating fragmented melody. When the music stops it is as if all life, all motion, stops, and a deep silence fills the land. Gradually, one by one, birds begin to sing, hesitantly at first, then joining one another. The wind rises and we hear the sound of a great forest moving and sighing like the sea. The sun shines warmly upon us, and we pause to listen to the vast orchestra of forest, bird and animal sounds rising from below. *Pause here.*

As we listen, a deer steps around the edge of the rocky shelf where we sit and, looking calmly at us for a moment, skips away down the path leading to the forest. A moment later a goat appears above our heads, scrabbling down over the steep rocks onto the path, nimbly following the deer. We hear the clicking of its hooves for a few moments, and then the sound fades. Out of the bright sunlight a shadow crosses our faces, and we look up to see the silhouette of a hawk hovering. Suddenly it falls out of the sky, striking down at great speed into the valley below us. With this third sign, we know that we must descend into the forest, and seek the source, the player of that wild music.

One by one we clamber down the steep path. It is not an easy way to travel, for it is full of jagged rocks fallen from the heights above. Only the faintest trail weaves between them, made by the passing of light agile creatures, and unaltered by human hands. Yet as we climb down, we see that many of the larger rocks have symbols carved into them, apparently at random, along the pathway. The marks vary – some are faint and worn, covered in lichen, while others are sharp and new as if cut recently. We pause before a huge boulder that blocks the path, leaving only a narrow gap between the rocky wall. Before we squeeze through this gap, we meditate upon the mark cut into the boulder. It is a deeply etched symbol, like a stylized lightning flash. *Pause here.*

Beyond the marker stone the path opens out and small bushes begin to grow around it. We smell rich resins and flower perfumes, and hear the humming of bees. The trail becomes wide and flat, covered in tiny plants and blue-green grasses. Just as it seems easy to travel, we find that it stops suddenly at the edge of a steep drop. Looking over this edge, we see that trees rise level with it, and there is a long drop down into the forest below. If we are to go further we must climb down through the tree branches, or jump.

In the distance we hear again the wild pipe music, and a faint sound of savage laughter, filled with joy and terror. The sound makes our hair bristle and our eyes water. The forest falls silent again, until one by one the birds begin to sing. The first sound is the ticking of a wren in the bushes close by, then other birds begin to call and fly. We hear gentle movement below, and see a huge herd of deer moving through the trees, travelling towards the sound of the laughter. Other creatures pass through the forest branches and along its floor; we cannot see them but mark their movement through the leaves and branches. They too are following the sound of the distant pipe and laughter.

We climb into the branches, and slowly make our way down to the forest floor. As we enter the trees we feel a strong sense of presence, of awareness, of identity. The forest knows that we have entered its branches. It is alive, and conscious that we have touched it. As we climb down the branches become wide and strong, and we see birds and squirrels looking at us, quite unafraid, as if no human hand has ever been raised against them. In a nearby tree a huge dun-coloured cat turns its yellow eyes upon us, then slowly leaps down out of sight.

We jump the last short distance from the great branches onto the forest floor, and find that it is covered with soft leaf mould. The forest wraps its presence around us, and the air feels warm, as if the great trees are radiating a subtle heat. Tiny random breezes blow between the trees, filtered down from the winds above that toss the branches to and fro. The light blurs and flickers from gold to green, dancing down from high above.

Within a few paces we come to the foot of a huge oak, so vast that it has a clearing around it. We gather at this tree, unsure of the way ahead, waiting to hear the sound of the wild music again.

Our sense of direction has become confused by the presence of the trees, and no animals are to be seen to give us any hint. We lean upon the rough trunk of the great oak tree, and set our backs against it for support. As we do so we feel a deep slow surge of life within the tree; its power seeps through our bodies into our bones. We slowly become at one with the oak tree and wait in silence and communion. *Pause here.*

The sky flows over us, seasons pass away, light to dark to light again, years become days, acorns fall and trees arise, each to shed seed again. The forest travels of it own will across the land: acorn, sapling, tree and acorn, moving ever onwards under the sun and stars. All trees are one tree, sinking deep into the earth and reaching far into the sky. Our human awareness fades away, leaving only a strange song floating through our minds:

> When I was nothing, nothing was I,
> All locked in the fruit of the tree,
> That raised me up to the summery sky,
> Then down on the ground to lie.
>
> And if you knew the same as I,
> You'd do as I have done,
> And raise your life unto the sky,
> And root in the earth and stones.
>
> Through the years I rooted and I grew
> And many men sought out my way
> And under my branches kings they slew,
> In the Moon and the Sun-marked days.
>
> I fall not, neither do I fail,
> My seed is like the rain
> That scatters far upon the ground,
> And flourishes forth again.
>
> And if you knew the same as I,
> You'd do as I have done,
> And raise your life unto the sky,
> And root in the earth and stones.

Out of this song the sound of a shrill pipe summons us, cutting through the tree-trance. Somewhere deep in the forest a Piper plays, and we remember that we must go to him.

We step away from the tree, and the deep contact fades, yet even now we feel the oak-awareness. Every oak in this huge forest is a child of the one oak tree. Now we are aware of the presence of many creatures moving close to us in the trees and undergrowth. There is no doubt which way to go, for we all travel the same path towards the Piper.

As we enter deeply into the forest, we see deer, goats and wolves travelling side by side. Tiny wild pigs scurry through the undergrowth, squealing shrilly. Many birds hop and flit from tree to tree. As we move we find that one creature comes close to each of us, choosing us unerringly, and leading us towards the Piper.

Still the wild music plays, and we feel our hair stand on end. Do we truly wish to meet the Player? Now we are within a great host of animals and birds, and enter a wide, tree-lined avenue. The sunlight shines down upon this grass-lined way, lighting and warming it. All around us is the breathing and scent of forest creatures, moving together as one, the cat and rabbit, the dove and deer, the hawk and wood pigeon. We see more creatures than we have ever imagined to exist in one gathering, and can feel the heat of their bodies, smell the scent of the breath. A great bear emerges from the trees, and a family of foxes walks beneath its paws.

At the end of the wide sunlit avenue is a clearing, and in the centre of that clearing we see a figure sitting upon a huge chair. The image is blurred in the bright sunlit, as the chair is a tree, and the figure is part-man part-animal, emerging from the tree. We look again, and see him lower his reed-pipe. He raises his head and laughs, a deep wild sound. All the living creatures pause and fall silent, flattening themselves to the ground as if bowing or worshipping. We also feel the urge to lower our heads and avert our eyes, and a sense of panic fills us, a fusion of ecstasy and terror, joy and pain. Then it passes, and the creatures rise and move forward again, bearing us gently with them. We all enter the great clearing, and dare to look upon the Piper.

Now we see him clearly, sitting upon a huge ancient tree stump. He is a horned man, with spreading antlers growing from his head, out of a profusion of wild shaggy red-brown hair. His body is lean and muscular, tattooed with many blue spirals. We slowly approach the tree-throne, and sit within the great circle of animals and birds that settle around the clearing.

In an endless unfathomable pattern creatures move toward the tree-throne. Sometimes they approach singly, sometimes in pairs or families. Around the throne remain a huge wolf, a doe and fawn, and a pair of crows, as if attending the Wild Lord. He touches each of the creatures as it reaches the foot of the throne, sometimes whispering to them, leaning forward, or taking them upon his lap. We feel a deep pulse of tenderness and love within his wild power as he blesses each creature. The clearing is silent; no sound comes from the assembled creatures except their breathing and their soft movement to and from the tree-throne. Their breath and gentle movements make a strange relaxing rhythm, a sound of rustling leaves and sighing. We feel this pulse within us, merging with the tree pulse, and the wild savage pulse, and the gentleness of the Wild Lord. The four forces twine together and unify. We feel that these creatures are one with us, and that we are one with them.

Now our own guiding creatures, our spiritual animals and birds, rise and approach the throne one by one. As they do so we are drawn with them, moving as they move into the presence of the Horned One. As we near him, we feel a surge of animal force radiating from him, wild, arousing, ecstatic. He touches the creature that has become our companion, and at his touch, we feel a powerful current of energy flow through our own bodies. This is the touch of the Horned One, Pan, Cernunnos, Wild Lord of the Animals. *Pause here.*

We feel our heads drawn up, and the Lord of the Animals looks each of us full in the face. His eyes are golden-yellow with deep black pupils. He looks directly through us, nothing can hide from him, and we are transparent to him. We feel fear and joy, deep grief and high exaltation, then his glance passes over us and he whispers to our creatures. As he whispers we hear a strange hissing whispering voice in our own ears. *Pause here.*

Now our companion creatures dig into the earth around the throne, and one by one bring us something. These are simple objects – leaves, a nut, a feather, a bone, other small, natural and materially worthless gifts. We receive these gifts, feeling that something of deep significance and value has been given, and slowly back away from the tree-throne and the presence of the Wild Lord. We sit and meditate upon our gifts, and feel the vast movement of the host around us. The warmth of their breath and bodies lulls us into a deep innocent rest, like the sleep of a child at home. Among the savage creatures in the great forest, in the presence of the Lord of Panic, we feel that we have come home. *Pause here.*

Through our peaceful sleep we hear the shrill sound of a reed-pipe, or faint echoing laughter, and the rush of bare feet dancing and leaping through fallen leaves. We emerge from our state of peace and realize that the clearing is empty. The Wild Lord and the living creatures have left us as we slept.

The sun beats down, the trees sigh and sway in the wind. We look upon the aged tree stump where the Horned One was sitting. A tiny clear spring seeps from its base, and we cross the clearing to this spring, and drink of its cold pure water. Now we walk back along the wide avenue, and follow it until it turns into a faint deer-trail through the forest. The way is now clear to us, as if we sense the animal tracks rather than seek a route with our minds. We make rapid progress back to the great oak tree. Briefly we touch the trunk of this tree, and see beyond it the spur of rock rising up out of the forest. As we look a figure seems to duck out of sight upon its peak.

Now we reach the foot of the great rock, and climb into the tree branches that will take us up to its edge. We reach the wide path and climb to the marker stone, easing our way around it onto the higher rocky path. At last we reach the platform where our journey began. Here we sit in silence and contemplate the gifts that we have received. Looking upon them they seem to have more than one form, and change subtly back and forward. *Pause here.*

The sky has turned red with the setting sun, and the peak of the hill casts a long shadow over us. A ray of light glitters from the highest rock above, and for an instant strikes upon a shard of rock in the centre of our circle.

It is a grey lump of rough stone with quartz veins and metallic colours running through it. We look upon this stone closely, and see many shapes and contours, subtle colours and patterns within it. We feel its substance, its nature, its essential being: stone. The landscape around us slowly fades away until we see only the stone, and we gradually return to the room in which we commenced visualization. Now we are in the Sacred Space that we have brought alive upon the Way of Merlin.

Let us return to our outer world, and carry with us the power and gifts that we were given in the forest by the Wild Lord.

Barinthus

Who knows well the way of sea and stars?
Who the strong hand upon the helm of passage?
Who guides the keel that plows the deep?
First ferryman, last light-bringer,
Blue cloak, white hair:
Wave-tops are your pathway,
Starlight your compass.
I who have been within your vessel
Not once but many times from star to star,
Bid you enter.
Oldest of the guiding gods
Wisest of the deep lords,
Eternal sea ruler.
Open is the Western Gate
Where the assembled company of worlds
Awaits the passenger you bring.

R.J. Stewart, 1985

CHAPTER
14

The Ferryman and
the Priestess

THE ORIGINS OF BARINTHUS

Reference to Barinthus is found in the *Vita Merlini*, where he is simply mentioned as the ferryman who bore the wounded Arthur to the Fortunate Isles for healing. His description is as one 'who knows well the way of sea and stars'. (A literary and mythic analysis of this reference in found in Appendix 7, for those who wish to pursue possible sources of Geoffrey's reference.)

In a deeper sense, we may find much of significance in this mysterious figure. Barinthus is a Ferryman of the Soul, bearing the undying king (Arthur) to the Otherworld. We may realize him as a mythic figure, for a number of gods throughout the world are of this type and function. In ourselves Barinthus is that function of consciousness that bridges, ferries, moves and relocates. Upon a transpersonal level, the Ferryman is that universal power of movement through the unknown towards new beginning. Thus he is a figure concerned with death and rebirth, not simply in a physical sense, but the psychic or inner death and rebirth that may occur during key transformation in our lives.

The primal powers of light and dark, male and female, are shown as guardians of the Sacred Spring (named Bladud and Aileron in the Creation Vision): these are the polarized energies that cycle within us and within all nature. In deeper definitions there is a tendency for the entities to separate and come in sequence: Barinthus, the Ferryman, transports us to the Otherworld, where Morgen, the Healer and Shape Changer, awaits.

THE VISUALIZATION

Sacred Space and Silence are first invoked.

We begin by visualizing a mirror. It is a plain mirror, with a simple wooden frame. First we look into this mirror, and see an image of ourselves. As we look, the image blurs and fades in and out of focus, and as it fades we sit in silence and dissolve our self-image within. *Silent pause here.*

Now the mirror is filled with a pearly light, constantly moving and changing. We pass through this light and emerge into a bare moonlit land. A narrow path stretches away before us, leading over hard rocks. The moon is directly ahead of us upon the horizon, and there is a faint pattern of stars high in the sky, with clouds moving slowly from our right to left. We set off along the path, and find that it rises slowly towards a crest of land on the horizon.

When we reach the tip of the rising land, we look down to a vast plain far below, with the dark line of the sea far away on the horizon. The distance is great, and we feel that we cannot cover it alone and on foot. The night grows cold, and we sit upon the ridge facing towards the distant sea, looking out over the great plain below. In the moonlight that comes and goes with the passing clouds, we see many things in the land below. *Silent pause here.*

Now our looking across the plain is gently disturbed: to each of us an animal or bird has come, and with complete calm and trust this creature looks us in the eyes. As we look back we feel the power of the creature take shape within us, and one by one we begin to descend to the plain below, moving with increasing speed until we feel nothing but the wild motion of our spiritual creature within us. We are becoming the creature, it is becoming us, and we are filled with a great exaltation. The land rushes past, and our sight seems clear in the dark. We see dwellings, cities, long open tracts of wildness, rivers, canals and farms. The huge coastal plain is laid out according to a pattern that we barely grasp as the animal power rushes through us and we travel to the sea. *Silent pause here, or suitable rushing music.*

We cut across the roads and canals, and follow a faint secret path that is unknown to the dwellers in this land. No one sees or hears us as we travel. Whenever we cross a great road or the bridge of a river or canal, we feel a current of energy flowing through it, as if it acts as a great artery for the power of the land. The path undulates but heads always to the sea. We can hear the sound of great breakers crashing on the shore, and suddenly find that we are passing over sand towards the shoreline.

Where the sea and land meet, we fling ourselves down upon the beach, and realize that we have come to a place where the Elements merge and separate. Air is in the ocean wind, Water in the seas, and Earth in the sand and rocks of the shoreline. Yet Air, Water and Earth mingle together in all of these, merging and separating. We seek for a sign of Fire in the night, and realize that in the stars above and within our own hearts and in our blood there is Fire. With this realization we see a beacon fire burst into flame not far from where we rest, and we walk along the tide-line towards its flames and sparks.

When we reach this fire, we see that it has been lit upon a wide block of black smooth stone, with a bowl-shaped hollow in its surface. The fire is dying down now, its logs and branches shooting streamers of sparks into the night wind. We see no sign of whoever lit this beacon fire, and suddenly realize that our animal companions have quietly left us.

From out of the shadows upon the great ocean a small boat appears. At first it seems only a dim shape upon the water, but then the light of the fire and shooting sparks reveal its size and shape as it comes to the shore. The boat has no sail or oars, and is made of black fabric or skin upon a light wooden frame. It rushes onto the beach, borne forward by a great wave, and seems to leap upon us. The surge of the tide bears it onto the sand, and there it remains, empty, waiting.

We know that if we are to cross the night ocean we must step aboard this frail vessel. One by one we climb aboard, and sit upon smooth worn boards. The next great wave whips the boat out to sea: we realize that it is double-ended, and the bow and stern are both sharp peaked. Looking back at the receding shore, we see the lights of a great city spread out across the plain, and realize that our animal guides must have led us by the secret way to avoid that place. Beyond the city is the dim shadow of a high ridge of land, and far beyond that again we see the faint shape of a high mountain, glowing faintly white as if topped by snow.

The wind and waves rise, and the little boat begins a rhythmic motion: a long climb up a wave, and fast fall down its back into the deep trough of black waters below. We see streamers and flashes of luminous colour in the wave troughs, and realize that the ocean is full of life. For a few moments a shoal of porpoise swims and leaps alongside the boat, then vanishes from sight as the wind blows harder towards the distant land.

As the shore recedes a mist gathers in the stern of the boat. It slowly becomes a faint figure with the waves and stars flowing through it. We now see an aged man with flowing white hair and beard. He steers the boat with a long elaborately carved pole. Now the shore is far behind, only seen as a glow of faint light upon the horizon, and a dim low shadow beneath the light. The Ferryman has become solid, and we see him radiate a clear flow of light, as if starlight emanates from within him. His simple robe is of a silver and blue, with moving spiralling patterns ceaselessly changing and swirling. His skin is a deep black, and his eyes are faint sky-blue, looking far beyond us to an unseen goal. At first he seems unconcerned and unaware of us, but as the boat climbs towards the crest of a huge wave, he slowly stands and looks at us.

As he stands he grows until he towers over us, bridging the space between the sea and sky. With one strong hand he steers the boat, and with the other he points back towards the shore, bidding us to look out just as the boat reaches its highest point on the wave crest. We look back to the dim shadow line and glowing light upon the horizon behind us, and for the briefest instant it seems that the ocean rises and swallows the land. The lights vanish, and a thick mist swiftly comes toward us, seeming to boil out of the sea like a living wall. The mist surrounds the boat until we can see nothing, but feel only the massive rise and fall of the great waves.

We feel the presence of the Ferryman Barinthus, yet can barely see his shape, now of human size, in the stern. In this mist all sounds fade into silence, and we meditate upon what we have seen and felt. In our meditations we reach out towards the land fall, the unknown place to which we travel. *Silent pause here.*

Suddenly the boat scrapes to a halt, and we are thrown forward and out onto a rocky beach. Immediately the boat is pulled back into the mist, and we are alone upon the unknown shore. We look round us, and see a faint light creeping through mist, revealing spiralling pearl-coloured patterns, shot through with rose and blue flashes. This soft light increases, and the mist begins to thin. We see that we are upon a small bleak island. It is bare but for two tall pillars of rough stone, standing close together on the beach. We walk towards these stones, and in the pearl light we look through the narrow gap between them. On the other side we see into a strange land. *Long pause here.*

Gradually we find ourselves drawing back from these visions of the Otherworld, and remember that we must soon return to our own world. But with this comes the realization that we may pass to and fro at will, and that our spiritual creature, and the presence of the Ferryman, enable us to make the crossings from one world to another.

Even as we find this knowledge, the scene between the stone pillars changes, and becomes a familiar room. We see that it is the room in which we began our journey, the dedicated Sacred Space aligned to the Four Directions. One by one, we pass through the pillars into our place of rest within the room. As the last one passes through, the gateway closes and vanishes: we realize that it is in the western Quarter.

Now we sit and meditate upon what we have experienced, fixing it in our minds. We particularly remember what we saw between the pillars, what people came to us in that vision, and what gifts, if any, were exchanged. *Pause here.*

Now let us return to outer life, carrying with us the power of motion inherent in our companion creatures and the sense of direction that we have gained from the Ferryman of the Stars.

MORGEN IN THE FORTUNATE ISLES

We begin by seeing a low archway with water flowing out of it. The water is hot and clouds of steam rise from its surface. The stones of the archway are coloured a rich orange-red, and the water has a distinct smell of minerals and steam.

As we look upon this archway we hear the rushing waters increase, and the cloud of steam builds into a thick fog. Peering through it we see movement within the cloud. Faint shapes appear and disappear in the depths. Suddenly the archway opens out and becomes a wide cavern with a deep river of hot water flowing out towards us from its depths. Through the rising steam we see a flickering light high up and far into the cave, and we begin to walk along the river bank towards it.

The way is smooth and level, shaped long ago by skilled workers in stone. As we walk along the river bank through the steam and shadow, the distant light brightens, and drawing close to its source, we see a flame burning high up towards the roof of the cave. As we approach this source of light, the sound of rushing water becomes louder, and as the steam billows out, it parts for a moment, and we see that we have arrived at a wall. It seems impossible to go any further. The wall is of dark red and green stone, encrusted with many minerals, and rises directly before us.

The hot waters fall from a slit high up in the wall, and over this narrow opening hangs a lamp. Looking upwards we see that the lamp is shaped like two dragons twining together, with their mouths issuing flame. It burns with a steady light, which is diffused through the moving steam. In this softened glow we look for a way forward. *Pause here for meditation.*

Out of the steam and shadow two figures slowly emerge from behind the waterfall. One is a man with long fair hair, the other is a woman with long dark hair. She wears a simple robe, while he wears a loin-cloth and cloak. Both have circlets around their heads. As these people come forward to meet us, the lamplight flickers across their faces, and they appear first light, then dark, then light again. The shadows that they cast through the steam take the form of huge wings, yet we see no wings upon their backs.

These are the King and Queen of the Sacred Spring, known in the Mystery of Merlin as Bladud and Aileron. They look closely at each of us, one by one, searching in our eyes for our true intent. To each of us comes either the King or the Queen of the Spring. We feel suddenly inspired to give a gift to either the King or Queen . . . something found spontaneously, something least expected, something we had not realized that we carried with us. *Pause here for meditation.*

One by one the gifts are received and passed into the shadows behind the waterfall. As the last gift is passed within, the dragon lamp flares up into brilliant light, then suddenly goes out. We are left in total darkness. Someone takes us by the hand, and we are led, unseeing, behind the curtain of steaming waters. We feel it fall upon our faces, wetting our skin and hair. The warmth and steam lull us into a relaxed and dreaming state for a few moments, until our unseen guides firmly pull us through. We feel a sense of disorientation, not knowing if we are walking or falling, but suddenly realize that we are now in a narrow passageway. We feel the walls close on either side, the floor beneath our feet, and sense that the roof is just above our heads. There is barely room to pass along this passageway, and we are drawn gently but firmly onwards by the hands that hold ours.

Gradually the sound of falling water fades away behind us, and the scent of minerals and steam is replaced by a faint smell of the sea. A current of air blows out of the darkness ahead of us, bringing with it the scent of salt and seaweed. We realize that the passageway has been gradually curving around to the right, in an ever-tightening spiral, and as we turn, a faint light appears. Turning still, the light increases until we see massive blocks of tight-fitting stones, carved with spirals, lines and serpentine patterns.

Around the last curve we emerge into brilliant light, like that of the sun at noon. We realize that our unseen guides have vanished, letting go of our hands when the light first revealed the walls. We emerge on the side of a hill, stepping out of an opening onto a grassy platform. We look out over a sea that reflects light from its blue-green water.

We are high up on a small island surrounded by sea. Below us curves a white shoreline, and lush green grass full of tiny flowering plants falls away steeply to the beach. Looking about we see ancient ritual stones of different heights and shapes, seemingly placed at random, some upright, others lying flat. The air is fresh and clean, and we breathe deeply. It fills us with a pure vitality, a surging force that rises to our heads. We know now that we have reached one of the Fortunate Isles. *Pause here.*

Now we step to the edge of the grassy platform and see that the path curves around the hill. To our right it descends, to our left it climbs steeply to the hilltop. As we look right and left, an animal suddenly runs up the path towards the top, moving so quickly that we barely have time to see what it is. We know instantly that we must follow this creature to the hilltop, and set off after it. Already it has run round the hill and out of sight.

As we climb the spiralling path, we see many islands in the brilliant sea. Some are small and rocky, while others are large and densely forested. We see islands filled with tiny trees bearing fruits and blossoms, and wide meadows of both green and ripe grain. Flocks of birds wheel and turn low over the islands, and in the sea we see the shadows of huge shoals of fish. Sometimes large creatures leap out of the depths to splash back into the water. In the distance we see the spouting of whales, and hear the eerie singing of seals from the shoreline below. The far horizon is lined with pillars of water vapour, rising from the sea into the sky above, as if drawn by an unseen power. The vapour fades into the brilliant light and vanishes, and suddenly we realize that there is no sun in the sky. There is clear brilliant light, but no sun.

We follow the path to the summit of the hill, and arrive at a tall standing stone of rough green rock. Carved into its side is a rough image, a tiny figure with radiating hair and outstretched arms. We walk around this stone, and find that it is surrounded by a circle of white quartz crystalline rocks, laid carefully to make a level circle its base.

At the foot of the stone is a wide deep basin of green rock. It is filled with clear water, and round its rim are scattered ears of grain. Some are coloured bright red, others are natural yellow-white, while a few are burnt black. One by one we bend and look into the basin. We are each moved to pick up a single grain of a particular colour and swallow it, then to drink of the cold water.

As we swallow the grain and drink the clear water we hear a deep distant sound from across the sea, as if a great horn is blown far away. From out of this sound comes the roaring of wind and the beating of wings. We see birds approaching us from each of the Four Directions. They begin as tiny shadows on the horizon, but approach rapidly, and within a few moments we see that they are nine swans. The beating of their wings mingles with the rising of great winds blowing upon us simultaneously from the East, the South, the West, and the North.

The winds pluck at us, and buffet us about. The east wind is cool and smells of spring flowers. The south wind is hot and smells of spices and rich perfumes. The west wind is mild and smells of ripening fruit. The north wind is icy cold and smells of wood-smoke and snow. Just as it seems that the winds will throw us from the hilltop, they suddenly cease. In the silence we hear the beating of great wide wings, and the nine swans land in a circle around us. As they land and fold their wings they transform into nine women. We see that they are sisters, alike and yet individual. They stand around us; we stand around the central stone. There is silence. *Pause here.*

From behind our backs we hear a faint chiming sound, a high crystalline tone, and we turn to look at the central stone. The stone has vanished, and in its place stands a tall woman, with arms upraised. She is Morgen, ruler of the Fortunate Isles, mistress of shape-changing and healing. Her hair is red and black reaching far below her waist. She wears a deep black robe and varicoloured cloak of birds' feathers. Her face is calm and commanding. *Pause here.*

Slowly the Nine Sisters begin to circle us. At first they move with a steady ritual step, circling to the right. As they move we feel a deep current of energy rise and rotate with them. We are drawn by this power, and begin to turn with them, circling within the circle of the Sisters. Now the speed of the dance increases. The seascape and distant islands blur in and out of focus, while the Nine Sisters seem to merge as one and then separate. Only Morgen remains still at the centre, her arms upraised, her eyes closed, her feather cloak billowing in the surge of energy raised by the dance, her hair slowly rising to fly outwards. Clouds roll in from the sea and gather in a seething mass above the hilltop. There is sudden darkness and a single blast of thunder with an immense lightning flash.

In the instant of this lightning flash the Nine Sisters pause in their dance, Morgen vanishes from the centre of the circle and rapidly appears and disappears in the East, the South, the North and the West. At each appearance she takes a different form, until from the West she vanishes, to reappear in the centre of the circle. She opens her eyes and smiles upon us.

Morgen lowers her arms and the clouds pass away overhead. The warm light of the clear sky shines upon us, and we feel a sudden ease. The Nine Sisters come towards us, and one by one we are each given a gift by a Sister, who seems to choose us without hesitation. We are bidden to sit around the edge of the quartz circle, facing inwards, and to contemplate the gifts that have been given.

As we sit Morgen comes to each of us in turn, and places her hands upon us. We sit in silence and receive her blessing, her power of healing and regeneration, her inspiration. *Pause here. Music should be played if possible.*

A faint musical sound rises from all around us, and we turn to see the Nine Sisters transform into swans and fly off over the brilliant sea. The light flashes from their wings, and in this flashing light we seem to see other islands that had been invisible to us before, with fine buildings and people upon them. This flashing vision fades, but we realize now that the sky is lit by many coloured lights, huge stars moving at great speed in complex patterns, weaving and radiating light far above.

Now Morgen walks around the outside of our circle, and points to the downward spiralling path. It is time to return. We slowly descend the hill path, and as we do we see ahead of us the animal that marked our ascent. For an instant it turns to look at us, and then vanishes around the corner. We reach the grassy platform and the entrance to the tunnel, and find the King and Queen of the Sacred Spring standing on either side of the opening. Now they are dressed in robes of brilliant colours, and their features seem subtly changed. They bid us enter the hill.

The light of the weaving stars over the Fortunate Isles fades as we turn the first curve of the passageway. We turn and descend slowly, and the sea-wind is replaced by the smell of steam and minerals. Ahead of us we see a dim red light, marking a small opening. At first we expect to find the waterfall, but see instead a shadowy unreal room. It looks like a dream room, vaguely familiar, insubstantial.

We reach the small opening, and the shadowy light changes, resolving into the image of a familiar room, the one in which we began our journey. One by one we pass through the gap, and choose a chair, a cushion, or some other place to sit. As the last of us passes through, the gap closes slowly, and we hear the faint sound of a distant chime.

Before we emerge fully into the outer world, let us pause and recollect what has occurred, recalling the gifts that we gave the Guardians of the Sacred Spring and the gifts that were given to us by the Nine Sisters. Through this exchange of gifts we entered the Otherworld, and remembering the Sister and the gift she gave us, we may return in meditation whenever we will.

Finally we recall the exact way and place in which Morgen touched us after the lightning flash, and the feelings that her power awakened within us.

Now our journey to the Fortunate Isles is over. We open our eyes, breathing steadily, and make ready to bring the power of that place out into our world, for healing and transformation.

Afterword

If you have worked through the various exercises, techniques, adventures, encounters and visualizations offered in this book, you will be attuned to the Way of Merlin. You will also have discovered that there are certain People, and certain meetings, that are not developed in the examples. Figures 8 and 9 will be helpful in building your own encounters through drama, visualization and meditation. The other techniques of working with Sacred Space, companion creatures, and natural entities such as springs and trees have within themselves a lifetime of potential.

Now that you have worked with the basics of the tradition, you will find that many potential patterns will manifest, both in your meditations and in your outer life.

The story of Merlin, like that of the once and future king, is unending. If we work with the land, with the energies, visions and interactions between ourselves and other beings that accompany us around the seasons, around the sun, we become part of that story. It gives us knowledge of the Wheel, and contains and reveals ways of liberation from it.

The story changes from century to century, from age to age. If we give any credence to *The Prophecies of Merlin*, we are drawing close to the ending of an age which will be marked by the Apocalypse of Ariadne. Yet the beginning, the Creation Vision, is eternally present within ourselves, within the Worlds.

The Way of Merlin begins and ends with the truth that we are at one with the land. If we can regenerate spiritually out of such a union, we may also regenerate the land. Where and what it will be is a mystery that we may bring out of the Weaving.

The Apocalypse
of Ariadne

From *The Prophecies of Merlin*,
based upon the translation by J. A. Giles

Root and Branch shall change place, and the newness of the thing shall pass as a miracle. The brightness of the Sun shall fade in the amber of Mercury, and horror shall seize the beholders. Stilbon of Arcadia shall change his shield; the Helmet of Mars shall call Venus.

The Helmet of Mars shall make a shadow, and the rage of Mercury shall exceed its orbit. Iron Orion shall unsheathe his sword; the marine Phoebus shall torment the clouds. Jupiter shall go out of his lawful path; and Venus shall forsake her appointed circuits.

The malignity of the star Saturn shall fall down in rain, and slay mankind with a crooked sickle. The Twelve Houses of the Stars shall lament the irregular excursions of their inmates.

The Gemini shall omit their usual embrace and will call the Urn (Aquarius) to the fountains. The Scales of Libra shall hang unbalanced, until Aries puts his crooked horns under them. The tail of Scorpio shall produce lightning, and Cancer quarrel with the Sun. The Virgin shall mount upon the back of Sagittarius, and darken her Virgin flowers.

The Chariot of the Moon shall disorder the Zodiac, and the Pleiades break forth into weeping. The Doorkeeper Janus will end his duty and close the gate, hidden in the cleft of Ariadne.

The seas shall rise up in the twinkling of an eye and the dust of the Ancestors be restored. The Four Winds shall fight, coming together with a dreadful blast, and their Sound shall reach to the Stars.

The astrological and mystical attributes of these verses are examined in detail in *The Prophetic Vision of Merlin*, R.J. Stewart (Penguin Arkana, 1986).

APPENDIX
2

The Creation Vision

From the *Vita Merlini*, tr. J.J. Parry (University of Illinois Press, 1925), ed. R.J. Stewart in *The Mystic Life of Merlin* (Penguin Arkana, 1986)

ELEMENTS AND CIRCLES

Meanwhile Taliesin had come to see Merlin the prophet who had sent for him to find out what caused wind or rainstorms, for both together were drawing near and the clouds were thickening. He drew the following illustrations under the guidance of Minerva his associate.

'Out of nothing the Creator of the world produced *four elements* that they might be the prior cause as well as the material for creating all things when they were joined together in harmony: the *heaven* which He adorned with *stars* and which stands on high and embraces everything like the shell surrounding a nut; then He made the *air*, fit for forming sounds, through the medium of which day and night present the stars; the *sea* which girds the land in four circles, and with its mighty refluence so strikes the air as to generate the *winds* which are said to be four in number; as a foundation He placed the earth, standing by its own strength and not lightly moved, which is divided into five parts, whereof the middle one is not habitable because of the heat and the two furthest are shunned because of their cold. To the last two He gave a moderate temperature and these are inhabited by *men* and *birds* and herds of *wild beasts*.

CLOUDS, RAIN, WINDS

He added clouds to the sky so that they might furnish sudden showers to make the fruits of the trees and of the ground grow with their gentle sprinkling. With the help of the sun these are filled like water skins from the rivers by a hidden law, and then, rising through the upper air, they pour out the water they have taken up, driven by the force of their winds. From them come rainstorms, snow, and round hail when the cold damp wind breathes out its blasts which, penetrating the clouds, drive out the streams just as they make them. Each of the winds takes to itself a nature of its own from its proximity to the zone where it is born.

ORDERS OF SPIRITS

Beyond the firmament in which He fixed the shining stars He placed the *ethereal heaven* and gave it as a habitation to troops of *angels* whom the worthy contemplation and marvellous sweetness of God refresh throughout the ages. This also He adorned with stars and the *shining sun*, laying down the law, by which a star should run within fixed limits through the part of heaven entrusted to it.

He afterwards placed beneath this the *airy heavens*, shining with the lunary body, which throughout their high places abound in troops of *spirits* who sympathize or rejoice with us as things go well or ill. They are accustomed to carry the prayers of men through the air and to beseech God to have mercy on them, and to bring back intimations of God's will, either in dreams or by voice or by other signs, through doing which they become wise.

The space below the moon abounds in evil *demons*, who are skilled to cheat and deceive and tempt us; often they assume a body made of air and appear to us and many things often follow. They even hold intercourse with women and make them pregnant, generating in an unholy manner. So therefore He made the heavens to be inhabited by *three orders of spirits* that each one might look out for something and renew the world from the renewed seed of things.

THE SEA

The sea too He distinguished by various forms that from itself it might produce the forms of things, generating throughout the ages. Indeed, part of it burns and part freezes and the third part, getting a moderate temperature from the other two, ministers to our needs.

That part which burns surrounds a gulf and fierce people, and its divers streams, flowing back, separate this from the orb of earth, increasing fire from fire. Thither descend those who transgress the laws and reject God; whither their perverse will leads them they go, eager to destroy what is forbidden to them. There stands the stern-eyed judge holding his equal balance and giving to each one his merits and his deserts.

The second part, which freezes, rolls about the foreshorn sands which it is the first to generate from the near-by vapour when it is mingled with the rays of Venus's star. This star, the Arabs say, makes shining gems when it passes through the Fishes while its waters look back at the flames. These gems by their virtues benefit the people who wear them, and make many well and keep them so. These too the Maker distinguished by their kinds as He did all things, that we might discern from their forms and from their colours of what kinds they are and of what manifest virtues.

The third form of the sea which circles our orb furnishes us many good things owing to its proximity. For it nourishes fishes and produces salt in abundance, and bears back and forth ships carrying our commerce, by the profits of which the poor man becomes suddenly rich. It makes fertile the neighbouring soil and feeds the birds who, they say, are generated from it along with the fishes and, although unlike, are moved by the laws of nature. The sea is dominated by them more than by the fishes, and they fly lightly up from it through space and seek the lofty regions. But its moisture drives the fishes beneath the waves and keeps them there, and does not permit them to live when they get out into the dry light. These too the Maker distinguished according to their species and to the different ones gave each his nature, whence through the ages they were to become admirable and healthful to the sick.

FISH

For men say that the *barbel* restrains the heat of passion but makes blind those who eat it often. The *thymallus*, which has its name from the flower thyme, smells so that it betrays the fish that often eat of it until all the fishes in the river smell like itself. They say that the *muraenas*, contrary to all laws, are all the feminine sex, yet they copulate and reproduce and multiply their offspring from a different kind of seed. For often snakes come together along the shore where they are, and they make the sound of pleasing hissing and, calling out the muraenas, join with them according to custom. It is also remarkable that the *remora*, half a foot long, holds fast the ship to which it adheres at sea just as though it were fast aground, and does not permit the vessel to move until it lets go; because of this power it is to be feared. And that which they call the *swordfish*, because it does injury with its sharp beak, people often fear to approach with a ship when it is swimming, for if it is captured, it at once makes a hole in the vessel, cuts it in pieces, and sinks it suddenly in a whirlpool. The *serra* makes itself feared by ships because of its crest; it fixes to them as it swims underneath, cuts them to pieces and throws the pieces into the waves, wherefore its crest is to be feared like a sword. And the *water dragon*, which men say has poison under its wings, is to be feared by those who capture it; whenever it strikes it does harm by pouring out its poison. The *torpedo* is said to have another kind of destruction, for if any one touches it when it is alive, straightway his arms and his feet grow torpid and so do his other members and they lose their functions just as though they were dead, so harmful is the emanation of its body.

ISLANDS

To those and the other fishes God gave the sea, and He added to it many realms among the waves, which men inhabit and which are renowned because of the fertility which the earth produces there from its fruitful soil.

Of these *Britain* is said to be the foremost and best, producing in its fruitfulness every single thing. For it bears crops which throughout the year give the noble gifts of fragrance for the use of man, and its has woods and glades with honey dripping in them, and lofty mountains and broad green fields, fountains and rivers, fishes and cattle and wild beasts, fruit trees, gems, precious metals, and whatever creative nature is in the habit of furnishing.

Besides all these it has fountains healthful because of their hot waters which nourish the sick and provide pleasing baths, which quickly send people away cured with their sickness driven out. So *Bladud* established them when he held the sceptre of the kingdom, and he gave them the name of his consort *Alaron*. These are of value to many sick because of the healing of their water, but most of all to women, as often the water has demonstrated.

Near to this island lies *Thanet* which abounds in many things but lacks the death-dealing serpent, and if any of its earth is drunk mixed with wine it takes away poison. Our ocean also divides the *Orkneys* from us. These are divided into thirty-three islands by the sundering flood; twenty lack cultivation and the others are cultivated. *Thule* receives its name 'furthest' from the sun, because of the solstice which the summer sun makes there, turning its rays and shining no further, and taking away the day, so that always throughout the long night the air is full of shadows, and making ice congealed by the benumbing cold, which prevents the passage of ships.

The most outstanding island after our own is said to be *Ireland* with its happy fertility. It is larger and produces no bees, and no birds except rarely, and it does not permit snakes to breed in it. Whence it happens that if earth or a stone is carried away from there and added to any other place it drives away snakes and bees. The island of *Gades* lies next to *Herculean Gades*, and there grows there a tree from whose bark a gum drips out of which gems are made, breaking all laws.

The *Hesperides* are said to contain a watchful dragon who, men say, guards the golden apples under the leaves. The *Gorgades* are inhabited by women with goats' bodies who are said to surpass hares in the swiftness of their running. *Argyre* and *Chryse* bear, it is said, gold and silver just as Corinth does common stones. *Ceylon* blooms pleasantly because of its fruitful soil, for it produces two crops in a single year; twice it is summer, twice spring, twice men gather grapes and other fruits, and it is also most pleasing because of its shining gems. *Tiles* produces flowers and fruits in an eternal spring, green throughout the seasons.

THE OTHERWORLD

The island of apples which men call 'The Fortunate Isle' gets its name from the fact that it produces all things of itself; the fields there have no need of the ploughs of the farmers and all cultivation is lacking except what nature provides. Of its own accord it produces grain and grapes, and apple trees grow in its woods from the close-clipped grass. The ground of its own accord produces everything instead of merely grass, and people live there a hundred years or more.

There nine sisters rule by a pleasing set of laws those who come to them from our country. She who is first of them is more skilled in the healing art, and excels her sisters in the beauty of her person. *Morgen* is her name, and she has learned what useful properties all the herbs contain, so that she can cure sick bodies. She also knows an art by which to change her shape, and to cleave the air on new wings like Daedalus; when she wishes she is at Brest, Chartres, or Pavia, and when she wills she slips down from the air onto your shores.

And men say that she has taught mathematics to her sisters, Moronoe, Mazoe, Gliten, Glitonea, Gliton, Tyronoe, Thitis, Thitis best known for her cither. Thither after the battle of Camlan we took the wounded Arthur, guided by *Barinthus* to whom the waters and the stars of heaven were well known. With him steering the ship we arrived there with the prince, Morgen received us with fitting honour, and in her chamber she placed the king on a golden bed and with her own hand she uncovered his honourable wound and gazed at it for a long time and made use of her healing art. Rejoicing, therefore, we entrusted the king to her and returning spread our sail to the favouring winds.'

APPENDIX
3

The Three Springs and the Purifying Goddess

From the medieval *Prophecies of Merlin*

Three springs shall break forth in the city of Winchester, whose rivulets shall divide the island (of Britain) into three parts. Whosoever shall drink of the first shall enjoy long life and never be afflicted with sickness. He that shall drink of the second shall die of hunger and paleness and horror shall be seen in his face.

He that shall drink of the third shall be surprised with sudden death, and it will not be possible to bury his body. Those that seek to escape this voracious death will try to hide it with several coverings, but whatever bulk shall be laid upon it shall receive the form of another body. For earth shall be turned to stones, stones into water, wood into ashes into water, if they are cast over it.

Then a Maiden shall be sent from the city of the forest, to administer a cure. Once she has practised her oracular arts, she shall dry up the poisonous springs by breathing upon them. Afterwards, when she has refreshed herself with the wholesome spring, she shall bear in her right hand the forests of Scotland (the wild North) and in her left hand the buttressed forts of London (the civilized South).

Wherever she shall go she shall make sulphurous steps, which shall smoke with a double flame. That smoke shall rouse up the Ruteni (ancient tribe) and shall feed the inhabitants of the deep sea. Tears of compassion will overflow her eyes, and she shall fill the island (of Britain) with dreadful cries.

These verses are examined in detail in *The Prophetic Vision of Merlin*, R.J. Stewart (Penguin Arkana, 1986).

APPENDIX
4

The Threefold Death

What was and is the Threefold Death? If we seek an answer in history, anthropology or folklore, we find that it was a ritual sacrifice. Versions of this ritual are found in myth and legend, and were central to the religions of the ancient world. In Celtic tradition we find a number of accounts of people undergoing multiple and magical or mysterious, paradoxical deaths.

For a host of convoluted reasons modern people find the idea of sacrifice repugnant. Christianity teaches that Christ's crucifixion replaces all other forms of sacrifice. Nevertheless, the crucifixion is one of many sacrificial deaths in world religion, and by no means unique or unusual. In a purely historical sense, early Christianity was merely a Jewish Messianic cult into which ancient ritual sacrifice had been incorporated. Such sacrifices were banned by the Roman Empire, as mystical cults tended to use this powerful theme in a revolutionary sense, declaring themselves free of the state. Only two religions were seriously banned by Rome – Christianity and Druidism – and both were proscribed and suppressed for their political revolutionary implications by a state that insisted on state-worship. Within this political framework, other religions were tolerated.

The practice of a special sacrifice connected to redemption, purification, and the vitality of the land and its people is at the roots of myth and religion, however, for it mirrors the sacrifice of the Creation of the Worlds.

In the Way of Merlin, therefore, as in many magical, mystical and spiritual paths, self-sacrifice plays an important part. As it is much misunderstood, and continually used as a conceptual means of suppression, we need to be clear on the subject.

The Threefold Death is represented by The Hanged Man in the Tarot, an individual who is at peace with all perspectives reversed. If we reverse the card, he becomes The Dancer, moving through an inverted world, a world standing on its head, water above, sky below. In the *Vita* this motif is found in an episode involving a youth who appears before Merlin in three disguises (see below). For each disguise, Merlin predicts a different death: falling, hanging and drowning. The youth is undefined, appearing as male, as female, and then as male again. The entire episode is a ritual drama from Celtic tradition. Eventually the youth grows to adulthood, and while out hunting falls from his horse over a cliff, catches his foot in a tree, and hangs with his head in the river – death by falling, hanging and drowning. In other Merlin legends the motif of the Threefold Death is directly associated with Merlin, for it is he who dies in this way. Geoffrey of Monmouth avoids this direct identification, presumably not wishing to be accused of heresy or paganism. He retains the legend in full, however, reporting it direct from bardic tradition.

The image of someone hanging upside down from a tree is one of sacrifice, and of willing self-sacrifice. In Celtic culture it was also connected to kingship and the power of the land. The sacred kingship of the ancient world involved the willing passage of an individual between worlds, through ritual death and rebirth. Something of this tradition is inherent in the Way of Merlin. The Youth of Three Disguises is The Fool in the Tarot, and later he grows to be The Hanged Man. He is also Merlin, you, me.

As The Fool the youth is neither male nor female, for he/she is the bisexual potential in each of us. This represents the human being in the Earth and Lunar World. The Fool is also the Divine Child, Mabon, at the centre of the spiral of Worlds and Beings.

The Threefold Death, however, bridges across all Three Worlds. The Dancer is free from the illusions of separation, but is freed only through a mysterious death. If we follow the Tarot imagery, we find that The Fool, through the sacrifice of becoming The Hanged Man, may become the Universe, an androgynous, fully-conscious being of perfect balance.

The Threefold Death: 1

Rydderch suddenly became sad at this accusation [of his wife's infidelity] and turned his face from her and cursed the day he had married her. But she, not at all moved, hid her shame behind a smiling face and said to her husband, 'Why are you sad, my love? Why do you become so angry over this thing, and blame me unjustly, and believe a madman who, lacking sound sense, mixes lies with the truth? The man who believes him becomes many times more a fool than he is. Now then, watch, and if I am not mistaken I will show you that he is crazy and has not spoken the truth.'

There was in the hall a certain boy, one of many, and the ingenious woman catching sight of him straightway thought of a novel trick by which she might convict her brother of falsehood. So she ordered the boy to come in and asked her brother to predict by what death the lad should die. He answered, 'Dearest sister, he shall die, when a man, by falling from a high rock.' Smiling at these words, she ordered the boy to go away and take off the clothes he was wearing and put on others and to cut off his long hair; she bade him come back to them thus that he might seem to them a different person. The boy obeyed her, for he came back to them with his clothes changed as he had been ordered to do. Soon the queen asked her brother again, 'Tell your dear sister what the death of this boy will be like.' Merlin answered, 'This boy when he grows up shall, while out of his mind, meet with a violent death in a tree.' When he had finished she said to her husband, 'Could this false prophet lead you so far astray as to make you believe that I had committed so great a crime? And if you will notice with how much sense he has spoken this about the boy, you will believe that the things he said about me were made up so that he might get away to the woods. Far be it from me to do such a thing! I shall keep my bed chaste, and chaste shall I always be while the breath of life is in me. I convicted him of falsehood when I asked him about the death of the boy. Now I shall do it again; pay attention and judge.'

When she had said this she told the boy in an aside to go out and put on woman's clothing, and to come back thus.

Soon the boy left and did as he was bid, for he came back in woman's clothes just as though he were a woman, and he stood in front of Merlin, to whom the queen said banteringly, 'Say brother, tell me about the death of this girl.' 'Girl or not she shall die in the river,' said her brother to her, which made King Rhydderch laugh at his reasoning; since when asked about the death of a single boy Merlin had predicted three different kinds. Therefore Rhydderch thought he had spoken falsely about the queen, and did not believe him, but grieved, and hated the fact that he had trusted him and had condemned his beloved. The queen, seeing this, forgave him and kissed and caressed him and made him joyful.

The Threefold Death: 2

Guendoloena remained sadly in the door watching him and so did the queen, both moved by what had happened to their friend, and they marvelled that a madman should be so familiar with secret things and should have known of the love affair of his sister. Nevertheless they thought that he lied about the death of the boy since he told of three different deaths when he should have told of one. Therefore his speech seemed for long years to be an empty one until the time when the boy grew to manhood; then it was made apparent to all and convincing to many. For while he was hunting with his dogs he caught sight of a stag hiding in a grove of trees; he loosed the dogs who, as soon as they saw the stag, climbed through unfrequented ways and filled the air with their baying. He urged on his horse with his spurs and followed after, and urged on the huntsmen, directing them, now with his horn and now with his voice, and he bade them go more quickly. There was a high mountain surrounded on all sides by rocks with a stream flowing through the plain at its foot; thither the animal fled until he came to the river, seeking a hiding place after the unusual manner of its kind. The young man pressed on and passed straight over the mountain, hunting for the stag among the rocks lying about. Meanwhile it happened, while his impetuosity was leading him on, that his horse slipped from a high rock and the man fell over a precipice into the river, but so that one of his feet caught in a tree, and the rest of his body was submerged in the stream. Thus he fell, and was drowned, and hung from a tree, and by this threefold death made the prophet a true one.

From the *Vita Merlini*, tr. J.J. Parry (University of Illinois Press, 1925), ed. R.J. Stewart in *The Mystic Life of Merlin* (Penguin Arkana, 1986)

The Hymn
of Jesus

Compiled from various sources and translations

He gathered us together and said: 'Before I am delivered over unto them we will hymn the Father, and so go forth to what lies before us.'

Then bidding us make as it were a ring, by holding each others' hands, with Him in the midst, He said: 'Answer "Amen" to Me.'

Then He began to hymn a hymn and say:

Glory to Thee, Father!
And we going round in a ring answered to Him:
Amen!
Glory to Thee, Word (*Logos*)!
Amen!
Glory to Thee, Grace (*Charis*)!
Amen!
Glory to you, Spirit!
Glory to you, Holy One!
Glory to your Glory!
Amen!
We praise you, O Father;
We give Thanks to you, O Light;
In Whom Darkness dwells not!
Amen!
I would be saved; and I would save.
Amen!
I would be loosed; and I would loose.
Amen!

I would be wounded; and I would wound.
I would be consumed for love; and I would consume.
Amen!
I would be begotten; and I would beget.
Amen!
I would eat; and I would be eaten.
Amen!
I would hear; and I would be heard.
Amen!
I would be understood; being all Understanding (*Nous*).
I would be washed; and I would wash.
Amen!
Grace leads the dance.
I would pipe; dance you all.
Amen!
I would play a dirge; lament you all.
Amen!
The one Eight in One sounds with us.
Amen!
The Twelfth Number above leads the dance.
Amen!
All whose nature is to dance, dance.
Amen!
Who dances not, knows not who comes.
Amen!
I would flee; and I would stay.
Amen!
I would adorn; and I would be adorned.
Amen!
I would be united; and I would unite.
Amen!
I have no dwelling; and I have dwellings.
Amen!
I have no place; and I have places.
Amen!
I have no temple; and I have temples.
Amen!
I am a lamp to you who sees Me.
Amen!

I am a mirror to you who understands Me.
Amen!
I am a door to you who knocks at Me.
Amen!
I am a way to you, a wayfarer.
Amen!
Now answer to My dancing!
Amen!
See yourself in Me who speaks;
And seeing what I do,
Keep silence on My Mysteries.
Understand, by dancing, what I do;
For yours is the Passion of Man
That I am to suffer.
You could not at all be conscious
Of what you suffer,
Were I not sent as your Word by the Father.
Seeing what I suffer,
You saw Me as suffering;
And seeing, you didst not stand still,
But were moved wholly,
Moved to be wise.
You have Me for a couch; rest upon Me.
Who I am you shall know when I depart.
What now I am seen to be, that I am not.
But what I am you shall see when you come.
If you had known how to suffer,
You would have power not to suffer.
Know how to suffer, and you have power not to suffer.
That which you know not, I Myself will teach you.
But as for Me, if you would know what I was:
In a word I am the Word who did dance all things, and
was not shamed at all.
'Twas I who leaped and danced.
But do you understand all, and, understanding, say:
Glory to you, Father!
Amen!

And having danced these things with us, Beloved, the Lord went forth. And we, as though beside ourselves, or wakened out of deep sleep, fled each our several ways.

APPENDIX
6

The Dark Man
and the Animals

From 'The Lady of the Fountain' in *The Mabinogion*
tr. Lady Charlotte Guest

'Sleep here to-night, and in the morning arise early, and take the road upwards through the valley until thou reachest the wood through which thou camest hither. A little way within the wood thou wilt meet with a road branching off to the right, by which thou must proceed, until thou comest to a large sheltered glade with a mound in the centre. And thou wilt see a black man of great stature on the top of the mound. He is not smaller in size than two of the men of this world. He has but one foot; and one eye in the middle of his forehead. And he has a club of iron, and it is certain that there are no two men in the world who would not find their burden in that club. And he is not a comely man, but on the contrary he is exceedingly ill-favoured; and he is the woodward of that wood. And thou wilt see a thousand wild animals grazing around him. Inquire of him the way out of the glade, and he will reply to thee briefly, and will point out the road by which thou shalt find that which thou art in quest of.'

And long seemed that night to me. And the next morning I arose and equipped myself, and mounted my horse, and proceeded straight through the valley to the wood; and I followed the cross-road which the man had pointed out to me, till at length I arrived at the glade. And there was I three times more astonished at the number of wild animals that I beheld, than the man had said I should be. And the black man was there, sitting on top of the mound. Huge of stature as the man had told me that he was, I found him to exceed by far the description he had given me of him. As for the iron club which the man had told me was a burden for two men, I am certain, that it would be a heavy weight for four warriors to lift; and this was in the black man's hand. And he only spoke to me in answer to my questions. Then I asked him what power he held over those animals. 'I will show thee, little man,' said he. And he took his club in his hand, and with it he struck a stag a great blow so that he brayed vehemently, and at his braying the animals came together, as numerous as the stars in the sky, so that it was difficult for me to find room in the glade to stand among them. There were serpents, and dragons, and divers sorts of animals. And he looked at them, and bade them go and feed; and they bowed their heads, and did him homage as vassals to their lord.

Then the black man said to me, 'Seest thou now, little man, what power I hold over these animals?' Then I inquired of him the way, and he became very rough in his manner to me; however, he asked me whither I would go? And when I told him who I was and what I sought, he directed me. 'Take,' said he, 'that path that leads towards the head of the glade, and ascend the wooded steep until thou comest to its summit; and there thou wilt find an open space like to a large valley, and in the midst of it a tall tree, whose branches are greener than the greenest pine-trees. Under this tree is a fountain, and by the side of the fountain a marble slab, and on the marble slab a silver bowl, attached by a chain of silver, so that it may not be carried away. Take the bowl and throw a bowlful of water upon the slab, and thou wilt hear a mighty peal of thunder, so that thou wilt think that heaven and earth are trembling with its fury. With the thunder there will come a shower so severe that it will be scarce possible for thee to endure it and live. And the shower will be of hailstones; and after the shower, the weather will become fair, but every leaf that was upon the tree will have been carried away by the shower. Then a flight of birds will come and alight upon the tree; and in thine own country thou didst never hear a strain so sweet as that which they will sing. And at the moment thou art most delighted with the song of the birds, thou wilt hear a murmuring and complaining coming towards thee along the valley. And thou wilt see a warrior upon a coal-black horse, clothed in black velvet, and with a pennon of black linen upon his lance; and he will ride unto thee to encounter thee with the utmost speed. If thou fleest from him he will overtake thee, and if thou abidest there, as sure as thou art a mounted warrior, he will leave thee on foot. And if thou dost not find trouble in that adventure, thou needest not seek it during the rest of thy life.'

Barintus

**From the *Rêvue Celtique* XXII pp.339ff
by Arthur C.L. Brown, 1901**

Geoffrey of Monmouth in his *Vita Merlini*,[1] written about 1148, introduces Barintus as the pilot who steered the ship in which Arthur was conveyed to the Fortunate Isles. There is no sign that Barintus is a monk, nor is the land to which he is the guide a Christian paradise. The only point insisted on by Geoffrey is that Barintus knew the waters and the stars.

It has been generally assumed,[2] without much reflection, that Geoffrey got his knowledge of Barintus from the well known introductory episode in the *Navigatio Brendani*.[3] A careful examination of the two passages, however, seemed to me to lead to directly the opposite conclusion. In the *Navigatio* 'Saint' Barintus is the head of a band of monks, and the voyage to the *Terra Repromissionis* that he undertakes, in company with his 'filiolus' Mernoc, is a reward for his piety. Furthermore the most that can be said is that Barintus suggests to St Brandan the idea of a voyage: he gives no directions for the way, much less acts as a guide or pilot familiar with the sea.

The Barintus episode in the *Navigatio* is useless for the narrative, and obscure and incoherent in itself. It must be a survival of something,[4] almost certainly therefore of some Celtic tradition. It seems to me evident that Geoffrey in the *Vita Merlini* has drawn his notion of Barintus from some such tradition and not from the *Navigatio*. Geoffrey could no doubt fabricate a clever story, but it is asking too much to suppose that he would have been at pains to strip Barintus of his ecclesiastical character and companions, associate him with Taliesin and Arthur, who are not mentioned in the *Navigatio*, and invent for him a *rôle* as pilot which is in accord with what probably must have been his position in Celtic legend.

We have an unmistakable indication of the existence of a Celtic tradition about Barintus. The life of Saint David, which was written in Wales thirty or forty years at least before the works of Geoffrey of Monmouth, [5] contains a curious story which, while it agrees with the *Navigatio* in bringing Barintus, here called St Barri, [6] into relation with St Brandan, cannot possibly be a mere adaptation from the Latin legend. The incident in outline is as follows: one day St Barri borrowed a horse from St David, and rode it across the sea from Wales to Ireland. After he had gone a long way he met St Brandan who '*super marinum cetum miram ducebat vitam*' and the two saints conversed together.

Zimmer, in his important study of the St Brandan legend, has compared this incident to other incidents of a similar character in the lives of St David and St Aidan, and has concluded that Barri must have been originally represented as riding a sort of fish or 'sea-horse'. [7] One naturally wishes to know how such a surprising adventure came to be attached to a saint. Zimmer contented himself with an unlikely suggestion, [8] and the matter, despite its interest, has not since been discussed.

I believe that to understand the source of this adventure one has only to read in the Irish Sagas the accounts of the sea-god Manannán mac Lir. He is regularly represented as riding [9] a 'sea-horse', and he especially frequented the waters between Wales and Ireland. [10] This is precisely the scene of the adventure of Barri and his fellow saints. We seem therefore to be in the presence of a local tradition which has survived after the pagan god, its original hero, has been forgotten. [11]

There is probably a special reason why this adventure is found attached to Barri. Barri or Barintus was, I venture to suggest, in origin, like Manannán, a sea-god [12] who in the Welsh lives and in the *Navigatio* has been changed into a saint.

To suppose that a pagan divinity has been transformed by later legends into a saint is not as difficult as it may at first seem. There is an excellent parallel in one of *The Mabinogion*, 'Branwen, Daughter of Llyr', where we find the old sea-god Bran, a giant who could wade through the sea from Wales to Ireland, called Bran the

Blessed (Bendigeit Bran). The Welsh *Triads* explain that he was a saint and the introducer of Christianity into Britain.[13]

Zimmer has shown[14] that Barintus is essentially an epithet or surname. It is the Irish *Barrfind*, sometimes written *Finnbarr*, which means 'fair-haired' or more literally 'white-topped'. A name more appropriate for a god of the hoary sea would be hard to find.[15]

It seems highly probable then that Barintus was in origin a god of the waters, and by consequence for the early Celts a god of the Land beyond the Waves, the Happy Otherworld. He may have been a fellow deity to Manannán,[16] or he may have been a mere manifestation of that god, who, noted for his delight in shape shifting, probably had different names according to his different appearances.[17] In the *Imram Brain*[18] Manannán is called 'the Fair Man' (*Fer find*) who rides over the 'white sea' (*find frismbein muir*). In the *Serglige Conculaind*, he is 'the horseman of the maned [or 'hairy'] sea' (*Marcach in Mara mongaig*).[19] It is not then difficult to suppose that he may have been known by the epithet 'Fair-haired' (*Barrind*).

Barintus' character as a kind of sea-deity well known in Celtic legend once admitted, the explanation of all that we are told about him works out with convincing completeness.

In *The Life of St David*, St Barri's ride on horseback across the sea is of course simply a survival of the old sea-god's power of riding the billows. The sea-horse has been partly rationalized into an ordinary horse, permitted by the miraculous power of the saint to tread the sea as on dry land.

In the *Navigatio Brendani*, the part played by Barintus is quite parallel to that taken by Manannán, or by one of Manannán's fellows, in many Celtic Otherworld tales. In these tales there is regularly an Otherworld messenger, who suggests to the hero the idea of a marvellous journey. Sometimes this mysterious visitor is a prince[20] of the Otherworld. Sometimes only an emissary[21] from such a prince appears. Once at least[22] the hero is persuaded to set out by the tale of a previous adventurer, who relates his experiences, somewhat as Barintus does in the *Navigatio*.

The Barintus episode, as it stands in the *Navigatio*, forms no integral part of the narrative. It is told quite in the mysterious style[23] of a Celtic Otherworld voyage. One is justified therefore in regarding it as a confused survival of some introductory incident like those just referred to.

In the *Vita Merlini*, Barintus, who steers the ship of Arthur toward the Otherworld, appears to have been in origin then a sea-god, a lord of the Land beyond the Waves, who, like Manannán in the tale of Ciabhan, conducted the voyager thither.[24] Later when his mysterious character was forgotten, he was represented as a pilot, and this was the form of the legend that Geoffrey knew. The rationalization of a sea-god into a famous navigator is a sufficiently natural process. We have for it one of the closest parallels imaginable. The thing happened very early to the famous Manannán. In *The Glossary of Cormac*[25] we read:

> ... Manannan mac lir, a celebrated merchant who was in the Isle of Man. He was the best pilot that was in the west of Europe. He used to know by studying the heavens, i.e. by using the sky, the period which would be the fine weather and the bad weather, and when each of these two times would change. *Inde Scoti* [the Irish of course] *et Brittones eum deum vocaverunt maris, et inde filium maris esse dixerunt*, i.e. Mac Lir 'son of sea', *et de nomine Manandan* the Isle of Man *dictus est*.

Substituting Barrind for Manannán, Geoffrey might almost have had these words under his eye when he wrote:[26]

> *Illuc, post bellum Camblani, vulnere laesum*
> *Duximus Arcturum, nos conducente Barintho*
> *Aequora cui fuerant, et doeli sydera nota;*
> *Hoc rectore ratis, cum principe, venimus illuc.*

Notes

1 Ed. Michel, 1837, p.37. Edition San Marte, *Die Sagen von Merlin*, 1853, p.299, verse 930.

2 C. Ferdinand Lot, *Annales de Bretagne*, XV, 534.

3 Ed. Schröder, 1871, p.3ff; Ed. Jubinal, 1836, p.1ff.

4 Such is the opinion of Zimmer, *Ztschr. für deutsches Alterthum*, XXXIII, 314. Cf. de Goeje, *Actes du 8e Congrès des Orientalistes*, I, i, 48.

5 For this date see Phillimore in *Y Cymmrodor*, XI, 128. The ms.

(Vespasian A, XIV, Cottonian, in the British Museum) is a collection of lives of Welsh saints. It was published by Rees, *Lives of the Cambro-british Saints*, Llandovery, 1853, see pp.132–3 (translation p.435). The text of the above incident has also been printed by the Bollandists, *Acta Sanct.*, Vol I for March, p.44, note d.

6   Cf. Zimmer, Kuhn's *Zeitschrift*, XXXII, 160.

7   *Ztschr. für deutsches Alterthum*, vol. XXXIII, pp.307–9 (1889). The life of St Aidan is found in the same ms. as that of St David.

8   Namely, that the episode originated in a misunderstanding by the Irish of a Norse 'kenning' according to which the early Vikings sometimes called a ship a 'sea-horse' (l.c., p.309).

9   In the *Serglige Conculaind*, Windisch, *Irische Texte*, 1880, I, 225, line 22, he is called the 'horseman of the hairy sea'. Cf. Nutt and Meyer, *The Voyage of Bran*, I, 10ff; the story of Ciabhan in the colloquy, O'Grady, *Silva Gadelica*, I, 177; and the Second Battle of Moytura, *Révue Celtique*, XII, 104; '*groig maic Lir la maur-ainfini*'; [numerous as] 'the Son of Ler's horses in a sea-storm'.

10   He was indeed the traditional lord of the Isle of Man, a place dimly confused with the Otherworld by the ancient Celts dwelling around the Irish Sea. See Henderson, *Fled Bricrend*, Irish Texts Society, II, p.142.

11   Thus Odin's 'Wild Hunt' survived with King Arthur as its hero. See Freymond, *Artus Kampf mit dem Katzenungetüm*, p.378–9, (Festschrift Gröber, Halle, 1899).

12   The idea that we have in Barintus a creature of the Otherworld is of course not new. Henri Martin, *Histoire de France*, Paris, 1857, I, 73, conjectured that Barintus was the Welsh Charon who conducted the souls of the dead to the underworld. He brought forward, however, no reasons for his idea, which seems to have been simply an inference from the *Vita Merlini*.

13   See Loth, *Les Mabinogion*, I, 67.

14   *Ztschr. für deut. Alterthum*, XXXIII, 314.

15   The epithet *find* (white) is so appropriate for a sea-god, that Meyer and Nutt have suggested that the name of Mongan, son of Manannán, comes from *Mong-find* (white mane). *Voyage of Bran*, II, 29 note.

[16] Finnbarr occurs in the *Colloquy* (O'Grady, *Silva Gadelica*, I, 199) along with Lir and Teigue and in *The Book of Fermoy* (Todd, *Irish MS. Series*, R.I.A. I, i, 47) along with Manannán as the name of a chieftain of the Túatha Dé Danann.

[17] For references to the shape-shifting habits of Manannán, see Meyer and Nutt, *Voyage of Bran*, I, 139, 198, etc. Mongan the reputed son of Manannán was really only a rebirth; the god under another name. 'Orbsen', still another name for Manannán, was noted by O'Donovan (translation of Cormac's *Glossary*, ed. Stokes, 1868, p.114).

[18] *Voyage of Bran*, I, ii.

[19] See note above.

[20] In the *Echtra Cormaic* (Windisch and Stokes, *Irische Texte*, III, i, 193ff), Manannán, in person, lures away Cormac. In the *Echtra Laegaire* (O'Grady, *Silve Gadelica*, I, 256–7) Fiachna himself invites Laegaire to his realm. So Arawn comes to meet Pwyll (Loth, *The Mabinogion*, I, 27ff). And Abartach, disguised as the Gilla Decair, lures away Dermot (*Silve Gadelica*, I, 257ff).

[21] For example, the 'Summoning Damsel' in *The Voyage of Bran* (ed. Meyer and Nutt, I, 2, cf. page 142).

[22] In the *Serglige Conculaind* (Windisch, *Irische Texte*, I, 218ff), where Laeg relates his journey in order to persuade Cuchulinn to set out. Cf. Chrétien's *Ivain*, where it is the tale of Calogrenant, a previous adventurer, that incites the hero to undertake his journey to the marvellous Fountain.

[23] Mernoc knows beforehand of Barintus' approach (a common incident in the Otherworld voyage, cf. *Voyage of Bran*, I, 30 and 62). The two embark in a boat that awaits them, and that travels (there is no mention of oars or sails) through a blinding mist to a marvellous land. Cf. the boat of glass in the *Echtra Connla* (Windisch, *Kurzgefasste Irische Grammatik*, pp.118–20), that of bronze in the *Serglige Conculaind* (*Irische Texte*, I, 210), the self-moving boat connected with Manannán's land in the story of Becuma (Summary in *The Book of Lismore* by Todd, R.I.A. Irish MS. Series, I, i, 38) and the mist through which Cormac journeyed to reach Manannán's 'Fort' (*Echtra Cormaic*, *Irische Texte*, III, i, 195).

[24] In the *Colloquy* (O'Grady, *Silva Gadelica*, I, 177), Manannán

appears to the voyagers who are on the point of being ship-
wrecked in a tempest. He takes them upon a dark-grey steed,
which he is riding, and conducts them, and their boat, to Tir
Tairngiri.

[25] I employ O'Donovan's translation (ed. Stokes, Calcutta, 1868,
p.114), which is based on the text of Stokes, *Three Irish
Glossaries*, London, 1862, p.31. Where the original is in Latin
I have allowed it to stand.

[26] *Vita Merlini*, ed. Michel, p.37, verse 930ff.

APPENDIX
8

Mabon, The Celtic Divine Child

Caitlín Matthews

Of the many archetypes in Celtic mythology, one of the most intriguing and evasive is that of Mabon, the Celtic Divine Child. In *Mabon and the Mysteries of Britain*,[1] I have identified many of the characters within *The Mabinogion* who manifest the Mabon archetype, but here I would like to range more widely and examine the evidence from a broader basis.

The core of Mabon's identity and function is embedded deeply in Celtic and Arthurian tradition and was obviously well known to earlier oral tradition, if the fragmentation of his archetype is anything to go by. Traces of his story appear in folk tradition and medieval romance. In the aptly named Breton text, the *Roman du Silence*,[2] there is a reference to two minstrels performing the *lai Mabon*, attesting to an extant medieval story. Unfortunately, the minstrels are not permitted to give us any verses in this text. Similarly a manuscript of the Shrewsbury School[3] speaks of a *lai* entitled *Rey Mabun*, but is as taciturn as the *Roman du Silence*. It is almost as though Mabon's story was so well known and ubiquitous that it is tacitly assumed the story bore no further repetition.

How a British Celtic archetype became the subject of a Breton *lai* is perhaps something we will never be able to trace with any exactitude. Where literary tradition takes over from oral tradition, written evidence runs out and we turn to archaeological backup. Mabon is the local name of the Romano-British deity, Maponus, to whom many dedications have been found in northern Britain, especially along Hadrian's Wall and the area of the Solway Firth.[4]

The characteristics of the British deity in the centuries before Rome may only be guessed at, but he certainly equated, in the Roman mind, with aspects of Apollo and Orpheus.[5] It is possible, though there is little evidence for this, that Maponus was the focus of a minor mystery cult among his Romano-British devotees. Closely associated with Maponus was the cult of the Matres, the Triple Mothers: a fact which should not surprise us, since Mabon is universally called Mabon, son of Modron – Son, son of Mother. The twin cults of Modron and Mabon were undoubtedly ancient before their classical overlay, and it is this primal tradition which we shall attempt to reconstruct.

The names 'Mabon' and 'Modron' are really titles, not personal names. They are remnants of a mystery tradition where these titles were applied to great divine archetypes, in much the same way as Demeter and Kore in Greek tradition have no personal appellation but are known as Mother and Maiden. This custom pertained in Celtic countries where heroes and chieftains swore a variation on this carefully phrased oath: 'I swear by the gods which my tribe swears by.' Such a formula obviated the use of a name. This caution sprang from the reverent custom of concealing the deity's name from the irreverent or uninitiated. Even today, the devout speak of 'Our Lord' and 'Our Lady' rather than the more familiar Jesus and Mary. It is possible that in the pre-Roman era one might have wandered the length and breadth of Britain swearing 'by the Son and his Mother' without any loss of understanding, each tribe holding a Mother and Son in reverence. Indeed, one might so swear today without any blasphemous intention.

It is this central premise that we must bear in mind, that the titles Mabon and Modron are applicable to various youths and their mothers, though certainly not arbitrarily and without warrant. This game of substitution can be played only with a select set of mythic pieces which bear traces of the original archetypes.

The earliest textual reference to the myth of Mabon appears in 'Culhwch and Olwen', one of the many sources appearing in a medieval compilation called *The Mabinogion*.[6] In this story, Culhwch falls in love with a giant's daughter, Olwen, but in order to win her he is set 39 impossible tasks by Olwen's father, Yspaddaden. Chief among these tasks is the finding of Mabon.

'Culhwch' is one of the oldest stories of *The Mabinogion*, stemming from an oral tradition which has its roots in the period immediately following that of the Dark Age Arthur, *c.* AD 537. It embodies traces of ancient, often lost, stories once prominent in proto-Celtic tradition. The story-teller gives a version of Mabon's story which betrays the manner in which a once-potent myth can be smoothed into folk-tale.

When Culhwch asks for information about Mabon he is told that the child was taken from between his mother and the wall when he was three nights old and that no one knows where he is now, nor indeed whether he is alive or dead. Mabon has departed from the memories of mankind, but the memories of animals prove more retentive, and it is to the animal kingdom that Culhwch directs his search. With him on this quest is Gwrhyr, an interpreter of animals' speech. They start with the blackbird.

The blackbird has not heard of Mabon, though she has pecked an iron anvil down to its wooden base, and she passes them on to the stag of the plains. He remembers a single sapling which grew to be a mighty tree, but even that has withered. He sends them on to the owl of the wood who has seen the triple growth and uprooting of the forest, but has never heard of Mabon. She passes them on to the eagle who has pecked the stars from the heights of a mountain until it is only a few feet high. He has never heard of Mabon, but has rumour of something via a salmon with whom he once battled. The salmon has never heard of Mabon, but has been troubled by a crying from the walls of Caer Loyw (Gloucester). The heroes mount on the salmon's back and are led to the walls where they ask the mystery question: 'Oh, who is it that there laments within a house of stone?'[6]

They receive the answer: 'It is Mabon, born of Modron's womb, within these walls alone.' Mabon is then brought out on Cai's back and liberated to help Culhwch fulfil the rest of his impossible tasks which will qualify him to marry Olwen.

In this story Mabon is very much a subsidiary character; a famous archetype which the story-teller has inserted into the narrative in order to give Culhwch his place among the older heroes. Much the same happens in later medieval romance, where Arthur occasionally makes a guest appearance in order to give the story authenticity within the Matter of Britain.

Nevertheless, the story-teller has preserved many elements of Celtic belief and practice. The long search through the agency of animals is closely associated with the transformatory sequence which most Celtic poets boast of having undergone. The poets Amergin[7] of Ireland and Taliesin[8] of Britain both claim to have inhabited various shapes. This must not be taken to mean a literal shape-shifting, any more than it necessarily implies a reincarnational memory.[9] More precisely, these poets speak of an initiatory sequence of realizations which every initiate of the bardic mysteries undergoes. In that moment of revelation, a complex web of imagery is presented in one vision. Like Celtic knotwork, everything in this vision is connected, leading to further interpretation. It may be the work of a lifetime to comprehend this sequence, which is really a visionary glyph of knowledge.

Forming a chain back to the beginning of time, the animals of Mabon's search each represent a species of knowledge and a non-linear age of time. Encoded both within these beasts and in the story of Mabon's finding is an inner history, an encyclopaedia of information and a direct experience of the worlds – both human and otherworldly. This chain of information is borne out from an evolutionary point of view, where each species of animal is part of life's history, each bearing some part of the genetic pattern of creation.

This, then, is the major source for Mabon's extant myth. We find other traces in the Welsh *Triads*,[10] the mnemonic verses which encapsulate sets of knowledge. Triad 52 speaks of Mabon as being one of three famous prisoners.[11] Both *The Mabinogion* and *The Triads* preserve the most persistent part of Mabon's myth – that he is imprisoned and released. Both these texts are the last remaining links with the tradition of Mabon as a native deity rather than the literary character which he later becomes. They retain his numinous power though neither is as informative as we would like them to be. Taking these texts alone, the paucity of evidence does not help us reconstruct, in even partial fashion, the lost myth of Mabon.

We are fortunate that the Mabon archetype found a vehicle of transmission which showed no signs of abating its progress: Arthurian legend. Any character lodged in the tales which comprise the Matter of Britain has been gifted with the kind of immortality associated with the ancient gods and heroes of British tradition. But what of Mabon? Is it possible to reconstruct something of his original mythos with any certainty? It is certain that the full power of Mabon's archetype has been lost to us, but it is likely that a once-potent god-form such as the Wondrous Child might well have left notable traces.

As Alwyn and Brinley Rees have stated in *Celtic Heritage*: 'Traditional tales used to be transmitted by a priestly order in the Celtic lands, and diverse blessings accrued to those who heard them related.'[12] It is in such traditional stories that the Matter of Britain found its roots. The myth of Mabon, perhaps once widespread, a story to be related as part of a seasonal ritual during the winter months, became merely the story of Mabon in later times. I write 'merely', but the hero-cycles which are told of semi-mortals like CuChullain, Fionn and others proved memorable in both oral and literary tradition. May we legitimately posit the existence of Mabon's archetype through a series of linked hero-stories?

The repertoire of a professional Celtic story-teller included the learning of some 350 stories in which individual heroes appeared in definable story-cycles. Thus the story-teller could relate the following tales about the hero's life: his conception, his youthful exploits, his adventures, his wooing of a maiden, his otherworldly voyaging, his hostings and raids; and finally, his woeful imprisonment, vision and lamentable death.[13] I propose to reconstruct here a similar hero-cycle applicable to Mabon's archetype, by juxtaposing stories of other heroes who share in some part of the Mabon mythos, or which they have inherited in the process of oral transmission. Such is the wealth of material scattered throughout both Celtic and Arthurian texts that such an experiment is possible. If Mabon represents x, the unknown factor, in this mythic equation, we must set something to work in his place and see what manner of revelation is given.

We are able to tell one story of Mabon's conception, or *compert*, as the Irish story-lists define it. For a Divine Child like Mabon we would expect to know of at least one otherworldly parent, and this is the case:

In Denbighshire there is a parish which is called Llanferres, and there is a Rhyd y Gyfartha (Ford of Barking). In the old days, the hounds of the countryside used to come together to the side of that ford to bark, and nobody dared to go to find out what was there until Urien Rheged came. And when he came to the side of the ford he saw nothing there except a woman washing. And then the hounds ceased barking, and Urien seized the woman and had his will of her; and then she said: 'God's blessing on the feet which brought thee here.' 'Why?' 'Because I have been fated to wash here until I should conceive a son by a Christian. And I am daughter to the King of Annwn, and come thou here at the end of the year and then thou shalt receive the boy.' And so he came and he received there a boy and a girl; this is Owein, son of Urien, and Morfydd, daughter of Urien. [14]

This Welsh story was preserved in oral tradition until the sixteenth century, and we may be sure that it tells the story of Mabon's conception, except, of course, that the story is told of Owain ap Urien, an historical character of the sixth century who was incorporated into Arthurian legend as Owain or Yvain, Arthur's nephew or cousin, according to some versions.

The fact that Owain's mother identifies herself here as a daughter of the King of Annwn is very significant, since a Triad [15] speaks of the parentage of Owain and Morfudd from Urien and *Modron, daughter of Afallach*. Both the folk story and the Triad obviously refer to the same tradition. Now, in Arthurian tradition, the wife of Urien is Morgan, Arthur's half-sister; [16] and Morgan is, in the earliest references, [17] the guardian of the realm of Avalon – Afallach being the original king of that paradisal island. Morgan is thus acting here in the role of Modron, and Owain in the role of Mabon.

Mabon's conception represents an intersection of linear time by paradisal dimension, for he is the child of earthly and otherworldly parents. Their meeting is the meeting of worlds, peoples, cultures brought into sudden alignment, and the Divine Child is born to mediate this set of encounters. The appearance of such a child, innocent and full of otherworldly knowledge, is the signal for a focalization of opposing powers. All that does not wish to change, all that wishes to maintain the existing order and impose its will upon the world, gathers itself against Mabon, whose very existence represents a threat.

It is not possible to reconstruct a full hero-cycle for Mabon. Of his *indarba* or imprisonment we have already heard in *The Mabinogion*, noting that this is the most prominent feature of his mythos. That the *indarba* should occur so early in a hero's career is quite extraordinary, for the implication in 'Culhwch' is that Mabon was stolen from his mother when he was a baby, though by the time of his liberation, he is grown to be a mighty hunter, capable of besting the fiercesome boar, Twrch Trwyth. This latter exploit represents Mabon's youthful deeds or *macgnimartha*; but perhaps Mabon's imprisonment is really of another order?

Within Celto-Arthurian tradition there are many instances of children being abducted, usually by otherworldly powers or in order to gain a special training. It is among stories of this kind that we can most authoratively see the half-covered trail of the Wondrous Youth, Mabon. There are two famous child abductions which bear obvious parallels with his myth, and a still more famous third: the abduction of Pryderi and Lancelot, and the obscure childhood of Arthur himself.

We learn that the abduction of Pryderi from his mother, Rhiannon, is caused by the enmity of Gwawl, an underworld noble who was once affianced to Rhiannon until Pwyll came to claim her. Gwawl was tricked into giving up his destined bride and humiliated by being put into a miraculous food-providing bag and beaten with sticks. For these blows he returns vengeance in one crushing attack: the abduction of Pryderi. It is not known how or where Pryderi is taken in the story; but, simultaneously, a British nobleman, Teyrnon, discovers that his own favourite mare has foaled. In previous years her foal had been stolen, and this night he keeps watch, for it is May Eve, the time when the otherworldly powers are most free to operate. He sees a gigantic claw come through the stable window to steal the foal and strikes at it. The foal is dropped and Teyrnon rushes outside to pursue the attacker. Finding nothing there, he returns to discover a newly born child in his stable alongside the foal. He keeps the boy and names him Gwri Golden-Hair.

The boy is, of course, Pryderi. He is raised by Teyrnon and his wife while Rhiannon silently suffers the ignominy of standing at the horse block where she must tell her story to every visitor, offering to bear each into the hall on her back: her punishment for having eaten her own child, for so she stands accused. Gwri is, however, recognized and brought back to his parents and Rhiannon is released from her punishment. Her son is acclaimed by her with the saying: 'My anxiety is over.' And so he is named, losing his secret childhood name, Gwri, and becoming Pryderi or 'anxiety' instead.[18]

I have dealt with the many ramifications of this story in *Mabon*,[19] where the obvious comparisons between Mabon and Pryderi are paralleled. Here we note that Pryderi's 'imprisonment' is really a fostering. He is cared for by an earthly, astute guardian who raises him and gives him a name to protect him from the otherworldly powers which threaten his existence. Pryderi is not abducted and imprisoned by his family's enemy, Gwawl, at this point, although this does happen in a later story when Pryderi is a man.[20]

Rhiannon is clearly shown to be a type of Modron in this story which best preserves the passion of Modron. Like the unnamed mother of Urien's children, Rhiannon is likewise the daughter of a king of an otherworldly realm, Annwn, the Underworld. She is likewise fated to marry a mortal man and bear a famous son. The symbolic attributes of Modron are distinct in Celtic tradition: she often bears twins, she is associated with the Underworld, and is often represented by horses, dogs and blackbirds or ravens. She suffers the loss of her child and undergoes a passion in this period similar to that of Demeter for Persephone, abducted into the realm of Hades,[21] or makes a lengthy search for her son, like the Blessed Virgin who loses her Son in the temple.[22] Great burdens are set upon the shoulders of Modron: those who lift them are the helpers and companions of the Great Mother, and they have their place in the freeing of Mabon from his prison.

The suffering mother is again a feature of Lancelot's own abduction. Indeed, the beginning of Lancelot's story is called 'The Tale of the Queen of Many Sorrows', where it tells of Lancelot's father, Ban of Benoic, who dies suddenly from the shock of seeing his castle burned by his enemies. His wife, Elaine, leaves Lancelot – still a babe in arms – on the ground and rushes to assist her stricken husband, only to turn back and see her son being embraced by a maiden who takes him away with her. She is none other than the Lady of the Lake. She takes him with her to her lake-domain where he is kept safe from attack by his family's enemies. The Lady does not name him, but calls him 'the Fair Foundling' or 'the Rich Orphan'. She raises him to be a knight and later arms and names him herself. He is then sent back into the world to avenge his father and restore the lands which had been stolen by his enemies. [23]

If we follow an earlier story of Lancelot's abduction, *Lanzelet*, [24] a twelfth-century text which undoubtedly drew on Celtic traditions absent from the *Prose Lancelot*, we find that Lancelot is taken into the Otherworld for the sole purpose of releasing the Lake-Lady's son from enchantment. This son is called Mabuz, and he has been cursed with cowardice by an evil magician called Iweret. Lanzelet is raised by the Lake-Lady to become an accomplished warrior – a late example of the Celtic tradition whereby boys were trained in war skills by women-warriors. [25] The Lake-Lady likewise arms and eventually names Lanzelet, although he remains nameless until he has accomplished her will, which is to kill the magician who cursed her son.

In this story, Lanzelet is almost a substitute for Mabuz. Mabuz himself is unable to move freely on his own behalf, for he is destined to live a strange existence within the Castle of Death – a prison in which he is trapped by the curse and a prison likewise for all knights who stray within its walls, for it renders them cowardly also. He is unable to make free use of his lands, realms analogous to the Lands of the Living in Celtic tradition, [26] for these are held by Iweret. When Lanzelet is released from his fostering, a fully trained knight, he starts to accomplish all that Mabuz would have done, had he been free. He kills Iweret and wins back Mabuz's lands, but for Mabuz there is no ultimate release, for his curse cannot be lifted. It is so that Mabuz's lands are awarded to Lanzelet who also marries Iweret's daughter. In this story, Lanzelet is clearly Mabuz's active 'twin' or substitute – they are, after all, foster-brothers. The author of the story has not fully comprehended the ancient tradition of Mabon's imprisonment but knows sufficient of the story to incorporate it in some manner. It is as though 'Mabon's prison' instead of being the 'place of

Mabon's imprisonment' has become 'the prison administered by Mabuz'. Lanzelet accomplishes the *macgimartha* or *slugard* of the Mabon-cycle in this story.

What of the third abduction of which we spoke? Mabon is closely associated with Arthur, who, according to Triad 52, undergoes a mysterious imprisonment:

> And one (Prisoner) who was more exalted than the three of them was three nights in prison in Caer Oeth and Anoeth, and three nights imprisoned by Gwen Pendragon, and three nights in an enchanted prison under the Stone of Echymeint. This Exalted Prisoner was Arthur. And it was the same lad who released him from each of these three prisons – Goreu, son of Custennin, his cousin.[27]

These references are encapsulations of stories which are lost to tradition, but which were clearly associated once with the disappearance and freeing of Mabon in Celtic imagination. There is a later tradition in which Arthur is 'lost'. He is conceived on Ygraine by Uther, who visits her in the shape of her husband, Gorlois: a transformation which is effected by Merlin, so that Uther is effectually a daemon or incubus.[28] Arthur is taken away after his birth by Merlin in order to be fostered by Sir Ector,[29] although his fostering in the land of Faery is spoken of by Layamon.[20] Arthur is thus hidden at the time of greatest danger to himself, during the interregnum between Uther's death and his own revelation as the rightful king who can draw the Sword from the Stone. The early part of Arthur's life parallels the Mabon archetype, but what of its latter end? Arthur is destined to weld Britain into a single country with himself as overlord. Nearly all his attempts to live a personal life are failures: he is at his strongest when he serves his country, who we can see as Sovereignty, the Goddess of the Land, who represents Logres or Britain.[31] He does not die, precisely, but is wounded and borne away into Avalon to be healed by Morgen.[32]

Both the abductions of Lancelot and Arthur are really fosterings, times of withdrawal and preparation for great exploits. From these and the other examples of our Mabon archetypes we can see some part of the pattern coming clear. The manifestations of Mabon's archetype betray distinct features: the child is born of a mortal and an otherworldly parent. He is lost or abducted shortly after birth – usually because he is a threat to the established order, or because he is in danger from enemies. He is raised secretly, usually in an otherwordly environment, where he learns deep wisdom and the skills for his destined task. He is released from his obscurity or prison by a character bearing characteristics similar to or more mature than himself[33] and is so enabled to start a life-cycle which proves to be redemptive, not personal. At the end of his life he does not die, but is withdrawn into a state of spiritual life.

We will see the latter part of this pattern more clearly from one of the closest exemplars of the Mabon archetype – Merlin. Merlin is born of a virgin and a daemon.[34] As Merlin Emrys, he is abducted by Vortigern's men, who are seeking for a suitable sacrifice to help sustain Vortigern's tower, which keeps tumbling down. This tower is a figure of the state of Britain – in collapse under an unlawful, bloody and treacherous king. The perfect sacrifice, say Vortigern's druids, would be a boy whose father is unknown.[35] Merlin Emrys fits this description perfectly. However, since he is a type of Mabon, there is more to him than first appears. He is the innocent child who can refute philosophers and make clear the state of the country. He reveals the true cause of the tower's collapse as being the two dragons which are imprisoned under its foundations. He reveals to Vortigern the true state of Britain both now and in the future in a series of brilliant prophecies.[36] Here we see revealed another part of Mabon's cycle, his *fis* or vision, wherein his inner knowledge of creation reveals itself to men.

Merlin Emrys prophesies and then helps establish the reign on the Pendragons: firstly Uther, and then Arthur. He is really their forerunner. This is significant in relation to Mabon, since an early Welsh poem[37] speaks of Mabon as 'the servant of Uther Pendragon': a single reference which helps us link Merlin's function as prophet with Mabon's own lost function as releaser and enabler.

We note that Merlin does not have a personal life. His function is to serve Britain and to act as prophet and adviser to kings. When his task is done, he is withdrawn to the realm of his unknown father, the Otherworld. Geoffrey of Monmouth speaks of his house with many doors and windows through which he can observe the heavens.[38] Merlin does not die, but voluntarily retires from the realm of men into his Otherwordly abode from which he can still remain in contact with Logres and from where certain people, sensitive to Merlin's role, can faintly hear the 'cri du Merlin'.[39]

Merlin's withdrawal from the world, like Mabon's imprisonment, has not always been perfectly understood by the later Arthurian romancers who have spoken of his entrapment by Nimuë, Vivienne or the Lady of the Lake.[40] Merlin's spiritual maturity is mistaken for senile infatuation, so that they tell of his revealing the method by which he can be trapped in his crystal tower, under his rock or in his thorn tree – those later representations of his place of retirement – to sinuous and treacherous damsels. These stories merely reveal the deterioration of the tradition. For in later stories Mabon similarly undergoes a diminution where, in Chrétien's *Erec*,[41] he becomes Mabonograin, a giant warrior, trapped within an enchanted garden where he is enslaved to a faery mistress whose domain he defends against all comers.

Both Merlin and Mabon's later commentators may stray from tradition, but they yet manage to retain aspects of older fragments which do not come down to us in any other way. From Merlin's story and from related tradition we can establish the archetypical Mabon death story or *aided* which appears nowhere else: the withdrawal of Merlin to his *esplumoir*.[42] Although there is one further example from late Arthurian tradition which has possibly inherited a vital part of Mabon's archetype: the character of Galahad.

The Arthurian tradition is exceedingly persistent. Whatever has been honoured, reverenced or sainted by holy custom remains embedded within the Matter of Britain, becoming mythologically subsumed in the variant texts. Their unravelling is the work of many scholars. We have seen how Mabon's archetype did not totally fade from the tradition but appeared in strange guises. It should come as no surprise to find that it resides in the highest flowering of the Arthurian legends – the Quest for the Grail.

The original Grail winner is Peredur or Perceval;[43] in him we find many broad traces of Mabon's archetype, as I have shown in my study of *The Mabinogion*. Galahad appears much later in the French texts and has always seemed to me to be a foreign usurper of Peredur's role. However, Galahad inherits not only the characteristics of Mabon but also those of Lancelot, his father, who, as Arthur's best knight, is directly descended from the Celtic original 'freer of the cauldron', Llwch Lleminawg.[44]

Galahad is conceived by Elaine, the daughter of the Grail guardian, Pelles, at whose behest and with the connivance of Dame Brisen, she appears to Lancelot in the shape of Guinevere, the only woman Lancelot desires.[45] In this mysteriously un-Christian conception of the most Christian knight, we see the ancient archetypal pattern emerging. Elaine, like Uther in Arthur's conception, acts the part of fantasy-being, a succuba. Her son, Galahad, is brought up surrounded by women in a monastery, just as Lancelot is raised by the totally female population of the Lake-Lady. He is brought to court by a holy man after his obscure youth and undertakes the quest for the Grail. What most people consider to be Galahad's worst features – his seeming priggishness and ultra-holiness – are revealed to be the simplicity and innocence of a man living a redemptive, not a personal life. His one function – the reason why he was born – is to reveal the potentialities of the spirit and release them, in the shape of the Grail. When this is achieved, he is withdrawn from the earthly sphere at Sarras, the Grail city, where his companions seem to see him die; but we must look on his death as upon Merlin's withdrawal to another mode of life. Like Merlin, who is aided by his sister, Ganieda, to withdraw into his last retreat,[46] so Galahad is enabled to make this transition through the mediation of the holy maiden, Dindraine;[47] as indeed Arthur is enabled to pass into Avalon through the mediation of Morgen.[48]

Here we see Modron's part in Mabon's hero-cycle; in whatever guise she takes, Modron appears at both the beginning and the end of his cycle. For Mabon is a servant of Sovereignty, of the Goddess of the Land. His service is to the land, a redemptive, not a personal life. He represents the truth and justice of the Goddess, his mother, from whom he comes and to whom he returns. He is, in fact, Sovereignty's son, when he appears as Mabon the Divine Child. His enemies always strive to imprison or sacrifice him because he is incorruptible, pure and discerning, but the truth remains that he cannot be overcome unless he voluntarily commits himself into the hands of his enemies.

We have traced Mabon's unfolding life and career from conception to withdrawal; what is his true purpose within our native mythology?

Mabon stands at the nexus of a threefold tradition. As a Celtic deity he is the joy of the Otherworld, the God of Youth and Delight. As a proto-Christian archetype, he is a Liberator of the Light, the Long-expected One who redeems the world. In non-religious, Arthurian tradition – which inherits elements of the two former ones – Mabon appears again as the perfect knight, conceived strangely, destined to free the waters of the wasteland and bring the Grail into manifestation through his offices.

The reason why Mabon cannot be found by one person's effort, nor from the testimony of one animal, is that he cannot be known by one single part of creation: he is the sum of creation. He is the Child of the Dawn, the First Born of the Mother. It is his task to harp creation into existence and to be the Shepherd of the orders of creations – birds, beasts and fish all answer to him. He exists from the beginning and can be found – in archetypal terms – within the terrestrial paradise. His mythos explicates this in other terms – he is known to be imprisoned, hidden or lost, just as our own innocence is lost. Whoever finds Mabon finds the primal source of truth and integrity. His mother, Modron, is the land, the goddess who guards the gates of death and living. An exchange takes place between them which is at the heart of native mysteries. [49]

Modron, for the sake of the land, permits Mabon to become lost to her. She enables his birth into the earthly realms by lying with a mortal man; in this way Mabon has dual divine and human citizenship. He is brought up secretly and taught all the skills which he will need. He forgets his origins but he remembers these at his initiation into manhood, when he enters the totemic tree of time where linear time is intersected by the otherworldly dimension. At this point he is given his earthly name, although he never ceases to be a Mabon. His mother watches over his career and either in person, or in the guise of messengers, encourages and helps him to fulfil his mission, which is to reconstruct the primal patterns of peace which exist endlessly in paradise but which are lost in the earthly realms.

The accomplishment of this pattern takes many forms: Mabon may appear as a warrior, hunting down whatever is corrupt; or as a poet/seer whose prophetic utterances show pathways through confusion; or as a sacrificial king, who brings justice to a war-torn land. He does not live a personal but a redemptive life. He upholds the honour of his mother in the persons of other women who represent her in the earthly realms, priestesses who mediate her influence and power; he is also a guardian of his mother's rights where she functions as Sovereignty – the Goddess of the Land – by wielding justice, truth and discernment in the administration of the land. He may act as the forerunner or adviser of a king. He is not permitted to perform rites of healing in his own right or for his own benefit, although he may enable others to do so. His part is to establish the patterns of peace, but others have to wield them. When these patterns are established, he must withdraw from the earthly realms and return to the paradisal Otherworld, where he is restored to his first condition, as the Son of Modron, the keeper of creation.

This archetypal pattern of Mabon's inner function has been drawn only from native sources and traditions, but it is not hard to see why the essential core of Christianity grafted so easily onto the existing mythos of the British Isles. There is almost no join, for the two traditions – Celtic, or proto-Celtic mythos and Christian mythos – flow together in an organic way. Ways of worship may change, but stories never.

The cycle of Mabon does not have to be forced to parallel that of Christ: they are the same mythic pattern. A seventh-century Irish poem attests to an intrinsic understanding of the Mabon archetype where it speaks of the Blessed Trinity as:

> Threefold God, three noble united Persons,
> Wonderful sole King of Heaven, infant, holy warrior. [50]

The horn which releases Mabon from his long imprisonment is blowing to assemble all peoples to a meeting place outside time to discover that the mediations of *all* traditions are valid, that they grow out of one another and will continue to do so.

The purpose of Mabon for our own time is the same as for all times: truth, justice and discernment are the heritage of all peoples; these are the means of healing the wounds of our earth and the pathways by which we may restore our lost innocence.

Notes

1. *Mabon and the Mysteries of Britain*, C. Matthews, Penguin Arkana, 1987.
2. *Roman du Silence*, L. Thorpe in *Nottingham Medieval Studies* V, II. 2761–5, 1961.
3. Shrewsbury School MS vii, fol. 200.
4. *Pagan Celtic Britain*, A. Ross, Routledge & Kegan Paul, 1967.
5. *A Traveller's Guide to Celtic Britain*, A. Ross, Routledge & Kegan Paul, 1985.
6. *The Mabinogion*, trans. Lady C. Guest, Ballantyne Press, 1910.
7. *Ancient Irish Tales*, T.P. Cross and C.H. Slover, Figgis, 1936.
8. *Mabinogion*, op. cit.
9. The story of Tuan mac Carill and Fintan, famous reincarnated Irish sages, reveal a similar pattern. Cf. Cross and Slover, op. cit.
10. *Trioedd Ynys Prydein*, trans. Rachel Bromwich, University of Wales Press, 1961.
11. Ibid.
12. *Celtic Heritage*, Alwyn and Brinley Rees, Thames and Hudson, 1961.
13. These are all species of stories which recur in the professional Irish story-lists. They are known, respectively, in Irish as: *compert*, *macgimartha*, *echtra*, *tochmarc*, *immram*, *slugard*, *rain*, *indarba*, *fis* and *aided*.
14. *Trioedd Ynys Prydein*, op. cit., p.459. It is perhaps significant to note that the greeting which Urien receives from Afallach's daughter is the same as the five-fold blessing found in some native British pagan rituals. A corrupt form of this blessing was collected in the Cheshire district:

Bledsian we thyn fote that habben brung thee in this weges [ways].

Bledsian we thyn cneo [knee] that sceol cneolin unto that sacren awltar.

Bledsian we thyn wame; withuten swilyke we willen nat by.

Bledsian we thyn breost forman in belte and in strang [beauty and strength]

Bledsian we thyn lippa that sceol spricka that sacren nama.

15 *Trioedd Ynys Prydein*, op. cit., p.185. Triad 70.
16 *Le Morte d'Arthur*, Sir Thomas Malory, University Books, 1961.
17 *Vita Merlini*, ed. and trans. J.J. Parry, University of Illinois Press, 1925. See also 38 below.
18 In most of the examples cited as archetypes of Mabon in this chapter, the hero, when a child, has a secret name which his replaced when he becomes adult; this usually happens at a juncture when he accomplishes his youthful exploits.
19 C. Matthews, op. cit., chapters 2, 4 and 9.
20 *Manawyddan, Son of Llyr* in *The Mabinogion*, op. cit.
21 *The Homeric Hymns*, trans. Apostos N. Athanassakis, John Hopkins University Press, 1976.
22 St Luke, chap. 2 vv. 41–52.
23 *Sir Lancelot of the Lake*, L.A. Paton, George Routledge and Co., 1929.
24 *Lanzelet*, Ulrich von Zatzikhoven, K.G.T. Webster, Columbia University Press, 1951.
25 *Warriors of Arthur*, J. Matthews and R.J. Stewart, Blandford Press, 1987.
26 His lands are called the Fair Forest and are described in terms familiar to anyone who has read accounts of *Tir mBeo* as the terrestrial paradise.
27 *Trioedd Ynys Prydein*, op. cit., p.140. In 'Culhwch and Olwen' in *The Mabinogion*, op. cit., there is a rare reference to Arthur's imprisonment when Glewlwyd, his porter, lists this as one of many adventures he has undergone with his king.
28 The daemon or incubus is of course a real otherworldly being, but Uther's assumption of another shape enables the conception of Arthur, who may be said to have an earthly mother and an otherworldly father.
29 Malory, op. cit., Book I, chap. 3.
30 *Arthurian Chronicles*, Ware and Layamon, trans. E. Mason, p.177, Dent, 1962.
31 I have dealt with Arthur's relationship to Sovereignty in the second of my two-volume study of *The Mabinogion*; *Arthur and the Sovereignty of Britain: Goddess and Tradition in The Mabinogion*, Penguin Arkana, 1989.
32 *Vita Merlini*, op. cit. (See also 38 below.)

[33] This part of Mabon's cycle I have identified as the Succession of the Pendragons cf. C. Matthews (1987).

[34] Wace and Layamon, op. cit., p.145.

[35] C. Matthews (1989). In my commentary of *Lludd and Llefelys* I have shown the many parallels of this sacrificial role.

[36] *The Prophetic Vision of Merlin*, R.J. Stewart, Penguin Arkana, 1986.

[37] *The Romance of Arthur*, ed. J.J. Wilhelm and L.Z. Gross, p.19, Garland Publishing Inc., 1984.

[38] *The Mystic Life of Merlin*, R.J. Stewart, Penguin Arkana, 1986.

[39] *Merlin*, ed. H.E. Wheatley, Early English Texts Society, p.692, 1869.

[40] *Studies in Fairy Mythology of Arthurian Romance*, L.A. Paton, Burt Franklin, 1960.

[41] *Arthurian Romances*, Chrétien de Troyes, D.D.R. Owen, Dent, 1987.

[42] Cf. John Matthews' essay 'Merlin's Esplumoir' in *Merlin and Woman*, Blandford Press, 1986.

[43] *The Mabinogion*, op. cit., and Chrétien de Troyes, op. cit.

[44] C. Matthews, op. cit., (1987), pp. 107–8, 156.

[45] Malory, op. cit., Book XI, chap. 2. I have examined the role of the dream-woman or succuba from her roots in the Sovereignty figures of Celtic tradition in *Arthur and the Sovereignty of Britain*, op. cit.

[46] *Vita Merlini*, op. cit. and 38 above.

[47] *The Quest of the Holy Grail*, trans. P. Matarasso, Penguin, 1969.

[48] *Vita Merlini*, op. cit, and 38 above.

[49] C. Matthews, op. cit., (1987), pp.177–86.

[50] 'Irish Origin Legends and Genealogy', Donnchadh O Corráin, in *History and Heroic Tale: A Symposium*, ed. T. Nyberg, Odensee University Press, 1985.

Notes to Main Text

1. R.J. Stewart, *The Prophetic Vision of Merlin* (Penguin Arkana, London, 1986) includes a full translation of and commentary upon the medieval *Prophecies of Merlin* as set out by Geoffrey of Monmouth.

2. R.J. Stewart, *The Mystic Life of Merlin* (Penguin Arkana, London, 1987) contains a translation of and detailed commentary upon the *Vita Merlini* of Geoffrey of Monmouth.

3. *The Merlin Tarot* (The Aquarian Press, Wellingborough, 1988) is a full colour deck of cards designed by R.J. Stewart and painted by Miranda Gray. The book describes the origins and use of the Tarot and the primal Tarot images and patterns inherent within the Merlin sources some centuries before Renaissance Tarot decks were first known.

4. Nikolai Tolstoy, *The Quest for Merlin* (Hamish Hamilton, London, 1986).

   See also Geoffrey Ashe, 'Merlin in the Earliest Records' in *The Book of Merlin* ed. R.J. Stewart (Blandford Press, Poole, 1988).

5. Geoffrey of Monmouth, *The History of the Kings of Britain*, various translations and commentaries, including the modern translation by Lewis Thorpe (Penguin, London, 1983).

6. *The Mabinogion*, various translations and editions, including Geffrey Gantz (Penguin, London, 1976). For commentaries see Caitlín Matthews, *Mabon and the Mysteries of Britain* and *Arthur and the Sovereignty of Britain* (Penguin Arkana, London, 1987, 1989).

7. Barry Fell, *America B.C.* (Pocket Books, USA, 1976).

8. R.J. Stewart, *Cuchulainn* (Firebird Books, Poole, 1988).
9. R.J. Stewart, *Celtic Gods, Celtic Godesses*, illustrated Miranda Gray and Courtney Davis (Blandford Press, London, 1990).
10. R.J. Stewart, *Creation Myth* (Element Books, Shaftesbury, 1989).
11. *Merlin and Woman*, ed. R.J. Stewart (Blandford Press, London, 1988).
12. J. Matthews and R.J. Stewart, *Legendary Britain* (Blandford Press, London, 1989).
13. Robert Kirk, *Walker Between Worlds*, modern English edition, ed. with commentary R.J. Stewart (Element Books, Shaftesbury, 1990).
14. Robert Graves, *The White Goddess* (various editions) is the modern classic of this information and of poetic bardic tradition. See also J. Matthews, *Taliesin* (The Aquarian Press, London, 1991); *Psychology and the Spiritual Traditions*, ed. R.J. Stewart (Element Books, Shaftesbury, 1990) includes chapters on animals in magical arts, psychology and counselling, and alchemy.
15. R.J. Stewart, *Where is St. George?* (Blandford Press, London, 1989, originally published Moonraker Press, Bradford on Avon, 1976, Humanities Press, New Jersey, USA 1977).
16. R.J. Stewart, *The Waters of the Gap* (Arcania/Ashgrove Publishing, 1990). A reprint with expanded Foreword of the 1980 Bath City Council edition of this book on the mythology and magic of Aquae Sulis.
17. The visualizations in this book, read by the author, are available from Sulis Music BCM 3721, London, WC1N 3XX.
18. R.J. Stewart, *Music, Power, Harmony* (Blandford Press, London, 1990) gives a detailed system and training programme of Elemental chants, vowel sounds, and musical patterns for the Four Direcions.
19. *The Welsh Triads* tr. Rachel Bromwich (University of Wales, Cardiff, 1961).
20. R.J. Stewart, *The Underworld Initiation* (The Aquarian Press, Wellingborough, 1986) gives examples of initiatory ballads and verses from oral tradition, and examines the Underworld tradition of psychic transformation.

Index

INDEX

Elements, the 15, 19, 20, 22, 30, 33-6, 38, 48, 49, 53, 63, 65, 75, 77, 78, 79, 80, 81, 82, 84, 85, 88-91, 98, 99, 103, 107, 114, 115, 116, 122, 129, 145, 149
England 14, 16, 26, 61, 122, 152
environment 14, 29, 41, 50, 65, 83, 88, 89, 91, 99, 119
Europe 11, 25, 27, 49, 61, 88, 89, 105, 139
Evangelists 97
evil 27, 28, 35, 41, 42, 105, 123, 125
exercises 9, 13, 31, 33, 34, 36, 106
eyes 126, 128, 134, 143, 145

falling 84, 86, 106, 134, 135, 147
feathers 143, 144, 147
Ferryman, the 122, 125, 146, 150
fertility 94, 99, 133, 150
fish(es) 27, 99, 102, 103
flies 99, 106
flowers 145, 146, 150
Flower-Maiden (wife of Merlin) 46
folklore 20, 27, 39, 44, 53, 55, 63, 98-100, 123, 148, 149
Fool, the 17, 21, 44, 75, 86, 112, 122, 138

Gabriel, Archangel 84, 97
Ganieda (sister of Merlin) 17, 34, 42, 120, 150
Gaul 105
gender 44, 45, 123
genitals 128
Gnostic 97, 140
Goddess, the 8, 13, 15, 16, 17, 26, 28, 29, 32, 36, 37, 39, 42-8, 50, 51, 63, 65, 66, 73, 75, 82, 92, 93, 94, 98, 99, 100, 104, 112, 116, 117, 118, 120, 122, 124, 132, 133, 135, 138, 140, 148, 150, 152, 154
grasshopper 99
Guendoloena (wife of Merlin) 34, 43

Hanged Man, the 44, 48, 75, 82
hanging 84, 86, 143
hawk 34, 104, 106
Hell 49, 123, 140
Hermit, the 62, 138, 151
hero 32, 49, 53, 93, 105, 117, 132, 139, 140
holism 10, 13, 14, 16, 20, 38, 45, 50, 52, 53, 55, 56, 57, 59, 65, 75, 119
Horus 105
hound 98, 103, 104

Igraine 16
Initiates 29, 124
Initiation 20, 22, 36, 46, 116, 139, 154
insects 99, 103
inspiration 15, 17, 26, 65, 100, 122, 127, 139
intuition 36, 65, 78, 81, 89, 90, 110, 111, 128
invocation 47
Isidore of Seville 99

Janus 51, 122, 132
Jersey 105, 154
Jesus 85, 149
Judas 149

Judge 9, 16
Judgement 78, 150

Kingship 92, 94, 95, 140, 149, 150

Leicestershire 122
London 41, 63, 105, 126, 129, 153, 154
Lyre 105

Mabinogion, the 26, 27, 106, 132, 153
Mabon 26, 105, 138, 139, 153
Madwoman 21
magic 12, 14, 15, 16, 29, 39, 40, 47, 48, 77, 88, 92, 93, 97, 117, 119, 122, 154
magician(s) 15, 22, 53, 62, 99
mandala 22, 81, 84
masters 9, 17
materialism 37, 57, 101
meditation 12, 17, 22, 30, 33, 34, 36, 37, 47, 49, 52, 55, 65, 78-80, 81, 84, 85, 89, 90, 93, 94, 95, 104, 106-9, 117, 125, 128, 133, 134, 135, 142, 143, 147, 148, 151
Metaphysics 122, 148
Michael, Archangel 84, 97, 105
Minerva 16, 26, 42, 43, 65, 150
Minotaur 132
mistletoe 92
Mithras 49
Modron 26
Monmouth, Geoffrey of 11, 16, 17, 25, 27, 43, 56, 64, 66, 99, 139, 149, 153
Morgan 28, 41, 42, 47
Morgana 28
Morgen 16, 28, 42, 47, 120, 125, 152
Morrigan 28, 98
Morrigu 28
mortal 47, 51
mysticism 12, 40, 93

oak 92, 93, 94, 95
octave 31, 124
octaves, resonance of 34, 66, 73, 79, 83, 87, 123, 132
Odin 27, 93, 98
Orpheus 27, 49
Otherworld 16, 17, 19, 39, 42, 51, 65, 79, 92, 95, 102, 123, 124, 125, 139, 150

Palestine 105
personae 32, 34, 35, 46, 112, 117, 118, 120
pig 34, 98, 101, 102, 104, 143-5, 147-8
Pleiades 104
Powers 15, 19, 28, 33, 38, 39, 40, 45, 46, 53, 59, 83, 85, 94, 98, 99, 103, 112, 116, 118, 119, 125, 129, 133, 138
Priest 152
Priestess 16, 120, 152
propaganda 32, 41, 43, 44, 45, 47, 48
prophecies 11, 14, 16, 20, 27, 42, 43, 44, 50, 62, 64, 66, 75, 81, 98, 99, 104, 112, 125, 132, 138, 153
prophecy 12, 15, 16, 17, 26, 27, 31, 32, 59, 64, 105, 106, 123, 128, 148, 149

239